THE CASE FOR GAY RIGHTS

THE CASE FOR GAY RIGHTS

FROM *BOWERS* TO *LAWRENCE* AND BEYOND

David A. J. Richards

University Press of Kansas

© 2005 by the University Press of Kansas

Published by the University Press of Kansas (Lawrence, Kansas 66049), which was
organized by the Kansas Board of Regents and is operated and funded by Emporia State
University, Fort Hays State University, Kansas State University, Pittsburg State University,
the University of Kansas, and Wichita State University

Library of Congress Cataloging-in-Publication Data

Richards, David A. J.
   The case for gay rights : from Bowers to Lawrence and beyond / David A. J. Richards.
     p. cm.
   Includes bibliographical references and index.
   ISBN 0-7006-1391-9 (cloth : alk. paper)
   1. Gay rights—United States. 2. Gays—Legal status, laws, etc.—United States. I. Title.
   KF4754.5.R525 2005
   342.7308′7—dc22

                                                        2005005522

British Library Cataloguing-in-Publication Data is available.

Printed in the United States of America

10 9 8 7 6 5 4 3 2 1

To my life partner, Donald Levy, with love

And remember, she said, that it is only when he discerns beauty itself through what makes it visible, that a man will be quickened with the true, and not the seeming, virtue—for it is virtue's self that quickens him, not virtue's semblance. . . .

This Phaedrus—this gentlemen—was the doctrine of Diotima. I was convinced, and in that conviction I try to bring others to the same creed, and to convince them that, if we are to make this gift our own, Love will help our mortal nature more than all the world.

—Plato, *The Symposium*

CONTENTS

PREFACE

What role does judicial review play in the development, recognition, and protection of basic human rights in the United States? What is the relationship of such judicial review to protest movements? This book offers a gripping insider perspective on the most recent chapter in this American story, the post–World War II struggle for gay rights and its impact on American constitutional law, focusing on two cases, *Bowers v. Hardwick* in 1986 (denying the protection of constitutional privacy to gays and lesbians) and *Lawrence v. Texas* in 2003 (overruling *Bowers* on this point).

The work tells this history, combining the personal and political, from the perspective of a leading constitutional scholar and a gay man, whose arguments over a period of thirty years gave expression to a resisting voice that influenced these constitutional developments. Developing such arguments enabled the author and others to find a sense of truthful voice that resisted injustice, making possible new personal relationships through the resonance afforded to that resisting voice by American constitutional institutions. The voice included appeals to philosophy, interpretive history, constitutional law, psychology, and literature, as a new voice required new methods and perspectives. This book shows how all these explorations made possible the struggle for resisting voice and its constitutional recognition that are the subject matter of this important work.

The book also shows how arguments for gay rights arose from the moral and political philosophy of liberalism and were allowed to be heard in the United States only after World War II as a consequence of the greater free-speech protection extended to various protest movements, including, for the first time in American history, a nascent movement for gay rights. As constitutional arguments, gay rights crucially built on the judicial recognition after World War II of the constitutional rights of religious minorities, people of color, and women. These developments included recognition of gender divisions as increasingly constitutionally suspect and an associated protection of the constitutional right to privacy for contraception and abortion.

The failure of the Supreme Court to extend such constitutional protection to gay/lesbian sex acts in *Bowers v. Hardwick* in 1986 crucially arose in a period of growing skepticism, on and off the Supreme Court, about the principle of constitutional privacy in general and its application in particular to abortion in *Roe v. Wade.* Justice Byron White's opinion for the Court in *Bowers* reflected this skepticism, and the dissents of Justices Harry Blackmun and John Stevens argued that this skepticism was unfounded and required extension of the principle of privacy to bans on gay/lesbian sex.

The Supreme Court reaffirmed the central principle of *Roe* in *Planned Parenthood of Southeastern Pennsylvania v. Casey* and in *Romer v. Evans* (1996) held unconstitutional a state constitutional amendment that rested on irrational homophobic prejudice. These cases suggested that the authority of *Bowers* was now in doubt. In 2003, in *Lawrence v. Texas,* Justice Kennedy, writing for five justices, overruled *Bowers;* Justice O'Connor concurred on equal-protection grounds.

There are two remaining issues of constitutional principle that will evolve in light of *Lawrence:* the increasingly suspect quality, as unconstitutionally discriminating, of sexual orientation and the constitutional recognition of same-sex partnerships, including same-sex marriages, reflected in recent state court constitutional opinions, federal legislation, and a proposed constitutional amendment hostile to such opinions. There are two compelling reasons for the treatment, as increasingly suspect, of sexual orientation: discrimination on these grounds is often based in religion and gender as suspect classifications, and should be suspect on such grounds. The argument for recognition of same-sex partnerships, including the right to marriage, rests both on the basic right involved and on the lack of compelling arguments that can justify depriving gays/lesbians of such recognition.

The book concludes with an investigation of the personal and political psychology of gay/lesbian resistance, and also the reactionary psychology that refuses to accept equal treatment of the rights of gays and lesbians, for example, the proposed constitutional amendment banning gay marriage. America is in transition between patriarchal and democratic culture, and gay rights is at the cutting edge of this transition, showing how far we have come and how far we have yet to go.

ACKNOWLEDGMENTS

The proposal for this book was first suggested by Michael J. Briggs, editor-in-chief of University Press of Kansas, to whom I am grateful for sensing, before I did, that it was a book that I could and should write. I am grateful as well for his quickly securing an able reader, Evan Gerstmann, whose comments were most helpful, and encouraging me to seek evaluations and advice from others as well. Two friends were particularly helpful to me, namely, Carol Gilligan (University Professor, New York University) and Nicholas Bamforth (fellow, Queen's College, Oxford University). Both of them read the entire manuscript and gave me detailed comments, urging me to retain and develop the attempt to connect the constitutional argument to my personal and professional life, a connection they regarded as important, original, and illuminating. Comments of Nicola Lacey were also helpful.

The book was researched and written over a summer, supported by a generous research grant from the New York University School of Law Filomen D'Agostino and Max E. Greenberg Faculty Research Fund.

1

THE PERSONAL AS POLITICAL

Shortly after the Supreme Court announced its decision in *Lawrence v. Texas*,[1] I received an unsolicited e-mail from a student I had taught some twenty years ago, a student I did not and do not know personally. The student had worked for the *New York University School of* Law *Law Review* on an article I had published after the Court's decision in *Bowers v. Hardwick*,[2] an article highly critical of the decision's reasoning and calling for its overruling.[3] The former student had remembered my argument and offered me warm congratulations on *Lawrence*, which overruled *Bowers*, noting the relatively short time between *Bowers* (1986) and *Lawrence* (2003). I was strangely moved by this e-mail because, amidst so much that distracts and trivializes in the demands of teaching and scholarship and administration in a major American law school, it recognized something deeply personal for me, a central ambition of my life as a constitutional scholar and my place, among others, in offering arguments over time that were in play in these decisions.[4] I was moved to be seen so clearly, in particular, by a student who shared history with me and saw me as a person, a moral agent in a certain history, which is a chapter in the larger history of American constitutionalism.

In fact, my work on these arguments had started much earlier, around 1974, when I left law practice to begin teaching, first at Fordham University Law School and then, three years later, at the New York University School of Law, where I have remained. At that time and for some time afterward, I wrote as one of very few such voices, certainly in American law schools, calling for the recognition of the human rights of gays and lesbians under American constitutional law.[5] I am thankful that there are now many other voices. I want to draw on this experience, personal as well as professional, from the beginning of my career thirty years ago until today to make clear

1

the role that arguments over basic American constitutional principles played in my life, as a gay man, as they have played in the lives of so many other gay Americans as well as other Americans struggling for recognition of their basic human rights under constitutional law. What were my motives and aspirations, and why did I turn to constitutional law as a way of constructing arguments that would meet my needs and the needs of so many others? What led me to resist? Is there a personal and political psychology here with a larger resonance in the human psyche that flourishes in and through resistance to injustice? What kinds of arguments did I, a member of a small and highly stigmatized minority (so stigmatized in the United States that until World War II and its aftermath of civil rights ferment it barely recognized itself as such), develop, and why were they reasonably appealing over some thirty years to growing numbers of citizens and, eventually, judges of our highest court? And what can my story tell us about American constitutional law, or law more generally, and its moral and political appeal?

Academic law in general and constitutional law in particular are often taught and written about in an excessively academic positivistic vein, as a stable body of self-interpreting doctrines or principles. Such an approach is as falsifying of law as would be an architecture that conceived of space as having only one or two dimensions. A close analysis of a constitutional development, such as the sodomy cases, brings out the multidimensionality of constitutional law as a humane normative enterprise that gives an acoustic to otherwise feeble, unjustly suppressed ethical voices that are strengthened by the resonance that law, properly developed, gives them. In many cases the law accords such voices and their claims a sense of being part of the constitutional community, no longer marginal, silenced, and dehumanized but recognizably human and humane.

This work is a study of constitutional history, of the developments that led to *Bowers v. Hardwick* and to its overruling in *Lawrence v. Texas*. My hope is that structuring my argument as a mapping of personal and constitutional history will bring alive to the reader the role that developments in constitutional law play in the lives of Americans (the personal as political), in particular, those who find uniquely in constitutional law an impartial forum of principle that hears and assesses their voice, testing them in terms of arguments of principle, sometimes in ways no other branch of American government does. The story is my own, but it reflects a larger pattern of thought and action in many others whose lives were fundamentally changed by the developments I discuss. I turn to personal history because it clarifies the struggle for voice from within the psyche of one among others who found within himself his own resisting voice, including exploring why I turned to a range of disciplines, including moral and political philosophy, interpretive history, constitutional interpretation, law, and, most recently, psychology, in order to do justice to this resisting voice. Why does a new voice require new methods?

The Struggle for Voice

I structure my argument in terms of the relationship between our psyches as persons and the role of voice (including struggles for voice) in giving expression to our psyches. Psyche is defined as "breath . . . ; hence, life (identified with or indicated by the breath); the animating principle . . . , the source of all vital activities, rational or irrational . . . , in distinction from its material vehicle."[6] A human psychology, thus understood, must take seriously the living of a human life from an inward sense of our emotions; consciousness and self-consciousness; bodies; and, of course, voice, including the gap between our feelings and knowledge of our feelings.[7] Anthony Damasio's *The Feeling of What Happens* importantly models our psychological complexity in terms of the metaphor of our experience of the unity in complexity of melody, harmony, and polyphony in music, "the music of behavior":[8] "You are the music while the music lasts."[9] Music, however, may not just be a metaphor for our psychological complexity. It may, as in the music of Giuseppe Verdi,[10] sometimes be our only way into feelings rooted in a suppressed voice we have but are not aware we have, and may indeed offer us a complex and subtle cultural form through which we are brought to self-knowledge of important emotions we hold within our psyches and how and why it is so difficult to acknowledge them. In such music we recognize a voice culturally suppressed in ourselves and experience a resonance for a voice that at least questions or can question such loss as the necessary foundation of our identity as men or women living under democracy.

My working hypothesis in the argument of this book is that, in appropriate historical circumstances, the construction of new forms of legal and constitutional arguments can be and are ways in which, analogously to the construction of voice in works of art, we not only recognize in ourselves a voice otherwise culturally suppressed but give expression as well to a voice that resists unjust forms of such suppression and that, appealing to values explicit and implicit in constitutional law, seeks and finds a resonance in the growing recognition of the justice of its claims. All these stages are reflected in the story I tell, which is specifically the story of a young man who, under the impact of the homophobic culture of his youth, certainly always knew his sexual orientation was gay but could not have acknowledged, let alone given expression, to such desires and feelings. My interest here is in exploring the role that the construction of certain kinds of moral and ultimately constitutional arguments, by myself and others, played not only in finding a voice expressive of my sexual psyche but, at the same time, thinking, writing, and speaking in a voice that resisted, as fundamentally unjust, the repression not only of the voice but of humane forms of life that give expression to such voice. I certainly do not believe that my own experience is either universal or universalizable: historically, gays and lesbians have found their voices and lived their lives in circumstances where such forms of public moral and legal argument were unthinkable, indeed savagely suppressed. But it is important to understand as well an experience, like mine and others', of a resisting ethical and constitutional voice that is increasingly common and that has been accorded, as the sodomy cases show, increasing respect and even acceptance not only by our judges but by citizens at large.

What organizes my argument is a narrative of voice, including experiments in personal and constitutional voice. It touches on autobiographical points, but only those essential to the larger narrative of personal and constitutional voice that is the subject matter of this book. The autobiographical facts, which I try to keep to a minimum (largely at the beginning and end of my argument), give a context for my story of voice, including the significant relationships out of which the struggle for voice arises and by which it has been supported and sustained. My arguments, even when highly abstract, arise from relationships and always return to relationships, which is a way of bringing alive what I believe motivates the kind of story I am telling, a story central, as I have come to believe, to the larger story of the role that resisting voice plays in the development and integrity of American constitutionalism.

How can this resistance happen? What does it tell us about the connections of our psyches to voice, connections that take the form of ethical and constitutional resistance that is widely stigmatized, marginalized, and even punished? What moves us to such forms of voice, and why and how do such voices enjoy growing appeal and even recognition? My story, while highly personal (even idiosyncratic), illuminates the larger American story of what moves us in a constitutional law that is, at its best, justly responsive to such voices.

My own struggle for voice has multiple dimensions: my family history, my undergraduate and graduate education (in which moral and political philos-

ophy were central preoccupations), my finding voice in a loving sexual relationship with my partner for some thirty years, and, very importantly, my
voice as a teacher and scholar of American criminal and constitutional law.
This, in turn, included various stages in the development of my teaching and
scholarly voice, including relationships to students, my colleagues, and the
larger constitutional and political culture. My life as a teacher and scholar of
law expressed itself in different voices over time: jurisprudential and philosophical; historical and constitutional; and, most recently, feminist and psychological and literary (in particular, exploring the links between personal
and political psychology in resisting injustice). These stages were a continuum,
and it would be a mistake to separate any one of them sharply from any
other. For expository convenience, I divide these stages of developing ethical voice into the three parts of this book: philosophy, law, psychology. But
all of them were expressions of my voice, rooted in my psyche, and thus
were as much ways of my finding and exploring my personal and ethical
voice as they were ways of seeking a resonance for personal and ethical voice
in the larger culture, whose dominant assumptions had been homophobic
(savagely repressing any such personal and ethical voice) because such voice
was unspeakable. It was, in Blackstone's words, "a crime not fit to be
named; *peccatum illud horribile, inter christianos non nominandum*"[11]—not
mentionable, let alone discussed or assessed. Philosophical argument has
always been central to my conception of human rationality and thus informs
my work in all areas. Philosophy itself has a history, and my interests in philosophy and history were there from the beginning. The uses of both philosophy and history in constructing new forms of constitutional argument
were thus wholly natural and quite productive developments in my voice.
And a growing interest in feminism, as pivotal to my teaching and scholarly
voice of ethical and constitutional interest, clarified the trajectory of my
work. The recent turn in my work to psychology and literature has brought
my struggle for voice full circle, clarifying the roots of resisting voice in family relationships I had not previously seen or understood, as I show at the
end of my argument. This psychology of resistance arose not only from
exploration of my own psyche, transformed, as it was, by the process of
resistance I describe at length in this book, but also from my experience of
the reactionary forces that the resisting voice of myself and others unleashed
in American politics. Bringing in this psychological dimension, as I do at the
end, tells a more complexly truthful story of how resistance unleashes reactionary repressive responses and enables us to explore and better understand
the balance between resistance and reaction in constitutional law and poli-

tics. My story is by no means a Whig history of inexorable progress but a complex history of the gains and losses of the moral agency of resisting voice in law and politics.

What was stable throughout this process is what explains much of its dynamic: living in a long-term, loving gay relationship, an experience of truthful voice in relationship that exposed the lies and violence on which cultural homophobia rests. Such homophobia is a political and constitutional evil directed precisely at denying and disrupting such relationships. An eye and an ear increasingly sensitive to such lies and violence clarify the forms of resistance to which I turned, including, as my argument shows, the view that equal recognition of same-sex relationships is a basic human right. It was because my voice arose from and was sustained by such a loving relationship that I began to look with growing skepticism at the reactionary forces that warred on such a relationship. Looking at the world through this prism strengthened a resisting voice that critically questioned a culture, resting on unjust gender stereotypes, that could not understand such relationships. All the forms of voice I explore in this book were ways of speaking in this resisting voice, a voice that compelled me both because it was more personally truthful to my experience of love as a basic human good, and because it more intelligently integrated my emotional and intellectual intelligence in offering compelling ethical and constitutional arguments against the fundamental injustice of homophobia.

Much of the argument of this book is about the construction of these ethical and constitutional arguments and the growing judicial and public recognition of their validity. But I also frame this discussion, as I have here, in terms of the underlying struggle for personal and ethical voice, which crucially explains how these arguments arose and why they have had any appeal at all. I will try to keep both discussions in some fruitful relationship to one another, but at some points one form of discussion will dominate the other. In fact, the truth of the matter is that both issues arose in my experience at the same time and were part of the same process. My hope is that this larger truth will inform the discussion throughout.

Personal History

Why did these issues first grip me in 1974? There had, of course, been the civil rights and antiwar movements, and now there was the feminist movement as well, and even gay resistance at Stonewall in New York City (for further discussion, see Chapters 3 and 4). I had certainly thought abstractly about homosexuality as an ethical issue during my undergraduate years at Harvard College[12] and, even more deeply, during the two years I studied moral philosophy at Oxford University,[13] leading to a doctorate in moral philosophy in 1971.[14] My tutorial study at Oxford with H. L. A. Hart is important to my story. I was attracted to study with Hart, in particular, because he had prominently defended in Britain the recommendations of the Wolfenden Committee, calling for the decriminalization of gay sex.[15] Hart's remarkable spirit particularly moved me as his student, though I only quite recently recognized what it was in Hart's own struggles with his sexuality that may have moved me subliminally in ways I did not then understand (I discuss these points further in Chapter 10). The subject absorbed me because I recognized my gay sexual orientation and wanted to know ethically whether I could live a moral life as a gay man. My assumption had long been that I could not. My studies in moral philosophy had led me to the conviction that I could,[16] but it was an abstract conviction that I did not connect to law study or to my life during my three years as a law student at Harvard Law School. The prominent gay law professor and advocate of gay rights, William Rubenstein, had some ten years later a very different experience of that distinguished law school, one involving not only law study but a rich gay personal life.[17] That, unfortunately, was not my experience; I was absorbed during those years in finishing my Oxford work (including preparing my dissertation for publication), by comparison to which law study seemed stale and sterile. One of the thesis examiners of my Oxford doctoral dissertation, R. M. Hare, powerfully objected (in a remarkably generous personal correspondence) to the rather grim Kantian treatment of personal love in my dissertation. People will think, he protested, that the way you treat love shows that you have never been in love. I deeply loved my family, but his point was about love of someone outside the family. On this point he was, in fact, quite right.

My interest in living a gay life arose when I moved to New York City to practice law with a Wall Street firm in 1971. I experimented, of course; sex was easy, relationships impossible, unthinkable (a world that heterosexual people, brought up in a culture that powerfully supports their loves, can barely understand or even imagine). What led me around 1974 to want to find a voice that could do justice to what I now believed, as an abstract matter, was meeting the man with whom I have shared my life from that time forward. Importantly, it was also at that time that I left practice to teach law, and the two choices (of lover and of profession) were connected. Certainly, my reasons for turning to study and writing about gay rights was not a professional decision (that is, a decision calculated to advance my career); indeed, from that point of view it was rather foolhardy (as various gay friends in law cautioned me at the time, arguing that a gay law professor should, as a matter of prudence, not write about gay issues). Though I know I paid a price in professional advancement, I have never really regretted my decision and, once having made it, pursuing it so doggedly. I feel like saying I had no choice, though choice it clearly was. My reasons were personal. What led me to it and sustained it was a sense of truthful voice in loving relationship that I was experiencing outside my family of origin for the first time in my life, and my growing sense that this voice and my relationship, based on it, were vulnerable to the homophobic forces around us and even in us. I thought this relationship could not endure, let alone flourish, unless we found a way to strengthen our voices, staying in touch with their truthfulness and learning the art and science of resistance—in particular to the lies about homosexuality that surrounded us, enveloped us like an insidious toxic miasma that we breathed at peril to our very psyches, to our lives. We could breathe only in a less polluted atmosphere, a cleaner environment that we had no choice but to try to foster. Resistance, for reasons I explain later (Chapter 10), was a psychological necessity for love.

I had been brought up in a loving, Italian American, piously Catholic family and had uncritically absorbed the homophobic teaching of its sexual morality, which was, of course, the general morality of the period. I had that voice very much in me, but I also had in me an ethical voice, grounded in my parents' remarkably egalitarian relationship and now in moral philosophy, and a truthful voice that arose from a loving gay relationship with a Jewish man. What compelled me personally was to understand these different voices and to bring them into some reasonable relationship to one another, which would include, eventually, bringing my beloved family (my parents and sister) into an honest relationship with me and my partner, with whom I lived from 1976 forward (my first article on gay rights was published a year later).[18] The year 1976 marked as well the Supreme Court's summary dismissal of a lower three-judge federal court opinion that had denied (2–1, Judge Robert Mehrige dissenting) that the constitutional right to privacy had any application to gay/lesbian sexuality, a dismissal and opinion that left me furiously indignant.[19] The personal and the political intersected in a sense of grievance at this assault on the right to love that most Americans assumed as an inalienable human right, and I knew my personal and professional life would require resistance to such injustice.

I could not have negotiated these intrapsychic complexities without the love of my partner, a ferociously intelligent, passionate, tender love that included something I very much needed: warm, intimate conversation with someone as learned in philosophy as I (my partner is an academic philosopher), and someone much more learned and experienced in psychology, psychoanalysis, and much else. His love also inspired courage, or, more accurately, was why courage seemed to be called for. We originally met as academics, through a mutual straight friend, to study issues of mutual concern, including the philosophy and psychology of love. As we studied and discussed philosophy and psychology, in particular Plato's *Symposium* and *Phaedrus* and Freud's works, we also closely studied one another. As we studied love, we fell in love. The question for me was how to understand my new experience of truthful voice in intimate relationship, how to protect, nurture, and strengthen this voice, in particular, against the lies about homosexuality that I and others had assumed axiomatically to be true. How had these lies achieved such a hegemonic power over our moral, political, and legal culture? How could something so personally and ethically valuable as gay and lesbian sexual love be subject to criminal penalties and be, at least in America, so apparently voiceless, supine, and abject? America, which endlessly celebrated companionate romantic love, had no place for my love. These questions haunted my relationship and my life, including my early, middle, and later professional life as a law professor.

Strengthening such a voice of resistance required, of course, the resonance I received from my partner, but it seemed that I might reasonably seek a resonance as well in the larger American culture, now alive with various protest movements that raised fundamental questions about the justice of American institutions and assumptions. I was now not only in a loving gay relationship but was a law professor, experiencing in teaching and writing a new kind of voice and authority and a new kind of audience. Law in the United States, unlike philosophy, was central to the political culture. I gravitated to teaching the courses central to my philosophical background, criminal law and constitutional law, but I saw, in both my teaching and my writing in these fields, resources for a new kind of voice that could not only speak to but be heard by the larger political culture, one rooted in my personal and ethical voice but that could speak and be heard in terms of basic constitutional principles of human rights that the civil rights movements had brought to the central stage of American political life. It was that search for voice and resonance, drawing on the authority of these principles, that led me to study and write about gay rights in an order that corresponds roughly to the structure of the argument of this book.

The beginning of my study was the political theory of liberalism that I had studied as an undergraduate and graduate student. It was that powerful political theory that had led in Great Britain to the pathbreaking 1957 recommendation of the Wolfenden Committee that consensual homosexuality be decriminalized (Parliament enacted the substance of their recommendations ten years later in 1967).[20] I begin my argument in Chapter 2 with the close study of this theory and why it seemed that it was not only defensible as a free-standing political theory but was also the normative political theory underlying American constitutional institutions, in particular, justifying the place of judicial review in such institutions.

If this was the best political theory of American constitutionalism, why had its requirements regarding the scope of criminal law in general and consensual homosexuality in particular been so little respected, either politically or personally? The key, I believe, was that important features of this political theory, in particular its demand for a robust principle of free speech, had not been the subject of serious judicial enforcement in the United States until after World War II. I argue in Chapter 3 that what made the post–World War II period the first in which arguments for gay rights were heard in the United States were important developments in the judicial protection of speech that were extended to such arguments.

Chapter 4 deals with important related developments in the post–World War II period in the judicial understanding and recognition of religion, race/ethnicity, and gender as highly suspect classifications. All these developments are rooted in arguments first made by the radical abolitionists in antebellum America, arguments that criticized American religious intolerance (for example, anti-Semitism), racism, and sexism as grounded in stereotypes that unjustly degraded whole classes of persons from their status as equal bearers of basic human rights. These developments afforded principles that could be reasonably developed to question American homophobia as well.

Chapter 5 turns to the close study, in light of the developments in Chapter 4, of the judicial protection of the right to intimate life. This right had importantly been recognized as one of those unjustly abridged by American cultural racism, but it was later importantly recognized in cases of the unjust abridgment of such rights on the basis of sexism as well. I closely study, in this connection, important elaborations of the constitutional right to privacy and its application to contraception and abortion services. It is the authority of these two decisions that was crucially in play as the background for the Supreme Court's examination of whether the right extended to gay/lesbian sex acts in *Bowers* and *Lawrence*.

Chapter 6 discusses in depth *Bowers v. Hardwick* as arising in a period of constitutional crisis about the continuing authority of decisions that recognized a constitutional right to privacy in the cases of contraception and abortion. The various opinions are closely parsed, in particular, in light of the division on the Supreme Court over the continuing authority of *Roe v. Wade*.

Chapter 7 turns to *Lawrence v. Texas*. I argue that *Lawrence* must be understood in the context of various cases decided after *Bowers*, in particular the Supreme Court's decisive reaffirmation of the central principle of *Roe* in *Casey* and its striking down in *Romer* of Colorado Amendment Two (forbidding laws that rule out discrimination on grounds of sexual orientation). Both these decisions clarified developing constitutional principles that required that *Bowers* be reconsidered and overruled.

Chapter 8 turns to the question, in light of *Lawrence*, of whether sexual orientation should be considered a suspect classification on the model of religion, race/ethnicity, or gender. I argue that there is an important ingredient of gender discrimination in homophobia but that religion also affords a secure basis for regarding discrimination on grounds of sexual orientation as highly suspect constitutionally.

Chapter 9 turns to the implications of *Lawrence* either for a more equal legal recognition of same-sex partnerships or for same-sex marriage. I place this question in the light of such developments in other countries and suggest that there are compelling constitutional arguments for extending marriage on equal terms to gays and lesbians.

Finally, Chapter 10, drawing on the earlier steps in my argument, offers a psychological perspective on what motivates resistance to injustice and on the reactionary politics such resistance elicits. I argue that we are in transition between patriarchal and democratic maturity, and the case for gay rights is at the incendiary cutting edge of that transition.

PART I
PHILOSOPHY

2

PHILOSOPHY

Why philosophy, let alone moral and political philosophy, as a starting point for thinking about issues such as gay rights and American constitutionalism? I believe philosophy is a natural place to start when there is the sense of a gap between one's own convictions and the conventional morality of society at large. This was certainly my own situation in the late 1960s. Philosophy appealed to me, as it has to so many others, because of its methodological Socratic individualism—the testing of one's own ethical convictions by the modes of argument innovated by Socrates and developed in a tradition that includes, among others, Plato, Aristotle, Hume, and Kant. Philosophy had had this appeal for me since my years of undergraduate and graduate study as a way of testing one's own convictions for their coherence, rationality, and reasonableness and, on this basis, affording a reliable standpoint of critical morality in terms of which one might understand and, when necessary, criticize the conventional morality.[1]

This method deeply engaged me as a way of finding and exploring an ethical voice independent of the homophobic conventional sexual morality of my childhood. Such conventions assumed that homosexual acts were unspeakable and thus in their nature brutally silenced any voice that might challenge their authority. Socratic philosophy was liberating of my voice because its discourse started in personal ethical conviction, never appealing to any authority outside that conviction. It thus gave me a way to find and explore an authoritative ethical voice that might reasonably question any form of conventional morality, including repressive sexual moralities, such as sexism and homophobia, that rested on the unjust repression of any reasonable questioning. For me, this method freed an ethical voice, making possible a freedom of mind that flourished long before I had brought that freedom to bear on my own life.

15

I had carried this method fairly far in terms of an abstract understanding that much of conventional sexual morality, including its homophobia, was unjustified. But the method took on a new meaning for me after I met my partner in 1974, when the ethical voice it made possible was brought into some working relationship with the sense of truthful voice in a loving relationship. If this relationship were to grow and deepen in the way we wanted, there had to be a closer connection between the more disassociated voice I had cultivated as a philosopher and the sense of embodied voice I found in intimate loving relationship. Philosophy had already made possible a freedom of mind that ethically questioned and indeed rejected homophobic sexual morality, thus rendering my mind open to sexual experiences I had once rejected as unthinkable. It was the experience of such sexual love in a relationship of emotional presence I had never had before that exposed to me how vulnerable such loving relationships are to an unjust culture that rests on the repression of any voice that speaks from the truth that love knows. The relationship for this reason empowered a voice that now, as an urgent personal and ethical matter, had to find ways to live a life centered in resistance to such injustice.

What perhaps made this more feasible for me and my partner was our common intellectual passion for philosophy and our sense of a new voice in ourselves, arising from our love, that neither of us had ever experienced before, certainly not in professional philosophy. Philosophy can be conducted in many ways, and the academic mode I had experienced at Harvard and Oxford was, to say the least, intensely, relentlessly agonistic, competitive, sometimes absurdly patriarchal, as well as more cruel than its educational or intellectual aims required. When I turned to philosophy in relationship to my partner, it was a conversation between equals animated by a fraternal sense of shared goals, including our erotic love for one another. Philosophy was as intensely critical as it had ever been, but it was now also as much listening as speaking, combining thought and feeling, patient, tender, a practice of voice in relationship implicitly, as I now see, developing an antipatriarchal way of a man relating to a man, what Carol Gilligan would call speaking in a different voice.[2] Socratic philosophy came alive for me as a way into deeper relationship, exploring new convictions and experimenting with a voice that might sustain them. Our sense of ethical and personal voice, as complementary, called for a resistance that could sustain our sense of truthful voice in relationship against what we increasingly saw as the lies about gender and sexuality that surrounded us. We could not sustain the terms of the relationship we wanted if we did not, each in our own ways, resist, and combine personal and ethical voice in a responsible resistance to what increasingly seemed to us to be the profound injustice that had afflicted gays and lesbians for much too long. Since we were intellectuals, the resistance called for new forms of thought and writing that might reasonably justify such resistance.[3]

Philosophy would play an important role for me because it appealed to the rational natures humans shared. A reasonable argument, in moral and political philosophy, was one that, consistent with the method of Socratic individualism, rationally examined the moral and political convictions all persons shared and thus might define a common moral point of view that all persons, as rational, could reasonably enter into if they chose, and perhaps did enter into whenever they thought responsibly about ethics and politics. Such a method appealed to me at this early point in my resistance because, if carried out responsibly, it might expand the circle of persons who gave my still frail voice of resistance that sense of reasonable resonance it needed to become stronger. Perhaps, also, such reasonable resonance might be the basis of a larger political and even legal resistance.

My sense of voice had been empowered by philosophy and the experience of personal life, but I needed now to develop that voice as a professor of law. My previous interests in philosophy had been largely personal and ethical, as a way of developing ethical views that rested on conviction independent of conventional morality. Now, however, as a law professor, I had to find a voice and audience in law, and I turned to legal and political philosophy as ways to find the voice and audience I was seeking.

There were two perspectives on legal and political theory that impressed me, from this perspective, as philosophically interesting. Both offered a liberal interpretation of the basic moral requirement: treating persons as equals. There were two components of this requirement that must be interpreted: first, a neutral theory of the good that allowed each person a scope of reasonable judgment to pursue his or her ends, whatever they were; and second, some metric in terms of which each person was to be treated as an equal. The first such interpretation was offered by utilitarianism, the second by contractualism.

Utilitarian Equality

The utilitarian interpretation of treating persons as equals uses pleasure and pain (or by preference satisfaction and frustration) as its basic normative terms. Both the components of liberal equality are given a sense in its terms.

On the one hand, this metric construes the neutral theory of the good in terms of whatever advances or frustrates one's interests and thus does not offer any judgment about what persons take pleasure in (or what causes them pain). It suffices for the utilitarian interpretation of neutrality that something gives a person pleasure or occasions pain. From this perspective, poetry is as good as push-pin.[4]

On the other hand, the utilitarian interpretation uses pleasure/pain as the metric in terms of which persons are treated as equals. The sense of equality is created by the same weight being placed on pleasure or pain wherever it occurs. This interpretation leads to the governing form of the utilitarian principle in ethics and politics: namely, that act or institution is right that leads overall to the net greatest aggregate of pleasure over pain in all the sentient beings affected.[5]

The enormous appeal of utilitarianism to liberal reformers, such as Jeremy Bentham and John Stuart Mill, was that it offered a critical morality (whatever maximizes utilitarian aggregation) that tied critical moral judgments to consequentialist investigations of what advanced or frustrated human interests. In particular, utilitarianism could draw sharp distinctions between the requirements of critical morality, thus understood, and those of conventional morality (what was regarded as acceptable or unacceptable by the dominant morality of one's culture). Bentham used this distinction, for example, to criticize the British criminal justice system, arguing that its conception of both what to punish and how to punish appealed to ideas of conventional morality that could not be justified in terms of utilitarian critical morality, and should on this ground be changed.[6] Bentham was one of the first legal philosophers to argue explicitly, albeit in unpublished papers, that the criminalization of consensual homosexuality was quite unjustified on such grounds.[7] John Stuart Mill developed the general framework of Bentham's thought into a particularly brilliant set of critical essays on British law, notably *On Liberty*[8] and *The Subjection of Women*.[9]

The argument of *The Subjection of Women*, for example, assumed the basic distinction between utilitarian critical morality and conventional morality. Mill was quite clear that British conventional morality, rooted in a long history of sexism, gave a weight to gender in depriving women of appropriate respect for basic rights; it regarded such deprivation as justified and indeed in the nature of things. But such claims of conventional morality were, for Mill, as unjustified on utilitarian grounds as the comparable arguments about race or ethnic differences in support of slavery or, after slavery, racism. Indeed, Mill offered a compelling case for persuasive analogies between the inadequate grounds on which slavery was once justified and the grounds on which what he regarded as a comparable subordination or subjection of women were justified in nineteenth-century Britain. In both cases, utilitarian critical morality must regard such alleged racial/ethnic or gender differences as not justified on the basis of any fairly tested differences under circumstances of freedom and equality.[10] Utilitarianism must condemn, as Mill and other utilitarians certainly did, treatment rationalized in terns of nonexistent differences, for such treatment fails to give equal weight to the pleasure and pain of women with that felt by men and all other sentient beings. Extending respect to women for their basic rights was thus called for on the ground of better realizing the net aggregate of pleasure over pain of all sentient beings.

The most brilliantly influential of John Stuart Mill's arguments was his defense of political liberalism in *On Liberty,* again on utilitarian grounds. Mill somewhat modified Bentham's understanding of utilitarianism by drawing on a distinction between higher and lower pleasures that did not, as Bentham did, regard poetry as being as good as push-pin.[11] Rather, Mill argued that rational persons, who have reflected on experiments in living with different ways of getting pleasure and avoiding pain, would accord greater weight to the exercise of certain kinds of intellectual, creative, and artistic pleasure than they would to pleasure not requiring the exercise of such competences, and that accordingly such pleasures should be accorded much greater weight than others in the understanding of what counted as the greatest net aggregate of pleasure over pain. Mill also added to Bentham's more static understanding of utilitarian aggregation a more dynamic view of cultural, political, legal, and economic change over time, appealing to "utility in the largest sense, grounded on the permanent interests of man as a progressive being."[12] In this view, a reasonable utilitarian critical morality would consult the evidence of history about which arrangements led to the discovery of more rational and less irrational ways of maximizing the net aggregate of pleasure over pain of all sentient beings over time. Mill thus interpreted the utilitarian principle in terms of identifying and supporting those arrangements that led to the greatest development, expression, and realization of a progressive understanding of human interests, for example, a feminist understanding of the interests of women on fair terms with the interests of men.

Mill's *On Liberty* powerfully used these modifications of Benthamite utilitarianism to support two arguments for a muscular constitutional and political recognition of basic rights of political liberalism, a robust right of conscience and free speech,[13] and a right of personal autonomy in actions.[14] I begin with free speech and then turn to personal autonomy.

Mill's powerful argument for a robust right of free speech appealed to values intrinsic to conscience and speech themselves as well as to consequentialist considerations. This is shown by the three arguments for a right to free speech that Mill identified: first, that freedom of conscience and speech allows truth to be spoken; second, that such freedom appropriately winnows the false from the true; and third, that such freedom ensures that persons develop mature rational faculties of thought and deliberation by learning to rebut the false. The first two arguments are consequentialist: free speech has two highly desirable consequences in terms of advancing truth and appropriately distinguishing the true from the false. Mill's sense of desirable truths is not narrowly scientific or technical; it includes the progressive testing of morally false, pernicious values such as racism and sexism, advancing a sense of utilitarian values based on reason. But his third argument for free speech is not consequentialist: it places a value on rational thought and deliberation independent of whether such thought and deliberation advance truth in the way that the other arguments do.[15] Mill fitted this independent sense of value into doctrinal utilitarianism by assigning it to the category of higher pleasures, which deserve much greater utilitarian weight than lower pleasures. But he gave free speech much greater weight than utilitarianism as such requires, giving it a value against all countervailing considerations: "If all mankind minus one, were of one opinion, and only one person were of the contrary opinion, mankind would be no more justified in silencing that one person, than he, if he had the power, would be justified in silencing mankind."[16]

The value Mill placed on free speech is close in weight and spirit to Kantian values of dignity, which are regarded by Kantians as not overridden by utilitarian considerations at all but only by competing values of dignity. Mill's argument for free speech, here as elsewhere, drew its normative power and appeal from considerations that cannot reasonably be accommodated by utilitarian argument.

The structure and content of Mill's argument for a liberal view of basic rights such as conscience and speech lead for similar reasons to the right of personal autonomy. Mill's argument again appealed to the important distinction between critical and conventional morality. A right of free speech is, as we have seen, justified because it ensures that conventional morality, often not justified on grounds of critical morality, is subject to precisely the criticism and reform it needs in order to be more justified on such grounds. Mill brilliantly argued that the same disparity (between critical and conventional morality) occurred in overcriminalization: the criminal law in Britain and elsewhere enforced conventional morality through criminal law that was unjustified on utilitarian grounds, unjustly subjecting human liberty to criminal and social sanctions that were cruelly in excess of any legitimate purpose of criminal justice. Mill argued that for the same reasons that liberalism requires respect for rights of conscience and speech, it also requires respect for the right of personal autonomy.[17] What Mill assumed here was that the same three subsidiary arguments he considered in the case of free speech (truth, winnowing the true from the false, the intrinsic value of rational thought and deliberation) applied to the right of personal autonomy in living one's life when the conventional morality that abridges these rights is unjustified on grounds of the critical morality of a progressive utilitarianism. The same role that free speech plays in the just criticism of conventional morality applies to the right of personal autonomy, leading to experiments in living that promote the values of a progressive utilitarianism.[18]

Mill offered a complex view of principles that govern when the right to personal autonomy applies. First, coercion is justified when required to share the reasonable burdens of securing justice, for example, obeying laws that create an equitable scheme of taxation or that secure opportunities on fair terms for persons otherwise subject to injustice (for example, laws forbidding discrimination on grounds of race or gender).[19] Second, assuming no such grounds of justice exist, it is a requirement for coercion that the act in question inflicts harm on assignable persons (for example, laws against killing or stealing).[20] Third, Mill denied the idea that if coercion of an act is neither required by justice nor required to avoid harm to other parties, the act might be subject to coercion solely on the ground that it inflicts harm on the agent.[21] His antipaternalism was undoubtedly shaped by his feminism, his concern that arguments of harm to self had often been unjustly used to claim that any deviation from women's traditional role was self-destructive in ways that warranted interference on paternalistic grounds. Finally, Mill denied, absent any of the considerations already discussed, that the mere fact that a majority of the population takes offense against a certain way of life (on the ground of conventional morality) can ever, in principle, be a ground for forbidding such a way of life.[22] Mill clearly meant these principles, sometimes summarized as the "harm principle," to impose constraints rooted in critical morality regarding when the state may legitimately forbid conduct.

The force of there being such a right of personal autonomy, for Mill, was that such considerations are required to justify abridgement of this right. Mere majoritarian offense can never be enough.

Mill's harm principle states an important principle of liberal political morality. Not all liberals will agree that Mill's formulation is its best expression; for example, liberals often regard paternalism as a just ground for interference when, other things being equal, the agent threatens an uncontroversial irreparable harm to self such as suicide.[23] There is also reason to question whether Mill's attempt to justify his principle on utilitarian grounds really did justice to his liberal conception of basic human rights. This is shown by the way in which Mill's arguments for rights of speech and autonomy depend, at crucial points, on nonutilitarian arguments about the intrinsic value of the dignity of exercising one's thoughts and speech as a reasonable person or living one's life as a morally independent agent in defiance of the unjustified claims of conventional morality.[24] Is there an alternative way of understanding the basis for Mill's principle?

Contractualist Equality

There is another plausible way of interpreting the twin demands of treating persons as equals: the neutral theory of the good, and a metric for judging when persons have been treated as equals. This alternative interpretation rejects pleasure and pain as the reasonable way of making sense of these demands because it is not sentience that grounds moral equality but our powers of moral personality, our responsiveness to rationality and reasonableness in our personal and ethical lives. Kant called these moral powers dignity and argued for a view of morality that tested principles, qua moral, in terms of whether persons could reasonably accept them as the ultimate standards incumbent on them and all other rational persons similarly situated.[25] In contemporary moral philosophy, contractualism interprets this conception in terms of the principles that all persons could reasonably accept as the ultimate standards in terms of which competing claims will be evaluated.[26]

Contractualist equality makes sense of the neutral theory of the good in terms of the fundamental normative weight it gives to dignity, the exercise of our powers of rational and reasonable choice and deliberation in deciding whether, when, and how to pursue our desires. This interpretation accords all agents a broad sovereignty over their thoughts and lives, as the neutral theory of the good requires.

But contractualist equality affords as well a compelling interpretation of the metric of equal treatment; namely, each person is to be treated as an equal with respect to the basic rights, opportunities, resources, and bases of self-respect that persons rationally require to advance their ends, whatever they are. Its interpretation is more reasonable than that offered by doctrinal utilitarianism because its metric, basic goods required rationally to live a life, more plausibly treats persons as equals than utilitarian's metric of pleasure and pain. Utilitarianism interprets moral equality in terms of an equal weighing of pleasures or pains (wherever they occur), which does not afford a morally reasonable interpretation of values of distributive equality that have weight independent of utilitarian aggregation.

Contractualist equality might also afford a more convincing moral justification for the great liberal rights John Stuart Mill aimed to justify: basic rights of conscience and speech and a right of personal autonomy. With respect to conscience and speech, its rationale for these basic rights brings out clearly the value of the dignity of rational deliberation that Mill's argument assumes but cannot explain on utilitarian grounds. And contractualist equality justifies as well a robust right of personal autonomy as a way of securing respect for the rational dignity of living one's life when conventional morality degrades persons by enforcing demands that have no basis in reasonable principles that persons could impose on one another as basic standards governing conflicting claims. Mill's harm principle can be regarded as giving a reasonable expression to these demands.[27]

Liberal Political Philosophy and Constitutional Law

I have so far discussed, as philosophy, two interpretations of treating persons as equals, as the basic demand of ethics in both legal and political philosophy. Of the two interpretations, contractualist equality seemed to me the more reasonable, but its appeal was that it gave an even more secure and plausible grounding to Mill's great argument for political liberalism than the utilitarianism that he mistakenly believed to be the basis for his views. But many features of Mill's pathbreaking arguments both in *On Liberty* and *The Subjection of Women* seemed to me of lasting importance, in particular the distinction between conventional and critical morality and the way in which a liberal critical morality arose from a protection of the dignity of persons against the unreasonable claims of conventional morality. Mill himself closely linked the liberalism of *On Liberty* with the feminism of *The Subjection of Women*, a connection I would later ground in a theory of moral slavery (explaining the unconstitutionality of extreme prejudices such as anti-Semitism, racism, sexism, and homophobia by the way they rest on unjust stereotypes that, in a vicious circularity, draw their appeal from the repression of the basic human rights of whole classes of persons).[28] It was on this basis that I would later argue that both sexism and homophobia rest on unjust gender stereotypes directed at suppressing any voice, whether of men or women, that reasonably challenged those stereotypes. But at this point in my thinking, my understanding of political liberalism centered on a view of the harm principle grounded in equal respect for persons, a principle that the criminalization of gay/lesbian sexuality clearly violated.

Within this framework I had come to believe and was now to argue at length that the legal treatment of consensual adult homosexuality egregiously violated basic human rights. But as I turned to research and writing on this issue, it seemed clear that not only was my argument an argument of moral philosophy directed to a more reasonable ethical view of homosexuality but that it also had and should have a larger political and legal resonance in constitutional democracies. Great Britain, a constitutional democracy, had appealed to a form of Mill's political liberalism when it decriminalized consensual adult homosexuality in 1967 at the urging, among others, of my teacher, the British legal philosopher H. L. A. Hart.[29] The United States was also a constitutional democracy, and it seemed plausible that the philosophical argument of basic human rights might have interpretive relevance in making arguments about how principles of American constitutional law should be understood and elaborated in contemporary circumstances. Indeed, whereas Mill's arguments had been addressed in Britain to a Parliament enjoying the powers of parliamentary supremacy, in the United States the argument seemed to be directed not only to political bodies but also to the judiciary enjoying powers of judicial review on the basis of a written constitution that protected basic human rights. But if the argument I wanted to make had a constitutional as well as an ethical grounding, why had the idea of basic constitutional rights in the United States not been connected to gay issues? Why had such arguments become even thinkable only quite recently? To answer this question, it seemed to me I had to connect liberal political theory to American constitutional history, which led to a growing interest in the history of resistance movements under democratic constitutionalism. This interest, combined with political philosophy, was crucially at the center of the constitutional arguments I was shortly to develop.

PART II
LAW

3

JUDICIAL REVIEW IN THE UNITED STATES AFTER WORLD WAR II: FREE SPEECH AND GAY RIGHTS AS A PROTEST MOVEMENT

How could ethical voice, now strengthened by a sense of truthful personal voice, connect to the larger political and constitutional culture of America in 1974 on an issue such as gay/lesbian rights? This was the question that preoccupied both my teaching and my writing as a young law professor.

Resisting Voice in History

While my background in moral and political philosophy would always be an important part of the way I thought about answering this question, it seemed important as well to bring this ethical voice (which, after all, I had achieved only after some long struggle) into some important relationship to the historical study of the struggle for ethical voice generally. My struggle for voice clearly was made possible by certain important historical developments (notably, the post–World War II civil rights movements in the United States), which suggested to me, as a working hypothesis, that my own struggle for ethical voice might be part of a much larger struggle for such voice that might be fruitfully connected to the interpretive enterprise of democratic constitutionalism in general and American constitutionalism in particular. The very fact that I now enjoyed a freedom to think, speak, and write about the evils of homophobia was made possible by a development in American constitutional principles of free speech that was historically (in the United States) remarkable.

My growing interests in history were motivated by two kinds of questions, which arose as subquestions in the larger question of how to connect my ethical voice of resistance to constitutional law. The first subquestion was one of explanation: Why was the discourse of gay rights so comparatively undeveloped in the United States? If its ethical foundations were as secure

27

as I had come to believe, why was there such a gap between critical ethical thinking and the conventional homophobic sexual morality that dominated American law and culture? The answer, I suspected, had to be sought in history, namely, as we shall shortly see, a history of how and why constitutional principles of free speech had only been extended to gay/lesbian protesting speech after World War II. My second subquestion was: What could the discourse of gay/lesbian rights learn from the comparable struggles for constitutional recognition of basic human rights of religious minorities, African Americans, and women? This question required an investigation of history to explain the gap between critical ethical thinking and conventional morality. It also suggested that historical investigation, conducted in a certain normative spirit informed by moral and political philosophy, might not just explain matters otherwise inexplicable but might itself be a way of discovering and understanding the nature and weight of the basic human rights that American constitutional democracy was intended to protect.

It was this historical method that I pursued in four books: *Toleration and the Constitution,*[1] *Foundations of American Constitutionalism,*[2] *Conscience and the Constitution: History, Theory, and Law of the Reconstruction Amendments,*[3] and *Women, Gays, and the Constitution: The Grounds for Feminism and Gay Rights in Culture and Law.*[4] What I discovered was the central role in American constitutionalism, both at its founding and in its historical development, of basic human rights such as conscience and speech that, in principle, extend respect for rights of free ethical voice to all persons, and that basic dehumanizing constitutional evils (such as extreme religious intolerance, slavery, racism, sexism, and homophobia), which I call moral slavery, could most reasonably be understood in terms of the unjust repression of the dissenting voices of those who would most reasonably protest such dehumanization. My research increasingly focused on the role protest movements had crucially played in the development of American constitutional doctrines and institutions, including the abolitionist movement leading to the Civil War and the Reconstruction Amendments and the later struggles (including the civil rights, antiwar, and feminist movements) over the interpretation of the Constitution, including the meaning of the great normative clauses of the Reconstruction Amendments. My working hypothesis had been that these protest movements, which had crucially shaped the development of American constitutionalism, could clarify the role that a movement of gay/lesbian protest might reasonably play in contemporary American constitutional recognition of the basic human rights of gays and lesbians. What I discovered through the historical method I pursued was that all such protest movements (including the gay/lesbian movement) could reasonably be understood not as unconnected eruptions of dissent but as grounded in the basic human rights that were owed all persons, as persons, under American constitutionalism, and that the grounds of their protests also appealed to the same principles of equal protection.

Basic human rights are, in their normative nature, owed universally to all persons. Accordingly, the interpretation of constitutional guarantees grounded in the protection of such basic human rights can be legitimate only when pursued in terms of arguments of principle that extend the protection of such rights universally to all persons. This argument plausibly explained and justified the role of judicial review under American constitutionalism (the power of judicial review was grounded in the protection of such arguments of principle), including why such constitutional interpretation was legitimate only when conducted in terms of arguments of principle. Such interpretation properly used historical argument in its discussion and evaluation of precedent when such argument contextualized and construed precedents in terms of whether and how they could be understood in terms of constitutional principles protecting basic human rights.

Understanding the role of free ethical voice in constitutional history and development offered a normatively powerful, historically validated model for the principles to which gay/lesbian resisting voice appealed, as a ground both for such voice and for the substantive constitutional claims the voice might reasonably make. If ethical voice had historically, after much struggle (including innumerable reactionary reverses), spoken and been heard in ways that more fairly extended basic constitutional rights, on terms of principle, to all persons, the ethical voice of gay/lesbian resistance might speak and be heard (subject to the same reactionary reverses) in the same way. A normatively guided appeal to history had shown me a way to find a place for gay/lesbian voices among the other voices that had challenged and transformed the understanding of American constitutional principles. There was not only an ethical case for gay/lesbian rights, grounded in moral and political philosophy, but a constitutional case, grounded in the constitutional principles of basic human rights owed to all Americans.

I draw on this analysis in this chapter and those that follow. I begin by addressing my first subquestion: Why do arguments for gay/lesbian rights come so late in the United States? and then turn to the forms such arguments took once they were allowed free play. I turn in later chapters to fuller discussion of how making the case for gay/lesbian rights drew upon the constitutional successes of other protest movements after World War II.

Why So Late?

My initial puzzle was why was there such a yawning gap between what moral philosophy and personal experience told me about gay sexuality and the homophobic assumptions of the dominant American culture. What I was later to discover, on the basis of my own historical researches into other protest movements, was that there had been the same yawning gap in the antebellum period between what the best ethical thought had come to believe in condemning American cultural racism and sexism and the dominant assumptions of that period, which were deeply racist and sexist. For example, dominant abolitionist thought, reflected in Abraham Lincoln's speeches and writings, morally condemned and urged the abolition of slavery, but such thought was notably racist, resisting the idea, for example, that people of color could and should live as equal citizens in the United States. Only a very small minority of radical abolitionists notably criticized both American cultural racism and sexism, views that were eventually to guide authoritative judicial interpretations of the meaning of the Reconstruction Amendments in the twentieth century after World War II.[5]

But once it became clear to me how far American constitutional law had come in recognizing the claims to human rights of people of color and women, I wondered why the rights of gays and lesbians were still so largely unrecognized in the United States in contrast to other nations, such as Great Britain.

There was certainly a time when gay Europeans looked to the United States as a beacon in the recognition of their rights, notably in the response of late nineteenth-century Europeans such as Oscar Wilde, Edward Carpenter, and John Addington Symonds to the poetry and prose of the American writer Walt Whitman. Both Wilde and Carpenter made what can only be called pilgrimages to visit Whitman, a man they regarded as a prophet of gay rights in a larger ethical conception of democracy. Whitman, however, wrote his great poem, *Leaves of Grass,* before the Civil War, a period in many ways remarkable for its openness to radical ideas and ways of life.[6] After the Civil War American openness narrowed sharply, as shown by the aggressive obscenity prosecutions not only against publication of Whitman's works but against Margaret Sanger's and Emma Goldman's early twentieth-century arguments for legal recognition of a right to contraception, among women's other human rights. Any serious argument for gay rights in the United States during the period at least up to World War II would have met with the same type of obscenity prosecution.[7] To the extent that some American cities, such as New York, were famous as congenial places for living a gay life, that life took place underground and did not raise its head or speak in a voice that publicly demanded legal recognition of basic rights on fair terms.[8]

In contrast, although Oscar Wilde was famously criminally prosecuted and convicted in Britain in 1898 for having gay sex, serious arguments for recognition of gay rights were made and published in Europe, notably the various books of Edward Carpenter in Britain and Magnus Hirschfeld in Weimar Germany.[9] The situation for gays and lesbians was by no means idyllic; in Britain, for example, it was very much a matter of public intolerance and private excess, at least among the upper classes.[10] It was no accident but practical good sense that led some of America's most creative writers, including the lesbian Gertrude Stein and the gay black novelist James Baldwin, to find their voices as American writers largely living in Europe. One could live a gay or lesbian life in America, but not *as* a gay or lesbian, let alone someone writing as a gay or lesbian (either in one's forms or one's subject matter) in a way arising from one's life and experience. Life for gays and lesbians was much freer and more tolerated in Europe, with the devastating exception of Nazi persecutions that, though largely directed against Jews, included gays as well. In the wake of World War II, despite massive police repression in Great Britain during the 1950s[11] and the post–World War II German government's denial to gays of any compensation for their incarceration in concentration camps and retention of "the antihomosexual legislation—the infamous section of the German Penal Code—under which the Nazis had originally incarcerated the men,"[12] European tolerance of gays eventually reasserted itself, and the development of constitutional institutions throughout Europe was eventually responsive to claims for recognition of their rights in ways summarized later.

It was only well after World War II that American constitutional institutions became more responsive even to hearing arguments for gay rights. After World War II the American judiciary, under the notable leadership of the Supreme Court of the United States, not only vindicated arguments for the unconstitutionality of state-sponsored racial apartheid, including antimiscegenation laws but, correlatively, expanded the protection of American constitutional principles of free speech to include not only arguments of the civil rights movement of Martin Luther King but other arguments and claimants as well.[13]

For gays and lesbians, much the most important such development was the Supreme Court's narrowing of what could count as obscene speech, which, as unprotected speech, was not subjected to close scrutiny under oth-

erwise applicable principles of free speech.[14] This narrowing of the definition of obscenity effectively limited prosecutions to hard-core pornographic
depictions of certain sorts, thus pushing anything else into the domain of
free-speech protection. That remainder included all of the speech protesting
conventionally repressive laws on sexuality and gender that had previously
been repressed, as obscene because unnatural. Such repression had been
aggressively directed against feminists, such as Sanger and Goldman, who
extended arguments for women's rights beyond rights of suffrage to include
rights to use contraceptives and much else.[15] It is no accident that serious
constitutional substantive privacy claims to rights to contraception and abortion were made possible by a broadening of free-speech protection to advocacy of such claims, previously subject to prosecution as obscene.

The most liberating consequence of the narrowing of obscenity law was
its empowering of public arguments for gay rights. Sanger had at least been
able to publish books calling for liberalization of contraception laws, even
prior to World War II,[16] but gays had been able to publish nothing because
any such advocacy was supposed so obscene as to be properly censored without implicating American principles of free speech. Now, for the first time in
the history of the United States, arguments for gay rights could be made
without censorship by the state, and this new freedom, in the wake of the
successes of the feminist movement with contraception and abortion,
undoubtedly energized gay voices arguing for a comparable recognition of
their rights. The movement for gay rights in the United States thus started,
in comparison to Europe, quite late.

The Emergence of Arguments for Gay Rights

The experience of World War II was an important catalyst both in advancing
the public mind of America toward recognizing stronger antiracist principles
and in unsettling gender roles (women entering the job market) as a preliminary to second-wave feminism. Many gay and lesbian Americans in military
service away from their homes, and in the context of serving with wider ranges
of persons of the same gender and sexual preference, experienced transformative opportunities for a new dissenting practice of gay life, including protests
on grounds of justice about the treatment of homosexuals in the military.[17]

In 1951 Donald Webster Cory argued in *The Homosexual in America*
that there were convincing analogies between such protests on behalf of
homosexuals and the claims of civil rights of other minority groups (blacks

and Jews).[18] Although Cory noted some other differences (the involuntary character of sexual preference,[19] lack of an associated philosophy of life,[20] not being rooted in the family[21]), he pointed to the crucial difference that "separates the homosexual minority from all others, and that is its lack of recognition, its lack of respectability in the eyes of the public. . . . As a minority, we homosexuals are therefore caught in a particularly vicious circle. . . . Until the world is able to accept us on an equal basis as human beings entitled to the full rights of life, we are unlikely to have any great numbers willing to become martyrs by carrying the burden of the cross. But until we are willing to speak out openly and frankly in defense of our activities, we are unlikely to find the attitudes of the world undergoing any significant change."[22]

Cory (a pseudonym[23]) thus identified an unjust culture that immunized itself from criticism of the vicious circularity of its degrading stereotypes[24] (drawing an express analogy to Du Bois on race[25]). American homosexuals needed (Cory argued) cultural heroes who would break the silence,[26] along the lines of a Carpenter[27] or an even more forthright Whitman.[28] They also simply needed a public culture in which they could find themselves represented as persons, one that fairly explored relevant history (for example, the Amerindians[29]), wrote truer fictional narratives (citing Gore Vidal[30]), and offered better speculative models for the proper place of homosexuality in nature and culture (citing Gide's *Corydon*[31]).

Against the background of the greater judicial protection of freedom of speech (including, as earlier noted, the constitutional narrowing of antiobscenity laws), some homosexual Americans were ready as early as 1951 to organize politically for gay rights. In that year the founding of the Mattachine Society in Los Angeles marked the beginning of what would grow into a nationwide effort. Henry Hay, an ex-communist, brought his organizational skills to bear on the new organization[32] and sought as well to develop an appropriate theory of the movement as a dissenting cultural minority. Importantly, Hay explicitly built upon Edward Carpenter's earlier work on the Amerindian homosexual role.[33] Other groups, including separatist lesbian organizations, would shortly follow.[34] By the 1990s there would be a wide range of such groups, including some specifically concerned with gay issues relating to the AIDS health crisis.[35]

Neither the antiracist civil rights movement nor second-wave feminism was initially hospitable to the claims made by such groups. Women in the civil rights movement had raised troubling questions about its sexism that were among the motivating sources of second-wave feminism. "The Civil Rights Movement was even more hostile to homosexuals than the wider society,"[36] as shown in its marginalization and stigmatization of two of its gay black leaders, Bayard Rustin and James Baldwin.[37] It is therefore not surprising that James Baldwin should have been subject to homophobic attacks from heterosexual male black leaders.[38] Betty Friedan notoriously stereotyped gay men in *The Feminine Mystique*;[39] as a leader of the National Organization for Women (NOW), she warned against the "lavendar menace"[40] and failed to support Kate Millett when her lesbianism was publicized.[41] Views, of course, later changed in response to growing challenges, on grounds of rights-based principle, by increasingly vocal gay and lesbian activists and their allies in the antiracist and antisexist movements.[42]

If the case for gay rights was to be understood and acknowledged, it would have to be made by gay people in their own voice and on their own terms, originating claims to their basic human rights to conscience, speech, intimate life, and work against the dominant moral orthodoxy that dehumanized, degraded, and marginalized them. By 1971, when Dennis Altman published his *Homosexual Oppression and Liberation* after the defining moment of the Stonewall resistance in 1969,[43] the central rights-based point was construed as a search for identity,[44] and analogies were drawn to the comparable identity-transformative struggles of women[45] (including consciousness raising[46]) and blacks.[47] Such a rights-based search required skepticism about the unjustly self-fulfilling stereotypes so fundamental to homophobia as well as racism.[48] For historical models of dissent, we should look to Allen Ginsberg's retelling in contemporary terms of Whitman's defense of homosexual love.[49] By 1982, Altman would be struck, following Susan Sontag, by analogies (first suggested by Proust[50]) between developments of gay and Jewish identity grounded in similar styles of critical moral independence[51] against comparable sectarian sexual mythologies (analogies to be pursued later).[52] The rights-based struggle for gay identity had forged a new kind of community and culture in which that identity could find personal and ethical meaning[53] (including writers such as Jean Genet, who wrote, unlike Proust and Gide, conspicuously as a gay man[54] and the development of serious work in history and social theory bearing on alternative cultural constructions of the homosexual role[55]). Increasingly, such claims were interpreted, by me among others, as grounding arguments of basic constitutional rights in America, Canada, and Europe.[56]

One important and illuminating form of that personal and constitutional-political struggle was making the case for gay rights in terms of rights-based feminism, using the insights forged by the just struggles for personal and ethical identity of women in general and lesbian women in particular. The poet and essayist Adrienne Rich powerfully explored, citing the Grimke sisters, the centrality to women's emancipation of independent moral voice[57] and the ways in which a still largely mythologically idealized conception of maternal gender roles (both mother-son and mother-daughter) unjustly subordinated that voice to the claims and needs of male supremacy.[58] Rich thus brought a rights-based feminism much more critically to bear on the heart of the traditional conception of gender roles that, since Catharine Beecher, had warred upon rights-based feminism. Beecher's normative conception basically rationalized women's gender subordination in terms of a complementary idealization of their moral superiority as self-sacrificing mothers.[59] Rich carefully analyzed, on the basis of her own experience as a wife and mother, both the profound sexuality of mothering, as an interest many women legitimately have,[60] and the unjust moral degradation inflicted on women by imposing on them a sectarian orthodoxy of compulsory motherhood (including when, how, and on what terms they have children),[61] including the unjust burdens of an idealized duty of maternal self-sacrifice.[62] Such "unchosen, indentured motherhood"[63] (including the sectarian conceptions of women's duty that support it[64]) stultified the complex personal and ethical aims of women's free moral personality and unreasonably burdened mothers and children with an unbalanced system of mother-dominated child-rearing[65] (a theme notably explored by other feminist social theorists and psychoanalysts as well[66]). Only a critical rethinking of the justice of such maternal gender roles would ensure women sufficient scope for their rational and reasonable moral powers, in personal and public life, so that children need no longer "live under the burden of their mother's unlived lives."[67]

Rich has generalized her argument about the need critically to reexamine women's gender roles (so that motherhood is no longer an enforced identity for women[68]) in two ways. First, contemporary feminism must rediscover the roots of the American feminist criticism of gender roles in the antiracism struggle,[69] in ways I shall later explore. Second, a rights-based feminism calls for the legitimacy of lesbianism as an option for women, precisely because it so fundamentally challenges unjust gender roles.[70] I focus here on the second point.

If the rights-based feminist struggle is a quest for identity in terms of respect for basic human rights against an unjustly enforceable orthodoxy of gender roles, lesbianism must be regarded as a legitimate feminist option for women precisely because it both is based on such basic rights and represents so fundamental a criticism of the sectarian orthodoxy. For Rich, the rights include not only the right to intimate life but basic rights to moral independence central to the feminist struggle of all women. In particular, such rights encompass the right morally to identify one's personality with other women in what Rich called a "lesbian continuum"[71] and to live a "lesbian existence"[72] centering on such moral identifications, which may or may not include sexual relations or having and raising children.[73] The important feminist issue is to foster both the wider exercise of such rights and cultural criticism that assists all women in their rights-based struggle. Much of the unjust sectarian orthodoxy rests, Rich argued, on compulsory heterosexuality, the insistence that women, to be women, must form a sense of self based on attachments to and dependence upon the authority of men.[74] Lesbianism, as a legitimate—indeed, desirable—feminist experiment in living morally empowers all women along both the dimensions (guarantee of basic rights and skepticism about traditional gender roles) central to their liberation from unjust moral slavery.

Nothing in Rich's argument requires that it be limited to lesbians as opposed to gay men, though she herself regarded her perspective as a step beyond general advocacy of toleration.[75] The case for gay rights crucially depends, for both men and women, on both the ingredients of Rich's rights-based case: its insistence on the range of basic human rights at stake and its skepticism about the legitimacy of enforcing a sectarian theory of normative gender roles. If lesbians may exercise such rights in desirable moral identifications with other women, then gay men may comparably exercise such rights identifying with both gay men and lesbians, both of whom embody ways of life that are critical of compulsory heterosexuality.[76] Indeed, both lesbians and gay men may deepen their understanding of the case for rights-based feminism, providing a reasonable perspective on and challenges to possibly stale and even oppressive feminist orthodoxies (some of them uncritical remnants of suffrage feminism) that must be rethought and reevaluated.[77] Certainly, relationships of love between gay men and between lesbians directly challenge the conception, perhaps central to traditional gender hierarchy and its conception of masculine and feminine identity, that love in its intimate nature cannot be between equals and that relationships between men or between women must be fraught with competition and hostility.[78] Very much to the contrary, such relationships embody a normative model for intimate life that apparently more fully develops features of egalitarian sharing in intimate life that are more often the theory than the practice of heterosexual relations.[79] And gay men, precisely because they do not sexualize women but nonetheless often have and form profound moral identifications with them, may contribute something unique to rights-based feminism: moral relationships with women not based on and therefore not distorted by sexual objectification.[80] It is controversial whether and how sexual desire embodies sexual objectification and whether, if so, it is necessarily a bad thing.[81] But it is certainly a good thing for rights-based feminism to legitimate relationships not only between women but between men and between men and women, all of which, in different ways, challenge the rights-denying evils of compulsory heterosexuality as the exclusive normative model for moral relationships between men and women. Rights-based feminism might, on such grounds, redefine its aims in terms of claims for the basic human rights of all persons (whether men or women) against all forms of politically enforced gender stereotypes that have unjustly usurped moral sovereignty over framing the meaning of gender in one's personal and ethical life. In fact, as we shall later see, it is precisely the unjust role of gender stereotypes in sexism, now constitutionally condemned in the United States, that plausibly explains why homophobia is and should be constitutionally condemned.

4

JUDICIAL REVIEW IN THE UNITED STATES AFTER WORLD WAR II: RELIGION, RACE, AND GENDER

Arguments for gay rights arose in the context not only of much more aggressive judicial protection of free speech but of growing constitutional concern for forms of invidious discrimination against religious minorities, persons of color, and women. These developments in constitutional analysis arose in response to protest movements, which can be traced back to the protests of the radical abolitionists in the antebellum period. Close historical study of these protest movements, including the common principles to which they appeal, illuminates, in ways I shall show in later chapters, how a gay/lesbian resisting voice reasonably drew on these principles to make the case for its constitutional claims. I begin with the forms of analysis that the radical abolitionists developed and then turn to their elaboration in the period after World War II.

Antebellum Radical Abolitionist Protest

When serious moral argument arose to question slavery, it emerged not from mainstream established churches but from usually quite heterodox religionists (for example, William Lloyd Garrison and Quakers) who not only questioned most views of the dominant established Christian churches but were famously antihierarchical in their conception of authority (sometimes allowing women to be ministers, a notable feature of the movements of American Quakers against slavery as well as sexism).[1] Their arguments brought a distinctive liberal political theory to bear on American politics, one that condemned American slavery, racism, and sexism. Its liberal political theory included both a robust principle of free conscience and speech and a principle that condemned the political force of irrational prejudice (such as extreme religious intolerance and racism). The two principles are related in the following way.

The principle of free conscience and speech rests on the argument for universal toleration that had earlier been stated, in variant forms, by Pierre Bayle and John Locke.[2] That principle forbade a dominant religion or group to unreasonably deprive other groups of their rights of conscience and speech. A prominent feature of the argument for toleration was its claim that religious persecution corrupted conscience itself. Such corruption, a kind of self-induced blindness to the evils one inflicts, is a consequence of the political enforcement of a conception of religious truth that immunizes itself from independent criticism in terms of reasonable standards of thought and deliberation. Paradoxically, the more the tradition becomes seriously vulnerable to independent reasonable criticism (indeed, increasingly in rational need of such criticism), the more it is likely to generate forms of political irrationalism (including scapegoating of outcast dissenters) in order to secure allegiance. The worst ravages of anti-Semitism illustrate this paradox of intolerance. Precisely when the dominant religious tradition gave rise to the most reasonable internal doubt (for example, about transubstantiation), these doubts were displaced from reasonable discussion and debate into blatant political irrationalism against one of the more conspicuous, vulnerable, and innocent groups of dissenters (centering on fantasies of ritual eating of human flesh that expressed the underlying worries about transubstantiation).[3]

The second liberal principle condemns the unjust force in politics of extreme religious intolerance such as anti-Semitism and any form of irrationalist prejudice that arises in the same way (because such irrationalist prejudices rationalize systematic violations of the first principle as well as other principles guaranteeing basic human rights). I call this pattern of structural injustice *moral slavery*, an analysis of how and why constitutional principles have progressively condemned a politics actuated not only by anti-Semitism but by ethnic prejudice (including racism), sexism, and, as I argue later, homophobia.[4] In all these cases, whole classes of persons have been traditionally excluded from the equal respect due to them through basic human rights such as conscience, speech, intimate life, and work on the grounds of dehumanizing stereotypes; yet the force of these stereotypes derived, in a viciously unjust circularity, from the tradition of subordination that refused to accord persons respect for their basic human rights. The claim of an analogy among such prejudices (for example, racism and sexism) is in the similar method of structural injustice inflicted in both cases, namely, "that others have controlled the power to define one's existence."[5] I call this injustice moral slavery because it culturally dehumanizes a category of persons (as nonbearers of human rights) in order to rationalize their servile status and roles. For example, the long history of Christian Europe's restrictions on Jews was rationalized by Augustine, among others, in the quite explicit terms of slavery: "The Jew is the slave of the Christian."[6]

It is an important feature of the struggle against any one form of moral slavery (for example, racism) that it tends, on grounds of principle, to link its protest to related forms of such slavery (for example, sexism), a point central to Garrison's politics of resistance, which condemned both racism and sexism as resting on a common structural injustice. For example, the American struggle against racism culminated not only in the constitutional condemnation of segregated education[7] but in antimiscegenation laws as well.[8] Antimiscegenation laws had come to bear this interpretation as a consequence of the Supreme Court's endorsement of the view of the unjust cultural construction of racism first suggested by Garrison's follower Lydia Maria Child in 1833[9] and importantly elaborated by Ida Wells-Barnett in 1892.[10] Wells-Barnett analyzed Southern racism after emancipation in these terms sustained by antimiscegenation laws and related practices, including lynching.[11] The point of such laws and practices was to condemn not only all interracial marriages (the focus of Child's analysis) but the legitimacy of all sexual relations (marital and otherwise) between white women and black men; illicit relations between white men and black women were, in contrast, if not legal, certainly socially acceptable, even normative. The asymmetry was rationalized in terms of gender stereotypes: a sectarian sexual and romantic idealized mythology of asexual white women and a corresponding devaluation (indeed, dehumanization) of black women and men as sexually animalistic. Illicit sexual relations of white men with black women were consistent with this political epistemology and thus were tolerable. Both licit and illicit consensual relations of black men with white women were not, and thus were ideologically transformed into violent rapes requiring lynching. The thought that could not be spoken, for it flouted the idealizing pedestal on which white women were placed, was that white women had sexual desires at all, let alone sexual desires for black men.

Both Harriet Jacobs (supported by Child as her editor) and Ida Wells-Barnett analyzed this injustice from the perspective of black women who had experienced its indignities at first hand. For example, the slave narrative of Harriet Jacobs, *Incidents in the Life of a Slave Girl*,[12] told the story, under the pseudonym Linda Brent, of the indignities she suffered under slavery, her moral revolt against them (leading to her hiding for seven years in a small garret), and her eventual escape north to freedom. Jacobs importantly examined the role of slave-owning women from the perspective of the slave. Her portrait of her slave owner's wife (Mrs. Flint) explored "her constant suspicion and malevolence."[13] Herself pridefully virtuous on her idealized pedestal of Southern womanhood, Mrs. Flint denied any virtue to a woman slave; indeed, "it is deemed a crime in her to wish to be virtuous."[14] The basis of marriage in a slaveholding family was hypocrisy and denial, treating white women contemptuously as pets on a very tight leash: "The secrets of slavery are concealed like those of the Inquisition."[15] To Jacobs's certain knowledge, Dr. Flint was "the father of eleven slaves,"[16] but the reality was known and not known; as Mrs. Chesnut confided to her diary: "Every lady tells you who is the father of all the Mulatto children in every body's household, but those in her own, she seems to think drop from the clouds or pretends so to think."[17] White slaveholding women themselves sustained this mythology by falsely idealizing their virtue and denigrating that of slaves, whose unjust situation, in Jacobs's view, made such virtue unreasonably difficult. Thus, Jacobs laid the foundation for later antiracist and antisexist analysis of the role that unjust gender stereotypes, based on abridgment of basic human rights, played in the dehumanization not only of black but of white women as well. It is resistance to such gender stereotypes that often makes possible resistance to forms of structural injustice.

The Quakers played a prominent role in destabilizing slavery as well as racism and sexism because their conception of religious and moral authority empowered ethical voices usually repressed and silenced by such patterns of injustice to speak in their own voices against the terms of the often interlinked ethnic and gender stereotypes that supported slavery as well as racism and sexism. Similarly, the democratic religion of Martin Luther King, Jr., rooted in the personal religion of his Baptist mother, found a new voice to protest injustice through nonviolence, a voice that empowered him and the movement he led to find and speak in their own voice against the unjust stereotypes that afflicted them and the injustices such stereotypes rationalized.[18] Such nonhierarchical forms of religious and moral authority have the role they do in challenging structural injustice because they empower the protesting voice that such injustice usually represses.

As the result of a long history of protest movements against such forms of structural injustice, basic principles of constitutional law, in the United States and elsewhere, now condemn, as I shall shortly elaborate, not only the use of racial and ethnic stereotypes to support laws but gender stereotypes as well. Such racism and sexism depend on a common structural injustice: rationalizing abridging the basic rights of whole classes of persons on the basis of stereotypes resting on such abridgment. It is through this mechanism of viciously circular rationalizations that cultural injustice is not recognized as what it is but is supposed to reflect on nature. The injustice of gender discrimination thus rests on gender stereotypes arising from the repression of any voice that would contest them, naturalizing the injustice as a matter of nature, not culture. Such unjust gender stereotypes express both unjust idealization (the woman on the pedestal) and denigration (any woman not on the pedestal) to remake reality in their image. Both such idealizations and denigrations invoke mythological images of sexuality (a good woman having no sexuality, a bad woman being sexual). Such mythology often rests on the repression of women's real sexual voice.

Constitutional Struggle, the Civil Rights Movement, and Abolitionist Antiracism

The mission of the Reconstruction Amendments was and should have been the inclusion, on terms of equal rights, of black Americans in the American political community now understood to be a moral community of free and equal citizens, not two nations divided by a culturally constructed chasm of intolerance and subjugation supported by law.[19] In 1896 in *Plessy v. Ferguson*,[20] the Supreme Court of the United States held state-sponsored racial discrimination to be consistent with the Equal Protection Clause of the Fourteenth Amendment, one of the more egregious examples of a grave interpretive mistake in the Court's checkered history. Similarly, in its earlier 1883 decision, *Pace v. Alabama*,[21] the Court had held that imposing stronger penalties for interracial, as opposed to intraracial, sexual relations was not racially discriminatory (since both white and black people were subject to the same penalty). The Supreme Court in both these opinions powerfully advanced the cultural construction of American racism. I begin with *Plessy* and the struggle leading to its overruling and then turn to *Pace* and its repudiation.

The interpretive issue in *Plessy* was whether there was a reasonable basis for the racial distinction that the state law used. The Court's decision can be plausibly explained, as Charles Lofgren has recently shown,[22] against the background of the dominant racist social science of the late nineteenth century.[23] The later development of this alleged science of natural race differences in moral capacity measured them in alleged physical differences (physically measured by brain capacity or cephalic indices);[24] these measures afforded a putatively scientific basis for making the allegedly reasonable judgment that the separation of races was justified. Segregation in transportation (the issue in *Plessy*) might thus discourage forms of social intercourse that would result in degenerative forms of miscegenation, and segregation in education would reflect race-linked differences in a capacity best dealt with in separate schools, as well as usefully discouraging social intercourse, etc.

The abolitionists had offered plausible objections to the scientific status of American ethnology, and similar objections were available at the time *Plessy* was decided in 1896. For example, Franz Boas had already published his early 1894 paper debunking the weight accorded race in the social sciences.[25] It is striking that the putative reasonable basis for *Plessy* was not, in fact, critically stated or discussed in the opinion but rather conclusorily assumed. Even in the circumstances of the state of the human sciences at the time of *Plessy*, the interpretive argument in the decision did not meet the standards of impartial public reason surely due all Americans. Americans had a right to expect more of their highest court than the conclusory acceptance without argument of controversial scientific judgments hostage to an entrenched political epistemology that protected the increasingly racist character of the American South. One justice (Justice John Harlan, a Southerner) powerfully made precisely this point in his dissent.

It is surely not without importance that Southern blacks during this period had been left by the federal government almost wholly at the mercies of Southern state governments; these governments had (in violation of the spirit of the Fifteenth Amendment) effectively disenfranchised them; certainly not afforded them adequate educational opportunity; and cast a blind eye on, when they did not actively support, the informal forms of terrorism (including lynching) used to intimidate blacks and prevent them from challenging their subjugated economic, social, and political position.[26] The Supreme Court, abandoning abolitionist ethical impartiality, supinely surrendered any semblance of morally independent critical testing in order to take instruction from bad and politically corrupt science to legitimate the further degradation of this already unconstitutionally victimized group. The political identity of the South, like its antebellum predecessor, immunized it from serious discussion of its greatest evil[27] and constituted its sense of political identity in racist subjugation. Consistent with the paradox of intolerance, such a failure of reason projectively fed on forms of political irrationalism (myth, factual distortion, deprivation of basic rights of conscience and free speech) based on the racist subjugation of its victims.

The consequences for the nation at large were felt not only in racist aspects of America's increasingly imperialist foreign policy but in the racist immigration restrictions on Asians and, after World War I, on Southern and Eastern Europeans.[28] If race and culture were in this period so unreasonably confused, it is not surprising that American intolerance, to the extent legitimated by betrayal of constitutional principles, should turn from blacks to non-Christian Asians or Catholic Latins or Jewish Slavs whose cultures appeared, to nativist American Protestant public opinion, inferior and (equating culture and race) therefore peopled by the racially inferior.

The long road to the overruling of *Plessy* by *Brown v. Board of Education*[29] in 1954 was the story of the critical testing and recasting of the assumptions that had made *Plessy* possible. The great change in these background assumptions was achieved through the mobilization of a constitutional movement of Americans, black and white, who kept alive the theory and practice of radical abolitionism during a period of resurgent national racism (culminating in patterns of lynching as well as the Atlanta race riots of 1906 and the Springfield, Illinois, riots of 1908) and finally founded the National Association for the Advancement of Colored People (NAACP) in 1910 to challenge such racism in radical abolitionist terms.[30] The ex-slave Frederick Douglass, who had been a central black abolitionist (and abolitionist feminist) in the antebellum period, played a central role in such antiracist resistance until his death (after attending a women's rights rally) in 1895,[31] and Ida Wells-Barnett similarly forged such resistance in the 1890s in her remarkable attack on Southern lynching and the racism it expressed and sustained. Anna Julia Cooper also defended a central role for black women in antiracist protest, "stepping from the pedestal of statue-like inactivity in the domestic shrine, and daring to think and move and speak,"[32] in her 1892 *A Voice from the South;* Cooper crucially grounded such rights-based protest in an elaboration of the argument for toleration.[33] Abolitionist antiracism (like abolitionist feminism) remained very much alive as a dissenting interpretive tradition during a deeply racist (and sexist) period of American history.

That tradition was powerfully deepened and energized by the scholarship and activism of W. E. B. Du Bois. His historical studies challenged the dominant, often racist orthodoxy of the age,[34] and his 1903 *The Souls of Black Folk*[35] offered a pathbreaking interpretive study of African American culture and the struggle for self-consciousness under circumstances of racial oppression[36]—"a world which yields him no true self-consciousness, but . . . this double-consciousness, this sense of always looking at one's self through the eyes of others, of measuring one's soul by the tape of a world that looks on in amused contempt and pity. One ever feels his two-ness,—an American, a Negro; two souls, two thoughts, two unreconciled strivings; two warring ideals in one dark body."[37] Du Bois also played a central activist role as director of publicity and research of the NAACP, editing *The Crisis* (Wells-Barnett attended the NAACP's biracial founding but withdrew in pique when her name was not included on a Committee of Forty on permanent organization).[38]

The founders of the NAACP believed that existing tactics for black advancement neglected issues of civil and political rights and reflected too moderate a position on economic issues. In addition to conducting lobbying efforts and publicity campaigns, the NAACP soon established a legal redress committee, in which figures like Charles Houston and Thurgood Marshall played central roles in the ultimately successful struggle to repudiate *Plessy* and *Pace*.[39] Such activism was sustained by and also fostered a growing civil rights movement that drew importantly upon both the black churches and colleges and the networks of women's groups.[40] Black Americans in the South and elsewhere asserted and were finally accorded some measure of national protection by the Supreme Court (reversing early decisions to the contrary)[41] in the exercise of their First Amendment rights of protest, criticism, and advocacy.[42] Martin Luther King, Jr., a towering figure in the later development of the civil rights movement to support and expand the abolitionist antiracist principle after *Plessy* was overruled,[43] brilliantly used and elaborated the right of conscience and free speech to protest American racism very much in the spirit of Garrisonian nonviolence; he thus appealed, as he did in his classic "Letter from Birmingham City Jail,"[44] for "nonviolent direct action . . . to create such a [moral] crisis and establish such creative tension that a community that has constantly refused to negotiate is forced to confront the issue."[45] Like Garrisonian radical abolitionists in the antebellum period, King demanded his basic human rights of conscience and speech to engage in reasonable public discourse about basic issues of justice, including criticism of the racist orthodoxy "that degrades human personality" and is therefore "unjust."[46] Now, however, the Supreme Court, in light of the Reconstruction Amendments, extended to the NAACP and King federal constitutional protection of basic free-speech rights of public voice and criticism. The consequences were those to be expected by the liberation, on fair terms, of culture-creating moral powers.[47] The racist orthodoxy of *Plessy*, no longer the enforceable measure of acceptable public discourse, was subjected to reasonable debate and criticism in the free exercise of their human rights by the groups previously subjugated. The interpretive foundations of *Plessy* could not withstand such reasonable criticism.

The pivotal figure in this criticism was a German Jew and immigrant to the United States, Franz Boas, who fundamentally criticized the racial explanations characteristic of both European and American physical anthropology in the late nineteenth century.[48] Boas argued that comparative anthropological study did not sustain the explanatory weight placed on race in the human sciences. In fact, there was more significant variability within races than there was between races.[49] Indeed, many of the human features, supposed to be unchangeably physical (such as the cephalic index), were responsive to cultural change; Boas had shown that the physical traits of recent immigrants to the United States had changed in response to acculturation.[50]

The crucial factor, heretofore missing from the human sciences, was culture; Boas made this point to Du Bois on a visit to Atlanta University that "had an impact of lasting importance"[51] on Du Bois's interest in black culture and its sources. Cultural formation and transmission could not be understood in terms of the reductive physical models that had heretofore dominated scientific and popular thinking. In particular, Lamarckian explanation—having been discredited by Mendelian genetics in favor of random genetic mutation—was not the modality of cultural transmission, which was not physical at all but irreducibly cultural. One generation born into a progressive culture could take no more credit for an accident of birth than a generation could be reasonably blamed for birth into a less progressive culture. In fact, cultures advance often through accident and good luck and through cultural diffusion of technologies from other cultures. Such diffusion has been an important fact in the history of all human cultures at some point in their histories. No people has been through all points in its history the vehicle of the cultural progress of humankind, nor can any people reasonably suppose itself the unique vehicle of all such progress in the future.[52]

Boas's general contributions to the human sciences were powerfully elaborated in the area of race by his students Otto Klineberg[53] and Ruth Benedict.[54] They argued that the explanatory role of race in the human sciences was, if anything, even less important than the judicious Boas might have been willing to grant[55] (Boas's student, Margaret Mead, suggested that the same might be true to some significant extent of gender[56]).

The most important study of the American race problem was not by an American but by the Swedish social scientist Gunnar Myrdal. His monumental *An American Dilemma*[57] brought the new approach to culture powerfully to bear on the plight of American blacks, who, from the perspective of the human sciences, were increasingly well understood as victims of a historically entrenched cultural construction of racism. In effect, the advances in morally independent critical standards of thought and analysis in the human sciences had enabled social scientists to make the same sort of argument that abolitionist theorists of race, such as Lydia Maria Child, had made earlier on largely ethical grounds.

This point of public reason was much highlighted in the American public mind by the comparable kind of racism that had flourished in Europe in the same period in the form of modern anti-Semitism. During this period both American racism and European anti-Semitism evolved into particularly virulent political pathologies under the impact of the respective emancipations of American blacks from slavery and European Jews from various civil disabilities keyed to their religious background.[58] In both cases, the respective emancipations were not carried through by consistent enforcement of guarantees of basic rights (in the United States, in spite of clear constitutional guarantees to that effect).

The characteristic nineteenth-century struggles for national identity led, in consequence, to rather stark examples of the paradox of intolerance in which the exclusion of race-defined cultural minorities from the political community of equal rights became itself the irrationalist basis of national unity. Strikingly similar racist theorists evolved in Europe to sustain anti-Semitism (Houston Chamberlain[59]) and in America to sustain racism against the supposedly non-Aryan (Madison Grant[60]). American constitutional institutions were, as a consequence, misinterpreted but nonetheless increasingly were the vehicle of organized black protest and dissent,[61] including the forms of protest I have already mentioned. Certainly American institutions did not collapse on the scale of the German declension into atavistic totalitarianism and the genocide of six million European Jews.[62] In both cases, however, the underlying irrationalist racist dynamic was strikingly similar: emancipation, inadequate protection of basic rights, a devastating and humiliating defeat that took the excluded minority as an irrationalist scapegoat.[63]

Boas's important criticism of the role of race in the human sciences had, of course, been motivated as much by his own experience of European anti-Semitism as by American racism; Boas forged his own self-respecting identity as a Jew against anti-Semitism as much as Frederick Douglass or Du Bois defined theirs as African Americans against American racism. The subsequent elaboration of his arguments by Klineberg, Benedict, and Myrdal had further raised the standards of public reason to expose both the intellectual and ethical fallacies of racism in America and Europe. In light of such criticism, the constitutional attack in the United States on the analytic foundations of *Plessy* began well before World War II in the litigation strategy undertaken by the NAACP to question and subvert the racist principle of "separate but equal" in the area of public segregated education.[64]

World War II itself, not unlike the Civil War, played an important role in stimulating the development of much more enlightened public attitudes on racial questions than had prevailed before. Not only did the distinguished military service of African Americans in both wars call for recognition of full citizenship, but the Allied victory in World War II raised questions about the state of American constitutionalism prior to the war not unlike those raised by the Reconstruction Amendments about antebellum American constitutionalism. The United States successfully fought that war in Europe against a nation that, like the American South in the Civil War, defined its world historic mission in self-consciously racist terms. The political ravages of such racism—both in the unspeakable moral horrors of the Holocaust of six million innocent European Jews and in the brutalities World War II inflicted on so many others—naturally called for a moral interpretation of that war, again like the Civil War, in terms of the defense of the political culture of universal human rights against its racist antagonists. In the wake of World War II and its central role in the Allied victory and in European reconstruction, the United States took up a central position on the world stage as an advocate of universal human rights. America was thus naturally pressed critically to examine not only at home but abroad practices such as state-sponsored racial segregation in light of the best interpretation of American ideals of human rights in contemporary circumstances.[65]

World War II played, as it were, a role in American moral and political thought of a kind of third American Revolution (the Civil War being the second[66]). American ideals of revolutionary constitutionalism were tested against the aggression of a nation, Nazi Germany, that attacked everything the American constitutional tradition valued in the idea and constitutional institutions of respect for universal human rights.[67] The self-conscious American defense of human rights against the totalitarian ambitions of Nazi Germany required Americans, after the war, to ask if their own constitutionalism was adequate to their ambitions.

In fact, the painful truth was what Boas and others had long argued, namely, that America had betrayed the revolutionary constitutionalism of its Reconstruction Amendments in ways and with consequences strikingly similar to the ways in which Germany had betrayed the promise of universal emancipation. Americans did not, however, have to reconstruct their constitutionalism in order to do justice to this sense of grievous mistake. Unlike the question that faced the nation in the wake of the Civil War, the problem was not one of a basic flaw in the very design of American constitutionalism. Rather, the issue was a corrigible interpretive mistake. The judiciary had failed to understand and give effect to the moral ambitions fundamental to the Reconstruction Amendments, namely, that the American political community should be a moral community committed to abstract values of human rights available on fair terms of public reason to all persons, not a community based on race.

The focus for such testing of American interpretive practice was, naturally, *Plessy v. Ferguson,* in which the Supreme Court had accepted the exclusion of black Americans from the American community of equal rights. But the intellectual and ethical foundations of *Plessy,* to the extent it had ever had such foundations, had collapsed under the weight of the criticism I have already discussed at some length. The idea of natural race differences had been thoroughly discredited as the product of a long American history of the unjust cultural construction of racism in precisely the same way that European anti-Semitism had been discredited. The Supreme Court, which in 1896 in *Plessy* could rationalize its decision as merely following nature or history, faced in the early 1950s a wholly different space for moral choice that Boasian cultural studies had opened up.

Thurgood Marshall in his argument to the Supreme Court for the NAACP morally dramatized this choice in terms of the blue-eyed innocent African American children indistinguishable in all reasonable respects from other children playing with them and living near them except for the role the Supreme Court would play in legitimating a constructed difference (segregated education) that enforced an irrationalist prejudice with a long history of unjust subjugation behind it.[68] The Supreme Court was compelled to face, on behalf of American culture more generally, a stark moral choice either to give effect to a culture of dehumanization or to refuse any longer to be complicitous with such rights-denying evil. Moral responsibility for one's complicity with evil could not be evaded. In effect, Marshall, as an African American, stood before the Court in the full voice of his moral personality as a free person and asked the Court either to accept its responsibility for degrading him as subhuman or to refuse any longer to degrade any person. State-sponsored racial segregation, once uncritically accepted as a reasonable expression of natural race differences, now was construed as an unjust construction of an irrationalist dehumanization that excluded citizens from their equal rights as members of the political community, and, as such, unconstitutional. In 1954 in *Brown v. Board of Education*,[69] the Supreme Court of the United States articulated this deliberative interpretive judgment for the nation by unanimously striking down state-sponsored racial segregation as a violation of the Equal Protection Clause of the Fourteenth Amendment.

In 1967 in *Loving v. Virginia*,[70] a similarly unanimous Supreme Court struck down as unconstitutional state antimiscegenation laws. Repeating, as it had in *Brown*, that the dominant interpretive judgments of the Reconstruction Congress could not be dispositive on the exercise by the judiciary of its independent interpretive responsibilities, the Court rejected the equal-application theory of *Pace v. Alabama* on the same grounds on which it had earlier rejected it in 1964 in a decision invalidating a state criminal statute prohibiting cohabitation by interracial married couples.[71] The Equal Protection Clause condemned all state-sponsored sources of invidious racial discrimination, and, the Court held, antimiscegenation laws were one such source. Indeed, the only basis for such laws was the constitutionally forbidden aim of white supremacy.

Antimiscegenation laws had come to bear this interpretation as a consequence of the Court's endorsement of the cultural theory of the rights-denying construction of racism first suggested by Lydia Maria Child in 1833 and importantly elaborated by Ida Wells-Barnett in 1892. Child had examined and condemned both American slavery and racism in light of the argument for toleration: basic human rights of the person were abridged on wholly inadequate sectarian grounds that Child, like other radical abolitionists, expressly analogized to religious persecution. Antimiscegenation laws violated the basic human right of intimate association on inadequate grounds, thus dehumanizing a whole class of persons as subhuman animals unworthy of the forms of equal respect accorded to rights-bearing persons. As we earlier saw, Ida Wells-Barnett, elaborating the role of the rights-denying sexual dehumanization of African Americans under slavery made clear earlier by Harriet Jacobs, analyzed Southern racism after emancipation as resting on a similar basis sustained, in part, by antimiscegenation laws.

The Feminist Movement and Constitutional Development

The struggle for recognition of a strong antiracist constitutional principle had implicit within it, as we have seen, a criticism of the racialized ideal of gender roles central to persistent patterns of American racism. The constitutional repudiation of antimiscegenation laws clearly reflected this criticism. Since the purpose of state-sponsored segregation was importantly to discourage even the possibility of such intimate relations, the unconstitutionality of segregation reflected this critical theme as well. Some of the most important exponents of this criticism had been black women, such as Harriet Jacobs and Ida Wells-Barnett, who spoke from within their own moral experience about the indignity this dehumanizing stereotype of black sexuality inflicted on them. The criticism was, in its nature, an assault upon the idealized conception of women increasingly central to suffrage feminism. For this reason, Ida Wells-Barnett was at loggerheads with a leading suffrage feminist advocate of this conception, Frances Willard.[72] Activist antiracist black women were for good reasons skeptical of a feminism rooted in such an ideology and would continue to be so for a long period.[73] Only a feminism itself skeptical of this ideology would have the promise of advancing both antiracist and antisexist principles in an acceptable way and thus engaging the moral convictions of black as well as white women.

Second-wave feminism arose on precisely such a basis. Betty Friedan's 1963 *The Feminine Mystique*[74] struck a responsive chord among American women, more of whom now worked outside the home than before,[75] when she critically addressed the idealized conception of gender roles and the force it had over women's lives.[76] Citing as precedent Elizabeth Cady Stanton's dissatisfaction with the demands of domesticity (leading to her role in the Seneca Falls Convention),[77] Friedan argued that American women in the post–World War II period experienced a comparable crisis of identity but over contemporary gender roles so impoverished that they "had no name for the problem troubling them."[78] Friedan spoke from her own personal experience of an advanced education that went unused in domestic life[79] and of the unjust epistemological power over women's consciousness and lives of the normative conception of gender roles that commentators invoked as the ground for pathologizing any feminist dissent.[80] A woman's problematic sense of herself, Friedan argued, was not to be dismissed or trivialized as merely psychologically personal and deviant, as perceived through the prism of this normative conception, when its political force was so demonstrably unjust. Otherwise, injustice would be the measure of the awakening sense of justice that alone might protest it. Friedan's criticisms of this normative conception, the feminine mystique, questioned not only its substance (making of femininity an end in itself,[81] or sex as women's exclusive career[82]) but its sectarian religious force,[83] which permitted no reasonable doubts to be raised[84] and fictionalized facts.[85] Indeed, using the very terms of the paradox of intolerance earlier noted, Friedan pointed to the polemical force of the ideology precisely when it was most reasonably open to doubt. She called this "the basic paradox of the feminine mystique: that it emerged to glorify women's role as housewife at the very moment when the barriers to her full participation in society were lowered, at the very moment when science and education and her own ingenuity made it possible for a woman to be both wife and mother and to take an active part in the world outside the home. The glorification of 'woman's role,' then, seems to be in proportion to society's reluctance to treat women as complete human beings; for the less real function that role has, the more it is decorated with meaningless details to conceal its emptiness."[86]

The general terms of the analysis are, of course, familiar from our earlier examination of the argument for toleration and its critical applications to American slavery and racism and, by the abolitionist feminists, to the subjection of women and sexism. What was so striking and original in Friedan's analysis was the way she plausibly applied it both to popular American culture and to the uncritical social scientists[87] who supported its cult of women's domesticity in the mid-twentieth century.[88] Friedan self-consciously saw herself quite rightly as in a similar position to leading advocates of abolitionist feminism such as Theodore Parker and Elizabeth Cady Stanton against the background of the way suffrage feminism had undercut their rights-based critique of American gender roles and thus reinforced women's moral slavery.[89] All the terms of the abolitionist feminist analysis of moral slavery were in place in Friedan's critique. The force of the sectarian ideology of gender roles rested on the abridgment of basic human rights to critical mind and speech,[90] associated rights to critical education,[91] fair terms for rights to intimate life,[92] and the right to creative work.[93] The result was the cultural dehumanization of women[94] in terms of an objectified sexuality[95] or biology.[96] Women's struggle was thus one for personal identity[97] on terms responsive to a morally independent basis to live a life from convictions of conscience, the voice within.[98]

Friedan importantly made reference early in her book[99] to Simone de Beauvoir's pathbreaking *The Second Sex*,[100] which had prominently explored analogies among anti-Semitism, racism, and sexism.[101] The terms of Friedan's analysis were drawn from a tradition, certainly familiar to her, that had recently applied all the terms of analysis used by her to the criticism of American racism; she acknowledged as much when she criticized the application of "separate but equal" to women's education (which had been struck down by the Supreme Court in 1954 as applied to the education of

African Americans) on the ground that such "sex-directed education segregated recent generations of able American women as surely as separate-but-
equal education segregated able American Negroes from the opportunity to
realize their full abilities in the mainstream of American life."[102] Friedan
used the analogy to address a constitutional culture on which "the black civil
rights movement had a very profound effect."[103] Gunnar Myrdal himself, at
the conclusion of his massive 1944 cultural analysis of American racism, had
noted that the status of women had been "the nearest and most natural analogy"[104] for those justifying slavery and racism and might be subject to similar rights-based criticism, as indeed the abolitionist feminists had urged.
Friedan's argument assumed the analogy, including the very terms of a personal struggle for moral identity and self-consciousness that Du Bois had
brought to the black struggle for a stronger antiracist constitutional principle of equal protection.

Friedan also assumed and used another critical principle that was central
to the stronger antiracist principle that the Supreme Court had accepted,
namely, the Boasian cultural science that had reframed issues from the pseudoscience of race to an unjust culture of racist subjugation. That principle
was plausibly applied not only to race but, as Myrdal suggested, to gender as
well. Boas had laid the foundations,[105] but his students Margaret Mead[106]
and Ruth Benedict[107] had elaborated the point. Indeed, such skepticism
about gender differences may first have been suggested by those skeptical of
the dominant suffrage feminist ideology of basic differences[108] that was then
extended to race differences.[109] The greater and earlier political success of
the racial case may be due to historical accident (an organized black movement that powerfully used the argument, a divided woman's movement
many of whom espoused physical differences), not to the underlying issues
of principle.[110] Friedan acknowledged Mead for having made a form of the
argument but then criticized her for not carrying it far enough.[111] Clearly,
the recent success of the argument in the racial area made it much easier to
deploy a form of it, as a matter of principle, in the criticism of the unjust cultural construction of gender. If *The Feminine Mystique* was about anything,
it was about that.

The dimensions of the analogy of principle became explicit in the moral
experience of the black and white women who participated in the civil rights
movement of the 1960s, as Sara Evans has made clear in her now classic
study of this period.[112] Drawing an explicit analogy to the transformative
experience of the Grimke sisters as pathbreaking abolitionist feminists,[113]
Evans noted how the struggle of black and white women to end racial dis-

crimination led women to develop a heightened consciousness of their own oppression. In the 1950s, the civil rights movement had grown in both confidence and sense of vision. Black women played major roles in this effort, from the actions of Rosa Parks and Jo Ann Robinson in starting the Montgomery bus boycott in 1955 to Ella Baker's part in giving birth to the Student Non-Violent Coordinating Committee (SNCC) in 1960.[114] As the civil rights movement became a central topic in American news media, Americans became sensitized to the existence of profound constitutional injustices (including racial segregation and antimiscegenation laws) that had been rationalized on grounds that denied whole classes of persons any decent respect for their basic human rights. Like their abolitionist feminist ancestors, many women who became active in this movement only came to a realization of the comparable injustices to which they were subjected when they experienced sexism from their male colleagues in the movement.

One group of women who realized the link between race and sex discrimination were young Southern activists who took part in the direct-action civil rights struggle of the SNCC. Both black and white, these women found their moral voice in the protests, including sit-ins; as one white woman later testified, "To this day I am amazed. I just did it."[115] For the white women, in particular, such activism constituted a moral revolt, similar in moral force to that of the Grimke sisters, against the idealized conception of white women central to Southern racism: "In the 1830s and again in the 1960s the first voices to link racial and sexual oppression were those of Southern white women."[116] These women, responsive to a Protestant sense of radical personal conscience and ethical responsibility, took as their model black women such as Ella Baker whose life realized in practice Anna Cooper's transformative model of "women in stepping from the pedestal of statue-like inactivity in the domestic shrine, and daring to think and move and speak."[117] In so doing, these white women spiritually exiled themselves from their own mothers in as radical a way as Angelina and Sarah Grimke's physical exile from the South, an experience, like the Grimkes', "exceptionally lonely, for it shattered once-supportive ties with family and friends."[118] Falling back upon personal resources they did not know they had, "they developed a sense of self that enabled them to recognize the enemy within as well—the image of the 'southern lady.'"[119] In contrast to Northern students who came and left the South, "southern white students were in an important sense fighting for their own identities."[120]

These white dissenting women were struggling with and against the idealized conception of white women's sphere that, as we have seen, enforced the correlative dehumanization of black men and women as sexually animalistic. No action more outraged this ideology than the idea of consensual sexual relations between white women and black men. Not only antimiscegenation laws but the whole structure of Southern apartheid were rationalized as measures directed against this ultimate mythological evil. The participation of white women in interracial cooperation protesting these and other such laws represented for many of their Southern white parents "a breakdown in the social order";[121] one such father, when his daughter announced "she wanted to leave school to work in a small-town black community accused her of being a whore and chased her out of the house in a drunken rage, shouting that she was disowned."[122] Within a movement of antiracist struggle led by Southern black men and women, such young white women had "to forge a new sense of themselves, to redefine the meaning of being a woman quite apart from the flawed image they had inherited."[123] Their struggle was the one Du Bois had earlier defined as the antiracist struggle for a new kind of identity and self-consciousness. They self-critically recognized that the struggle for racial equality called for fundamental changes in gender roles, including what they now recognized and condemned as a conspicuously sectarian, religiously based moral "defense of white women's sexual purity in a racist society [that] held them separate from and innocent of the 'real world' of politics."[124]

The catalyst for the development of a rights-based feminism, on the model of abolitionist feminism, was the pervasive attitudes of male supremacy within SNCC that these women encountered. Their self-critical development and support of antiracist principles had required them to question and reject traditional gender roles, regarding "the term 'southern lady' . . . [as] an obscene epithet";[125] they thus asserted their own human rights to conscience, speech, intimate life, and work against a sectarian racist orthodoxy that had traditionally abridged these rights. Now, within SNCC, these hard-fought personal rights were again at hazard; rights of conscience and speech were subordinated in decision-making, rights of intimate life compromised by expectations that women would automatically acquiesce when men asked them to sleep with them, rights of work abridged by limiting them to the sphere of housework.[126] More and more of these young women began to talk with one another about their common experiences. Initially, the hope was that simply pointing out the problem in an anonymous memorandum would bring change.[127] Stokely Carmichael's rebuttal, "The only position for women in SNCC is prone,"[128] led them to conclude that they must be assertive in defense of their own rights as they had been—together with men—in the struggle for racial equality.

Increasingly, their moral experience in this rights-based struggle led them to link the two causes directly. In a summation of their thinking addressed to women in the peace and freedom movement, Casey Hayden and Mary King declared in the fall of 1965 that women, like blacks, "seem to be caught up in a common-law caste system that operates, sometimes subtly, forcing them to work around or outside hierarchical structures of power which may exclude them. Women seem to be placed in the same position of assumed subordination in personal situations too. It is a caste system which, at its worst, uses and exploits women."[129] The identity-transforming struggle for a moral independent exercise of basic rights, which had led them "to think radically about the personal worth and abilities of people whose role in society had gone unchallenged before,"[130] required the same analysis and criticism of "the racial caste system" and "the sexual caste system."[131] Failure to extend the criticism of racial caste to sexual caste reflected, Hayden and White argued, the depth of the injustice of the sexual caste system and the dimensions of the problem of remedy. In particular, they pleaded for open discussion of these issues among women, creating "a community of support for each other so we can deal with ourselves and others with integrity and can therefore keep working,"[132] thus identifying the centrality to rights-based feminism of the praxis of consciousness raising.[133] As the development of the Black Power movement made it increasingly difficult at this time for white and black women to cooperate across racial lines, the white women veterans of the civil rights struggle took such sentiments into the student movement, the antiwar movement, and the like, becoming in the process the cutting edge of second-wave feminism as itself a civil rights movement.[134] The emerging feminism of these women and of Betty Friedan centered feminist discourse, in a way it had not been since the abolitionist feminists, in the criticism, on rights-based grounds, of the normative gender roles that had theretofore, under the impact of suffrage feminism, largely been immunized from such criticism. Rather than idealizing these gender roles as the source of a higher morality, on the model of a Catharine Beecher or Frances Willard, the roles themselves (including their idealization) were now critically examined in the light of morally independent values of human rights. A new centrality was accorded to both the appeal to basic human rights (conscience, free speech, intimate life, and work) and to the lack of the kind of compelling secular public justification constitutionally required before such rights might be abridged. It was such fundamental criticism of gender roles (already, as we have seen, an ingredient of the stronger antiracist principle that many black and white women now defended) that made normative space available on which black and white women could reasonably aspire to find common ground.[135] The very terms of rights-based feminism required white women to raise questions about racialized ideals of gender[136] and suggested as well that the integrity of both the stronger antiracism and antisexism arguments rested on common principles of nondiscrimination that should be pursued together.

In all of this, the civil rights movement was the impetus both for the new forms of substantive argument women now made and for women organizing themselves into a civil rights movement. It was also indispensable in preparing the constitutional mind of the nation for greater concern for related issues of constitutional justice, and indeed urging the judiciary interpretively to recognize such claims. The Supreme Court of the United States would both respond to and encourage such claims in two areas: condemning as suspect the use of gender as a ground for unequal treatment and extending basic human rights on fair terms to women. I begin with the first development and then examine the second in the next chapter, focusing there on the judicial elaboration of the constitutional right to privacy.

The struggle constitutionally to recognize sexism as evil crucially called for a skepticism about the role such unjust gender stereotypes played in our political life. Judicial concern along these lines was first suggested in 1971 in *Reed v. Reed*,[137] representing a sharp turn from the very different approach taken in 1948 by Justice Felix Frankfurter for the Court in *Goesaert v. Cleary*[138] and in 1961 by Justice Harlan in *Hoyt v. Florida*.[139] In the latter two cases the Court invoked the traditional conception of gender roles as the reasonable basis for its decision upholding the exclusion of women, in the one case, from bartending and, in the other, from jury duty. In *Reed v. Reed,* the Court unanimously struck down, as an unconstitutional violation of equal protection, a state's mandatory preference for men over women in the appointment of the administrator of a decedent's estate. The state had defended the statute as a way of eliminating an area of controversy (and the need for a hearing) between relatives otherwise equally qualified. Chief Justice Warren Burger, writing for the Court, conceded that the state's purpose was "not without some legitimacy"[140] but nonetheless struck down the statute because it drew a distinction that was "the very kind of arbitrary legislative choice forbidden by the Equal Protection Clause of the Fourteenth Amendment."[141] In light of *Goesaert, Hoyt,* and previous cases, such a choice, based on traditional normative gender roles, would appear to have a rational basis, perhaps one that could be relevantly rationalized further in terms of statistically significant differences in the experience of men (in the public world of business and affairs) and women (in a largely domestic life) that the acculturation in traditional gender roles had produced. The doctrinal oddity of *Reed* was its claim that without heightening the standard of review as it would for a suspect class like race[142] or a fundamental right like voting,[143] it could find such a statute irrational when almost all comparable cases, subjected to a rational-basis view, had been upheld as valid.[144] The legislative classification in *Reed* was no less overinclusive or underinclusive than many other such statutes and was, on this basis, no less rational.[145] The result in *Reed*, however doctrinally anomalous, suggested growing judicial skepticism about the place traditional gender roles had been permitted to enjoy in the interpretation of equal protection.

The extent and basis of such judicial skepticism were clarified in 1973 in *Frontiero v. Richardson*,[146] in which the Court struck down (8–1) a federal law permitting male members of the armed forces an automatic dependency allowance for their wives but requiring servicewomen to prove that their husbands were dependent. Justice William Brennan, writing for himself and Justices William Douglas, Byron White, and Thurgood Marshall, interpreted *Reed v. Reed* as calling for heightened scrutiny for gender classifications, and indeed defended applying to gender at least the level of scrutiny accorded race. In support of such scrutiny, Justice Brennan acknowledged the nation's "long and unfortunate history of sex discrimination,"[147] which was "rationalized by an attitude of 'romantic paternalism' which, in practical effect, put women, not on a pedestal, but in a cage."[148] As evidence of the degree to which "this paternalistic attitude became so firmly rooted in our national consciousness,"[149] Brennan cited Justice Joseph Bradley's concurring opinion in *Bradwell v. State*[150] that had made Catharine Beecher's normative theory of gender roles the measure of women's shriveled human and civil rights. In defending the analogy between race and gender, Brennan observed:

> As a result of notions such as these, our statute books gradually became laden with gross, stereotyped distinctions between the sexes and, indeed, throughout much of the 19th century the position of women in our society was, in many respects, comparable to that of blacks under the pre–Civil War slave codes. Neither slaves nor women could hold office, serve on juries, or bring suit in their own names, and married women

traditionally were denied the legal capacity to hold or convey property or to serve as legal guardians of their own children. . . . And although blacks were guaranteed the right to vote in 1870, women were denied even that right—which is itself "preservative of other basic civil and political rights"—until adoption of the Nineteenth Amendment half a century later.[151]

To further support the analogy between gender and race, Justice Brennan also pointed to "the high visibility of the sex characteristic," which, "like race and national origin, is an immutable characteristic" frequently bearing "no relation to ability to perform or contribute to society."[152]

In a footnote, Brennan conceded "that when viewed in the abstract, women do not constitute a small and powerless minority" but emphasized that "in part because of past discrimination, women are vastly underrepresented in this Nation's decisionmaking councils. There has never been a female President, nor a female member of this Court. Not a single woman presently sits in the United States Senate, and only 14 women hold seats in the House of Representatives. And, as appellants point out, this underrepresentation is present throughout all levels of our State and Federal Government."[153]

Brennan concluded "that classifications based on sex, like classifications based upon race, alienage, or national origin, are inherently suspect, and must therefore be subject to strict judicial scrutiny."[154] Subjecting the statutory classification to this standard, Brennan found that its claimed purpose, administrative convenience (more spouses of men than of women are likely to be dependent), did not justify use of the gender distinction when a more individualized assessment of dependence was available at little cost and was likely to save the government money on balance (many wives of male servicemembers would fail to qualify for benefits under an individualized test).[155]

Four other justices concurred in Brennan's judgment for the Court, but on the rational-basis standard of *Reed v. Reed*. Justice Lewis Powell, writing for himself, Chief Justice Burger, and Justice Harry Blackmun, argued that *Reed* "abundantly supports our decision today"[156] without adding "sex to the narrowly limited group of classifications which are inherently suspect."[157]

A majority of the Supreme Court finally agreed in 1976 in *Craig v. Boren*[158] that gender classifications were subject to heightened scrutiny, an intermediate level certainly stronger than rational basis but not as demanding as the strict scrutiny accorded to race. Justice Brennan, writing for the

Court, characterized this heightened scrutiny as applying both to the purpose and the means-end reasoning of the statute: "Classifications by gender must serve important governmental objectives and must be substantially related to achievement of these objectives."[159] The statute in question in *Craig* drew a gender distinction between men and women in drinking age (men at twenty-one, women at eighteen), allegedly on the ground that statistical evidence suggested higher rates of drunk driving and traffic injuries for men. On its face, the statute, in contrast to *Frontiero* and related cases of blatantly unconstitutional sex discrimination against women,[160] gave women an advantage over men. Brennan's analysis framed the constitutional issue in terms of the role gender, as a cultural stereotype, played in the statute. Assessing the statute in terms of appropriately heightened intermediate scrutiny, the Court accepted the legitimacy of the state's ostensible purpose for the statute, traffic safety,[161] but found its means-end reasoning constitutionally defective, in particular, the role statistical evidence played in rationalizing the use of a legislative classification in terms of gender.

The problem was not merely doubt about the accuracy of the statistical evidence. Even taking the most reliable such evidence presented, the statistics on driving while under the influence established that 0.18 percent of females and 2 percent of males were arrested for this offense. The Court conceded that although "such a disparity is not trivial in a statistical sense, it hardly can form the basis for employment of a gender line as a classifying device."[162] The point was not only that a 2 percent correlation hardly makes gender a reliable proxy for drinking and driving, for the use of gender would be constitutionally problematic even if it were much more accurate. The basis for the gender distinctions used in *Reed v. Reed* and *Frontiero v. Richardson* may be much more statistically reliable measures of, in the one case, relevant business experience and, in the other, dependency but were nonetheless problematic.[163] The constitutional evil, rather, was giving expression through public law to the unjust political force that a gender stereotype has traditionally enjoyed, often, as a consequence, creating reality in its own unjust image. Brennan made this point about age-differential laws such as that in *Craig* in terms of the degree to which unjust social stereotypes may themselves distort the statistics: "'Reckless' young men who drink and drive are transformed into arrest statistics, where their female counterparts are chivalrously escorted home."[164]

The analogy to race and ethnicity was, Brennan argued, exact:

If statistics were to govern the permissibility of state alcohol regulation without regard to the Equal Protection Clause as a limiting principle, it might follow that States could freely favor Jews and Italian Catholics at the expense of all other Americans, since available studies regularly demonstrate that the former two groups exhibit the lowest rates of problem drinking. . . . Similarly, if a State were allowed simply to depend upon demographic characteristics of adolescents in identifying problem drinkers, statistics might support the conclusion that only black teenagers should be permitted to drink, followed by Asian-Americans and Spanish-Americans. "Whites and American Indians have the lowest proportions of abstainers and the highest proportions of moderate/heavy and heavy drinkers" [citing study].[165]

We would not permit the use of even accurate statistics to justify racial, ethnic, or religious classifications in such cases for the same reasons that gender classifications should not be permitted on such a basis. The classifications themselves reflect a long history of unjust and unconstitutional treatment that has shaped reality in its image. Laws can no more constitutionally give expression to such classifications than they can to the facts such classifications have shaped. Brennan thus took the argument he had earlier made in *Frontiero* about the unjust force that a rights-denying conception of gender roles had been allowed to enjoy in American public law and culture (including its stark endorsement by members of the Supreme Court) and applied it to the unjust gender stereotypes such a conception had sustained. Such unjust gender roles and stereotypes included the idealized image of women's higher morality on the pedestal, rationalizing, as it did, abridgment of basic rights and opportunities. To condemn the political imposition of such gender roles was to condemn as well the cultural stereotypes such roles enforced on reality. From this perspective, not only men but women suffered from the political enforcement of such stereotypes, which have rested on a rights-denying, dehumanizing idealization from which women in particular have suffered.

The constitutional standard of heightened scrutiny of gender classifications has certainly moved the constitutional treatment of gender closer to race. Heightened scrutiny is not, however, strict scrutiny. Although many gender classifications have, as we have seen, been struck down, others have survived, albeit sometimes by narrow majorities. In *Michael M. v. Superior Court*,[166] for example, the Court, 5–4, accepted the constitutionality of a state's statutory rape law that subjected a man, but not a woman, to criminal liability for intercourse with a female under eighteen and not his wife largely on the ground that women, in contrast to men, bore the risks of pregnancy. And in *Rostker v. Goldberg,*[167] the Court ruled, 6–3, that Congress could limit registration for the draft to men on the ground that women, in contrast to men, were excluded from combat.

The recent case *United States v. Virginia,*[168] however, suggests that the Supreme Court may be raising the level of scrutiny for gender much closer to that of race. In striking down the exclusion of women from the Virginia Military Institute, the Court invoked the standard of whether the justification for exclusion was "exceedingly persuasive";[169] was quite skeptical of the weight accorded putative gender differences as a rationale for the exclusion;[170] and expressly invoked an important racial case, *Sweatt v. Painter,* as a relevant analogy for the unconstitutionality of "separate but equal" in the realm of gender.[171] If so, the result in cases such as *Michael M.* and even *Rostker* may now be constitutionally problematic.

5

THE CONSTITUTIONAL RIGHT TO PRIVACY

As we have seen, as recently as 1961 the Supreme Court had unanimously affirmed as the measure of women's rights and responsibilities their ascribed status "as the center of home and family life."[1] Even the three justices who had dissented from the enforcement of this conception in 1948 assumed that, in principle, truly benign legislation protective of women would be constitutional.[2] However, subsequent cases have interpreted relevant constitutional principles in a very different way that gave expression to and indeed forged a constitutionally enforceable conception of the rights of women on the rights-based principles central to second-wave feminism. The argument of toleration, applied as the abolitionist feminists did to both racism and slavery, suggested dimensions of argument that would focus on both the basic human rights that have been unjustly denied and the inadequate sectarian grounds that rationalized such abridgments.

It is fundamental to the kind of criticism that the argument for toleration has brought to American racism and sexism that the political power of these ideologies rested on dehumanizing cultural stereotypes that abridged basic human rights of moral personality, including basic human rights such as conscience, speech, and intimate life. Systematic abridgment of these rights is a fundamental insult and indignity because of the role the free exercise of such rights plays in self-respect and in our creative moral freedom to originate claims and reasonably to forge and sustain the cultural forms of life that give enduring personal sense and moral meaning to living as a responsible moral agent. Persons systematically deprived of such rights in a constitutional community such as the United States that otherwise respects such rights are denationalized as both persons and citizens: useful as tools are useful, lovable and amusing as pets are, but not equal subjects of rights and responsibility and thus members of the constitutional community. Accordingly, any serious

63

attention to such injustice requires correlative attention to guaranteeing each of these basic rights on equal terms.

The tradition of rights-based feminism, from Wollstonecraft to Sarah Grimke to Lucretia Mott to Elizabeth Cady Stanton, has given central weight, consistent with the centrality of the inalienable right to conscience in the argument for toleration, to claims for equal rights to conscience and correlative rights to equal educational opportunity (including, as Wollstonecraft argued, integrated public education[3]). For Grimke and Mott, the argument focused on the equal right of women to be scholars, theologians, and ministers and thus to bring their moral independence to bear on the criticism of misogynist Bible interpretation and the political power it had unjustly been allowed to enjoy; Stanton published *The Woman's Bible* very much in this spirit.[4] Women in nineteenth-century American culture had used constitutional guarantees of religious liberty to forge, as Grimke and Mott did, abolitionist feminist dissent within a religion such as Quakerism that traditionally accorded a more central role to women in the works of conscience.[5] They also used such guarantees to generate and foster either highly personal forms of spirituality, such as that of Sojourner Truth,[6] or religious organizations such as Shakerism, Christian Science, and spiritualism.[7] But the censure of Stanton by the suffrage movement she had founded[8] suggests the degree to which suffrage feminism had compromised the argument for toleration that had made it normatively possible, cramping the scope of acceptable feminist conscience to the sectarian measure of a Frances Willard.[9]

An important background condition for the emergence of second-wave feminism after World War II was thus not only the increasing numbers of American women who worked[10] but the formative cultural importance of the increasingly powerful insistence of the Supreme Court during this period that, consistent with the guarantees both of religious free exercise and against a state religious establishment in the First Amendment, the state not engage in or support what in contemporary circumstances was sectarian religious teaching but extend respect to all forms of conscience, secular and religious.[11] Although these doctrinal developments did not deal specifically with issues of gender or gender roles, they affirmed principles that imposed limits on legitimate state power in the enforcement of sectarian purposes that were of generative importance in the constitutional legitimation of new forms of conscientious dissent, both antiracist and antisexist, that rested on such grounds. We can see the impact of such protest on the elaboration of the constitutional right to privacy by the U.S. Supreme Court.

I have now examined at some length the role that the abridgment of basic human rights of intimate life played in the racist dehumanization of African Americans both under slavery and in later patterns of state-supported segregation and antimiscegenation laws. It was a symptom of the depth of the comparable dehumanization of women that the very proposal of a right of intimate life based on gender was the subject of obscenity prosecutions (including, for their advocacy of the right to contraception, Emma Goldman and Margaret Sanger). Against this background, the struggle for a rights-based feminism could reasonably be measured by how seriously American constitutional culture would be willing to take the protection of so basic a human right.

The judicial elaboration and protection of the constitutional right to privacy can be traced to two cases that survived the otherwise discredited *Lochner* era of wrong-headed judicial intervention in matters of economic policy, namely, *Meyer v. Nebraska*[12] and *Pierce v. Society of Sisters*.[13] Both cases were described as protecting the role of parents in family relationships from the standardizing hand of the state, which failed to accord the constitutionally required weight to the place of parents in the formation and transmission of values, a function that was not, without compelling reason, to be commandeered by the state. That the underlying right in question extended to sexual relations, leading to procreation, was implicit in *Skinner v. Oklahoma*,[14] striking down, on equal-protection grounds, a state law requiring compulsory sterilization for some crimes but not others.

In 1965 the Supreme Court in *Griswold v. Connecticut*[15] constitutionalized the argument for a basic human right to contraception that had been persistently and eloquently defended and advocated by Margaret Sanger for well over forty years, a decision that Sanger lived to see.[16] The Court first recognized the right in *Griswold* for a married couple but subsequently extended it to all persons, married or single,[17] adults or sexually active teenagers.[18] The Court extended the right to abortion services in 1973 in *Roe v. Wade*[19] to married and unmarried women (and reaffirmed its central principle in 1992[20]), protecting as well the right of minors to an abortion without parental consent.[21] I discuss *Roe v. Wade*'s application to gay/lesbian sex in the next two chapters.

Sanger's and Goldman's arguments for the right to contraception were very much rooted in rights-based feminism. Sanger's opponents certainly made that point very clear. When her then husband, Bill Sanger, was convicted of obscenity for distributing one of his wife's publications, the judge emphasized that the dispute was over woman's role: "Your crime is not only a violation of the laws of man, but of the law of God as well, in your scheme to prevent motherhood. Too many persons have the idea that it is wrong to have children. Some women are so selfish that they do not want to be bothered with them. If some persons would go around and urge Christian women to bear children, instead of wasting their time on woman suffrage, this city and society would be better off."[22]

Sanger's and Goldman's arguments had two prongs, both of which were implicit in the Supreme Court's decisions in *Griswold* and later cases: first, a basic human right to intimate life with contraception as an instance of that right; and second, the assessment of whether laws abridging such a fundamental right met the heavy burden of secular justification that was required.

The basis of the fundamental human right to intimate life was, as Lydia Maria Child, Stephen Andrews, and Victoria Woodhull had earlier made clear,[23] as basic an inalienable right of moral personality (respect for which is central to the argument for toleration) as the right to conscience. Like the right to conscience, it protects intimately personal moral resources (thoughts and beliefs, intellect, emotions, self-image, and self-identity) and the way of life that expresses and sustains them in facing and meeting rationally and reasonably the challenge of a life worth living—one touched by enduring personal and ethical value. The right to intimate life centers on protecting these moral resources as they bear on the role of loving and being loved in the tender and caring exfoliation of moral personality, morally finding one's self, as a person, in love for and the love of another moral self.

The human right of intimate life was not only a central right in the argument for toleration central to American constitutionalism but a right interpretively implicit in the historical traditions of American rights-based constitutionalism. In both of the two great revolutionary moments that framed the trajectory of American constitutionalism (the American Revolution and the Civil War), the right to intimate life was one of the central human rights the abridgment of which rendered political power illegitimate and gave rise to the Lockean right to revolution.[24]

At the time of the American Revolution, the background literature on human rights, known to and assumed by the American revolutionaries and founding constitutionalists, included what the influential Scottish philosopher Francis Hutcheson called "the natural right of each one to enter into the matrimonial relation with any one who consents."[25] Indeed, John Witherspoon, whose lectures James Madison heard at Princeton, followed Hutcheson in listing even more abstractly as a basic human and natural right a "right to associate, if he so incline, with any person or persons, whom he can persuade (not force)—under this is contained the right to marriage."[26]

Accordingly, leading statesmen at the state conventions ratifying the Constitution, both those for and against adoption, assumed that the Constitution could not interfere in the domestic sphere. Alexander Hamilton of New York denied that federal constitutional law did or could "penetrate the recesses of domestic life, and control, in all respects, the private conduct of individuals."[27] Patrick Henry of Virginia spoke of the core of our rights to liberty as the sphere where a person "enjoys the fruits of his labor, under his own fig-tree, with his wife and children around him, in peace and security."[28] The arguments of reserved rights both of leading proponents (Hamilton) and opponents (Henry) of adoption of the Constitution thus converged on the private sphere of domestic married life.

The founding generation assumed that the Constitution would not reach matters of intimate life, such as marriage and divorce, because those matters would be within the competence of the states, not the federal government. Since the Bill of Rights of 1791 only imposed enforceable constitutional constraints on the national government, it makes sense that they would not have included the right to intimate life among the specifically guaranteed rights in the Bill of Rights, as it was not a matter in which the government had any competence; it would, however, certainly have been assumed that it was among the unenumerated rights protected by the guarantees of the Ninth Amendment. The matter appeared in a very different light, however, after the experience of the growing antebellum constitutional crisis, culminating in the Civil War and the victory of the Union, leading to the Reconstruction Amendments.

At the time of the Civil War, the understanding of marriage as a basic human right took on a new depth and urgency because of the antebellum abolitionist rights-based attack on the peculiar nature of American slavery; such slavery failed to recognize the marriage or family rights of slaves,[29] and indeed inflicted on black families the moral horror of breaking them up by selling family members separately.[30] One in six slave marriages thus was ended by force or sale.[31] No aspect of American slavery more dramatized its radical evil for abolitionists and Americans more generally than its brutal deprivation of intimate personal life, including undermining the moral authority of parents over children. Slaves, Theodore Weld argued, had "as little control over them [children], as have domestic animals over the disposal of their young."[32] Slavery, understood as an attack on intimate personal life,[33] stripped persons of essential attributes of their humanity. My colleague Peggy Davis has powerfully made the point that it was the racist attack on the intimate life of slaves that was at the very heart of the atrocity of American slavery and the abolitionist political morality that condemned slavery.[34] It was precisely because the Southern states had abridged so fundamental a human right that the abolitionist political morality, which underlies the Reconstruction Amendments, required enforceable constitutional principles that would protect this right against both state and federal power.

It is against this historical background (as well as background rights-based political theory) that it is interpretively correct to regard the right to intimate life as one of the unenumerated rights protected both by the Ninth Amendment and by the Privileges and Immunities Clause of the Fourteenth Amendment, as Justice John Harlan may be regarded as arguing in his concurrence in *Griswold*.[35] The Supreme Court quite properly interpreted the Fourteenth Amendment in particular as protecting this basic human right against unjustified state abridgment and, as Sanger and Goldman had urged, regarded the right to use contraceptives as an instance of this right. The right to contraception was, for Sanger and Goldman, a fundamental human right for women because it would enable them, perhaps for the first time in human history, reliably to decide whether and when their sexual lives would be reproductive. Respect for this right was an aspect of the more basic right of intimate life in two ways. First, it would enable women to exercise control over their intimate relations with men, deciding whether and when such relations would be reproductive. Second, it would secure to women the right to decide whether and when they would form the intimate relationship with a child. Both forms of choice threatened the traditional gender-defined role of women's sexuality as exclusively and mandatorily procreational and maternally self-sacrificing and were resisted, as by Bill Sanger's judge, for that reason.

But, this human right, like other such rights, may be regulated or limited only on terms of public reason not themselves hostage to an entrenched political hierarchy (for example, compulsorily arranged marriages[36]) resting on the abridgement of such rights. For example, from the perspective of the general abolitionist criticism of slavery and racism, the proslavery arguments in support of Southern slaveholders' treatment of family life were transparently inadequate, not remotely affording adequate public justification for the abridgment of such a fundamental right.

These arguments were in their nature essentially racist:

"His natural affection is not strong, and consequently he is cruel to his own offspring, and suffers little by separation from them."[37]

"Another striking trait of negro character is lasciviousness. Lust is his strongest passion; and hence, rape is an offence of too frequent occurrence.

Fidelity to the marriage relation they do not understand and do not expect, neither in their native country nor in a state of bondage."[38]

The blind moral callousness of Southern proslavery thought was nowhere more evident than in its treatment of what were in fact agonizing, crushing, and demeaning family separations:[39]

"He is also liable to be separated from wife or child . . . —but from native character and temperament, the separation is much less severely felt."[40]

"With regard to the separation of husbands and wives, parents and children, . . . Negroes are themselves both perverse and comparatively indifferent about this matter."[41]

The irrationalist racist sexualization of black slaves was evident in the frequent justification of slavery in terms of maintaining the higher standards of sexual purity of Southern white women.[42] Viewed through the polemically distorted prism of such thought, the relation of master and slave was itself justified as an intimate relationship like that of husband and wife that should similarly be immunized against outside interference.[43] In this Orwellian world of the distortion of truth by power, the defense of slavery became the defense of freedom.[44] Arguments of these sorts rested on interpretations of facts and values completely hostage to the polemical defense of entrenched political institutions whose stability required the abridgment of basic rights of blacks and of any whites who ventured reasonable criticism of such institutions.

If the antebellum experience of state abridgments of basic rights must inform a reasonable interpretation of the Privileges and Immunities Clause,[45] the protection of intimate personal life must be one among the basic human rights thus worthy of national protection. The remaining question is whether there is any adequate basis for the abridgment of so basic a right, namely, in the case of contraception, the right to decide whether or when one's sexual life will lead to offspring, indeed, to explore one's personal sexual and emotional life as an end in itself.

That abridgment can be justified only by a compelling public reason, not on the grounds of reasons that are today sectarian (internal to a moral tradition not based on reasons available and accessible to all). In fact, the only argument that could sustain such laws (namely, the Augustinian[46] and Thomistic[47] view that it is immoral to engage in nonprocreative sex) is not today a view of sexuality that can reasonably be enforced on people at large. Such a view may once have made reasonable sense when there was massive infant and adult mortality and a correspondingly desperate need to have large numbers of children, at least some of which might survive to perform needed tasks in a basically agrarian way of life. But such a context is no longer present in industrialized societies with modern health care and growing worries about overpopulation, and enforcing such a procreational model of legitimate sex in contemporary circumstances is now unreasonably anachronistic. Indeed, many people regard sexual love as an end in itself and the control of reproduction as a reasonable way to regulate when and whether they have children consistent with their own personal and larger ethical interests, those of their children, and those of an overpopulated society at large. The question of having children at all is today a highly personal matter of genuine choice, not social or moral necessity, certainly no longer governed by the perhaps once compelling secular need to have children for necessary work in a largely agrarian society with high rates of infant and adult mortality.[48] From the perspective of women in particular, as Sanger and Goldman made so clear, the enforcement of an anticontraceptive morality on society at large not only harms women's interests (as well as those of an overpopulated society more generally) but impersonally demeans them to a purely reproductive function, depriving them of the rational dignity of deciding as moral agents and persons, perhaps for the first time in human history, whether, when, and on what terms they will have children consistent with their other legitimate aims and ambitions (including the free exercise of all their basic human rights). Enforcement of such a morality rests on a now conspicuously sectarian conception of gender hierarchy in which women's sexuality is defined by a mandatory procreative role and responsibility. That conception, the basis of the unjust construction of gender hierarchy, cannot reasonably be the measure of human rights today.[49]

Similar considerations explain the grounds for doubt about the putative public, nonsectarian justifications for laws criminalizing abortion. Antiabortion laws, grounded in the alleged protection of a neutral good life, unreasonably equate the moral weight of a fetus in the early stages of pregnancy with that of a person and abortion with murder; such laws fail to take seriously the weight that should be accorded a woman's basic right to reproductive autonomy in making highly personal moral choices central to her most intimate bodily and personal life against the background of the lack of reasonable public consensus that fetal life, as such, can be equated with that of a moral person.[50] Society has a legitimate interest in giving weight at some point to fetal life as part of making a symbolic statement about taking the lives of children seriously and caring for them, analogous to the symbolic interest society may have in preventing cruelty to animals or in securing

humane treatment for the irretrievably comatose, to advance humane treatment of persons and ensure that such issues are properly understood. But
such interests do not constitutionally justify forbidding abortion throughout
all stages of pregnancy.[51] Rather, such interests can be accorded their legitimate weight after a reasonable period has been allowed for the proper scope
of a woman's exercise of her decision. The *Roe-Casey* doctrine of allowing
criminalization only at viability may be regarded as making this point: giving reasonable freedom to women to choose to have an abortion, subject to
making a decision by a time that for many marks legitimate symbolic concerns for valuing children.

The moral arguments for the prohibition of abortion cluster around certain traditional conceptions of the natural processes of sexuality and gender.
Once, however, one takes seriously the notion that fetal life is not a reasonable public value sufficient to outweigh the right of reproductive autonomy,
the argument for criminalizing abortion is not a constitutionally reasonable
argument for regarding abortion as homicide but a proxy for complex background assumptions often no longer reasonably believed in the society at
large, namely, a now controversial, powerfully sectarian ideology about
proper sexuality and gender roles. From this perspective, the prohibitions
against abortion encumber what many now reasonably regard as a highly
conscientious choice by women regarding their bodies; their sexuality and
gender; and the nature and place of pregnancy, birth, and child rearing in
their personal and ethical lives. Carol Gilligan's important study of women
making the abortion choice clarifies the way in which *Roe* supported women's
ethical voice, not ceding to society or the state an authority it lacks.[52] The
traditional condemnation of abortion fails, at a deep ethical level, to take
seriously the moral independence of women as free and rational persons,
lending the force of law, like comparable anticontraceptive laws, to theological ideas of biological naturalness and gender hierarchy (expressed in
mythological conceptions of women as idealized asexual mothers and infi-
nitely self-sacrificing) that degrade the constructive moral powers of women
to establish the meaning of their own sexual and reproductive life histories.
The underlying conception appears to be at one with the sexist idea that
women's minds and bodies are not their own but the property of others,
namely, men or their masculine God, who may conscript them and their
bodies, like cattle on the farm, for the greater good. The abortion choice is
thus one of the choices essential to the just moral independence of women,
centering their lives in a body image and aspirations expressive of their moral

powers. It is a just application of the right to intimate life, because the right to the abortion choice protects women from the traditional degradation of their moral powers, reflected in the assumptions underlying antiabortion laws.

In the background of the laws at issue in all these cases lies a normative view of gender roles. That is quite clear, as I earlier suggested, in the case of *Griswold v. Connecticut,* less obviously so in *Roe v. Wade.* On analysis, however, the little weight accorded to women's interests and the decisive weight accorded to the fetus in antiabortion laws make sense only against the background of the still powerful traditional conception of mandatory procreational, self-sacrificing, caring, and nurturant gender roles for women; it is its symbolic violation of that normative idea that imaginatively transforms abortion into murder. The enforcement of such gender stereotypes through law is, as we earlier saw (Chapter 4), now condemned as constitutionally suspect for reasons analogous to those that render racial/ethnic classifications constitutionally suspect. Just as the constitutionally suspect quality of racial classifications influenced the recognition of the unconstitutionality of antimiscegenation laws, the suspect quality of gender stereotypes justly shaped as well the unconstitutionality of both anticontraception and antiabortion laws, both of which presume, on grounds of mythological gender idealizations (asexual good women) and denigrations (sexual bad women) rooted in injustice, to tell women what their role and nature are.

6

BOWERS V. HARDWICK

Bowers v. Hardwick must be discussed, analyzed, and criticized in its historical context. As I have now discussed at some length, in the post–World War II period, under the impact of various protest movements, the Supreme Court of the United States interpreted basic constitutional principles, including guarantees of basic rights as well as equal protection of laws, to give fuller protection to the claims of religious minorities, people of color, and women. There was, I have argued, a connection of deeper principle between two such developments: those striking down the use of racial/ethnic and gender stereotypes that reflected the history of cultural dehumanization I have called moral slavery, and those extending basic human rights on fair terms to groups afflicted by that history. The connection is this: the evil of moral slavery is to dehumanize a whole class of persons from their status as full bearers of basic human rights (such as conscience, speech, intimate life, and work). That evil has two dimensions: the unjust ground (moral slavery) on which persons have not been accorded their basic rights, and the abridgment of their basic rights on such inadequate grounds. These two dimensions are mirror images of one another. The growing constitutional concern for this evil in the post–World War II period accordingly took two forms: the striking down as unconstitutional of certain grounds for laws or policies (suspect classification analysis under the Fourteenth Amendment) and the corresponding protection of basic human rights that had been unjustly denied on such grounds. It was on such grounds that the Supreme Court struck down laws reflecting unjust racial/ethnic stereotypes and also struck down laws that abridged the basic right to intimate life on such grounds (for example, the antimiscegenation cases). Similarly, the Court's growing skepticism about gender as a suspect classification for the same reasons as race/ethnicity was reflected in its recognition of various basic rights

73

of women, among which prominently was the right to intimate life reflected in the constitutional privacy cases.

For reasons discussed earlier, the gay/lesbian protest movement, at least in the United States, came relatively late in these historical developments. Although there had been a long history of protest by people of color and women in the United States (dating back at least to antebellum radical abolitionism), the voice of gay protest, though given brilliant expression in the poetry and prose of Walt Whitman, had been brutally repressed and marginalized until the developments in the robust judicial protection of free conscience and speech in the post–World War II period, and then appeared relatively late. America was, for this reason, much more culturally homophobic than Britain and many European nations, many of which had decriminalized gay/lesbian sex long before *Bowers* in 1986 or *Lawrence* in 2003—France and the Netherlands as early as 1810, Belgium in 1867, Italy in 1889, Spain in 1932, Scandinavian countries between 1930 and 1970, Britain in 1967, Germany in 1968–1969.[1] Indeed, five years before *Bowers,* the European Court of Human Rights held that laws proscribing gay/lesbian sex acts were invalid under the European Convention on Human Rights, a decision authoritative in all countries that are members of the Council of Europe (twenty-one nations then, forty-five nations now).[2] Nonetheless, despite American cultural homophobia, it was clear to me and other gays and lesbians by 1974 that we could reasonably build on constitutional developments in other areas, that our protesting voice had a just place in the constitutional principles Americans, under the leadership of the Supreme Court, had come to regard as basic. That is to say, by this time in American constitutional history, the arguments of liberal political philosophy that had led me ethically to question traditional homophobic moralism had now been recognized as underlying the best interpretation of basic constitutional rights such as conscience, speech, and intimate life and associated guarantees of equal protection of laws. How could such a constitutional development not be extended on fair terms to gays and lesbians as moral persons entitled to respect for their basic human rights (the personal as the political)? It was now a question of showing by reasonable arguments that the gay/lesbian protesting voice must, on grounds of principle, be accorded just recognition in terms of these rights and guarantees, which are, of course, the birthright of all Americans.

It was clear to me, as to others, that the starting point for our arguments for such recognition must be the constitutional right that more than any other was brutally denied to gays and lesbians: the right to be free of criminal sanctions directed at the sexual lives of consensual adult homosexuals. There was reason to believe that such arguments, appealing to already judicially accepted principles of constitutional privacy and equal protection, might be given a just hearing by a judiciary committed to arguments of principle as the ground for the legitimacy of its powers of judicial review in the United States. For example, the highest state court of New York, the New York State Court of Appeals, had accepted in 1980 arguments I and others had made to recognize that the right to privacy protected by the New York State Constitution rendered New York's sodomy statute unconstitutional.[3] If good state courts had accepted such arguments, why not the Supreme Court?

The problem was that by the time the issue was posed to the Supreme Court of the United States in *Bowers v. Hardwick* there had been increasingly politicized criticism of the Supreme Court's application of the constitutional right to privacy to abortion services in *Roe v. Wade* in 1973, which showed itself in the increasingly conservative appointment of judges to the Supreme Court who might overrule *Roe*. Although a majority of the justices still supported the principle of *Roe* at the time *Bowers* came before the Court, it was not clear, with new judicial appointments, that this majority would last for long, and clearly the criticism of *Roe* had an impact on members of the Court when they considered *Bowers*.

It is important to be clear that some of the constitutional criticism of *Roe* came from otherwise liberal constitutional scholars who, as a matter of democratic politics, believed that abortion should be decriminalized in the United States. The notable intellectual leader of these scholars was Professor John Hart Ely. Ely had conceded that there was a plausible interpretive case to be made for the legitimacy of *Roe,* based on the text and history of the Constitution, but he argued that a sound understanding of judicial review in the modern world required that when a result was not commanded by specific texts, the judiciary should exercise its power of judicial review over democratic politics only when its review secured a democratically more representative politics. Ely's models for such legitimate judicial review were the Warren Court's decisions in both racial and reapportionment cases. Since African Americans had been historically deprived of the weight they deserved in American politics, it was legitimate for the Supreme Court to strike down the use of racial classifications used to disempower them, as in state-supported racial segregation; in contrast, Ely defended the use of racial classifications in ameliorative affirmative action programs because such programs did not disempower but fairly empowered African Americans. Malapportionment in electoral districts unfairly accorded some persons more political power than others, and the judiciary had performed an appropriate role in striking down such malapportionment, thus securing a fairer system of political representation.[4] Ely's theory questioned the very legitimacy of the principle of constitutional privacy, in contrast to other constitutional scholars, such as Charles Fried and Kent Greenawalt, who objected not to the principle of constitutional privacy in general but rather to its application to abortion services (in light of the problem of fetal life), as opposed to contraception and consensual homosexuality.[5]

Ely's theory of legitimate judicial review explained and justified important decisions of the Warren Court but questioned the legitimacy of later decisions that had extended suspect classification analysis from race/ethnicity to gender and the related constitutional privacy cases, such as *Roe v. Wade*, that extended the basic right of intimate life to women (*Griswold* was, for Ely, more acceptable because it rested on more specific constitutional guarantees of privacy in the home). Women had had an effective right to vote for a long time, not crippled in their political power, as African Americans had been, by egregious failures of state officials to allow them to vote. Moreover, women were a majority of the population, and thus had enormous potential democratic political power, if they chose to exercise it, to right any wrong inflicted on them, including any unjust discrimination on grounds of gender and decriminalizing abortion services, a political direction in which states were moving before *Roe v. Wade*. The backlash against *Roe* would not have occurred if democratic political processes had been respected, and, Ely argued, there was no good reason why the Court should not have respected such processes in cases crucially involving women.[6]

Ely's argument is enormously problematic as constitutional theory, marginalizing, as it does, central principles of American constitutionalism such as the religion clauses of the First Amendment.[7] But it shows how broad was the questioning of *Roe* among otherwise liberal-minded Americans, usually men. Even if we accept the application of the right to constitutional privacy as a wholly legitimate development within American constitutional law, as the Supreme Court now clearly does, there are reasonable questions to be raised about the way in which the Court in *Roe* struck the balance between its identification of a basic constitutional right and the compelling state purposes that might justify the abridgment of such a basic right. Why, if fetal life is accorded weight as potential life, should the operative line be drawn at viability as opposed to a range of other points at which the fetus develops moral relevant features, for example, sentience, or brain activity? Why not draw the line (which determines when criminalization will and will not be constitutional), if not earlier, later? Ultimately, three justices of the Supreme Court, all appointed by Republican presidents who claimed to be prolife, decided not to restrike the balance struck by the Court in *Roe,* reaffirming the core principle of *Roe* that abortion could not be criminalized before viability but allowing more regulation before that point than the *Roe* Court had allowed. But these issues were still open at the time that *Bowers* came to the Supreme Court and undoubtedly made the case interpretively more difficult for prochoice justices than it should have been.

The facts of *Bowers v. Hardwick* were these. The Georgia criminal statute was an act-defined statute, applying by its terms to sexual acts of sodomy defined as when a person "performs or submits to any sexual act involving the sex organs of one person and the mouth or anus of another,"[8] subject, upon conviction, to a term of imprisonment of not more than twenty years. In August 1982, Hardwick was charged with a violation of this statute with another man in the bedroom of Hardwick's home. After a preliminary hearing, the district attorney decided not to present the case to the grand jury. Hardwick then brought suit in the U.S. District Court challenging the constitutionality of the statute insofar as it criminalized consensual sodomy between adults. Although the district court dismissed the suit for failure to state a claim, the Court of Appeals for the Eleventh Circuit reversed. The Supreme Court granted certiorari to resolve a conflict among the circuit courts on this issue and reversed the judgment of the Eleventh Circuit in a 5–4 judgment. The opinion for the Court was written by Justice Byron White, in which Chief Justice Warren Burger and Justices Lewis Powell, William Rehnquist, and Sandra Day O'Connor concurred. Chief Justice Burger and Justice Powell filed concurring opinions as well. Justice Harry Blackmun filed a dissenting opinion, in which Justices William Brennan, Thurgood Marshall, and John Stevens concurred. Justice Stevens also filed a dissenting opinion, in which Justices Brennan and Marshall joined.

Justice White's opinion for the Court certainly suggested a general skepticism about the constitutional right to privacy rooted in his dissent in *Roe v. Wade* and perhaps in the worries about *Roe* suggested by liberal constitutionalists such as John Hart Ely and others. This was shown by the fact that White's arguments applied more plausibly to constitutional privacy generally than, as he disingenuously suggested, only to the expansion of the constitutional right to privacy to gay/lesbian sex. White was not, however, in a position to overrule the entire line of constitutional privacy cases, so he made his critical point rather unreasonably by postulating: "We think it evi-

dent that none of the rights announced in those cases bears any resemblance
to the claimed right of homosexuals to engage in acts of sodomy that is
asserted in this case."[9] Nothing could be less evident, as at least two of the
leading constitutional privacy cases, *Griswold v. Connecticut* and *Roe v. Wade,*
rest on a right to conduct one's intimate sexual life without procreating,
which is exactly the constitutional principle Hardwick appeals to. We can see
what White's quarry really is (namely, constitutional privacy itself) when we
consider the two arguments he offered for identifying basic rights: namely,
those so implicit in ordered liberty that justice could not exist if they were
sacrificed, and those deeply rooted in the nation's history and traditions.[10]
White believed neither argument would justify protecting acts of consensual
sodomy because historically sodomy had always been criminal in the United
States. Indeed, even making such an argument "is, at best, facetious."[11]
The same point could be made about *Griswold* and *Roe,* both of which
departed from a long history hostile to the legitimacy of nonprocreational
sex, but White was not in a position to overrule these cases, which clearly
stand for a principle that regards criminalizing nonprocreational sex as a
constitutionally unacceptable purpose in contemporary circumstances.
What White's argument, with all its polemical excesses, came to was insisting on a distinction among cases when there was no reasonable distinction
worth making.

White put his point about not expanding constitutional privacy to cover
gay/lesbian sex in terms that echoed Ely's theory of the legitimacy of judicial review: "The Court is most vulnerable and comes nearest to illegitimacy
when it deals with judge-made constitutional law having little or no cogniz-
able roots in the language or design of the Constitution."[12] Once again,
White is making an objection to the principle of constitutional privacy itself,
questioning the legitimacy of judicial inference of a right when no such right
is expressly guaranteed, in contrast to the rights of religious liberty and free
speech. It is correct, in this view, to protect enumerated rights but wrong to
protect unenumerated ones, as if our tradition draws a sharp line between
these, when in fact both the Ninth Amendment of the Bill of Rights and the
Privileges and Immunities Clause of the Fourteenth Amendment offer us
text, history, tradition, and political theory that expressly and for compelling
reason deny that the protection of enumerated rights should in any way prejudice the protection of unenumerated rights.

All these points had been cogently made by Justice Harlan: there is quite
clear text and history in the Bill of Rights of 1791 (notably, the Ninth
Amendment) rejecting the inference that rights specifically protected by the

Bill of Rights exhausted the rights worthy of protection. In any event, there was a very good reason why the right to intimate life would not have enjoyed specific protection under the Bill of Rights, namely, the fact that questions of marriage and divorce were clearly not federal but rather state matters, and the Bill of Rights was addressed only to federal powers. There is abundant history and text in the Reconstruction Amendments, which clearly are directed against state power, demonstrating that the rights guaranteed by them included the basic right to intimate life. The Reconstruction Amendments, which ended American slavery and condemned, inter alia, the cultural racism that supported it, reflected an antebellum abolitionist political morality that regarded one of the worst atrocities of American slave-holding culture as its abridgment of the rights of slaves to marry or to have custody of their children. It was against this background that Harlan argued that the Privileges and Immunities Clause of the Fourteenth Amendment clearly protected the right to intimate life, as a constitutional right rooted in a basic human right, and that any abridgment of such a basic right must satisfy at least the same heavy burden of secular justification required for the abridgment of other such basic rights, for example, the right of religious liberty. It is quite consistent with that text and history that the Supreme Court of the United States might strike down abridgments of so basic a right no longer supported by the kind of burden of justification we require, as it did in *Griswold v. Connecticut.*

There is as reasonably compelling a tradition of respect for the right to intimate life in the United States as there is a tradition of respect for the rights to conscience and speech, and the judiciary may be as uniquely positioned to secure respect, on grounds of principle, for the right to intimate life as it has been to secure respect for variant religious and irreligious interpretations of the right to conscience and the expansive forms of conscientious speech that now enjoy unprecedented protection. There is certainly no good reason of political theory for regarding a right such as that of intimate life as a lesser right than the right of conscience or free speech: such ties of intimate life are as central to what makes us human, and thus bearers of human rights, as our conscience or our expressiveness. The Founders of the U.S. Constitution would not have understood a distinction among such rights, and our historical experience in the antebellum period shows clearly how important abridgment of the right to intimate life was to a growing American understanding of the atrocity of slavery. We may say, paraphrasing Lincoln on slavery,[13] that if the right to intimate life is not a basic right, then nothing is. Accordingly, exercises of the power of judicial review are legitimate if we regard the institutional task of the judiciary to be a forum of principle in which persons may reasonably be heard for claims that they should enjoy on equal terms basic human rights owed to all persons. There was, from this perspective, something Orwellian in Justice White's appeal to legitimacy in *Bowers*. In the unfortunate spirit of Justice White's opinion in *Bowers v. Hardwick*, it was legitimate for the Court to extend a basic right such as intimate life to all forms of heterosexual coupling but to dismiss such claims as illegitimate precisely when they come from a class of persons (gays and lesbians) whose rights of intimate life have been egregiously abridged by a cultural tradition that, until well after World War II, refused even to allow their ethical voices to be heard. Judicial review makes the moral contribution to contemporary constitutional understanding that it sometimes indispensably does when it gives a fair hearing to the previously unjustly silenced voices of Americans who make claims to the basic principles of American constitutional law. White's appeal to legitimacy in *Bowers* was a parody of this mission.

Another way of understanding White's argument would be to interpret it as urging different styles of judicial interpretation when constitutional rights are specifically protected, and when such rights are more inferential. It was certainly not the first time the Court had taken this general approach to how history matters in constitutional interpretation. For example, in *Williams v. Florida*,[14] Justice White wrote the opinion for the Court interpreting how the constitutional guarantees of a jury in criminal cases, which date from the Constitution of 1787 and the Bill of Rights of 1791, should be interpreted in the twentieth century. There was, of course, an available original interpretation of "jury": namely, a jury was the historical institution assumed by the Founders in 1787 and 1791, consisting of twelve persons and requiring unanimity as its rule of decision. White expressly rejected this interpretation, arguing that the jury guarantee should be interpreted in terms of a more abstract intention: a reasonably representative group of one's peers, sufficiently large to resist intimidation from judges and prosecutors but not so small as to discourage dialogue, that would be required to interpose its judgments of guilt or acquittal between a criminal defendant and the state authorities who are criminally prosecuting him or her. This mode of interpretation appealed to Justice White precisely because it released the interpretive judgment of the contemporary Supreme Court from an unreasonably slavish tracking of how the Founders would have applied a constitutional term in their historical context. The appeal of a more abstractly connotative approach is that it allows a contemporary generation to construe a constitutional term reasonably in light of current facts and circumstances. For example, Justice White could assess whether in contemporary circumstances the essential purposes of the jury guarantee might be realized with a somewhat smaller jury size (say, nine instead of twelve) or by a decision rule less demanding than unanimity (say, two-thirds).

One way of understanding Justice White's illegitimacy claim in *Bowers v. Hardwick* is that whereas specific guarantees called for this abstractly connotative approach, an inference of a constitutional right, such as constitutional privacy, should stay closer to its original history. The problem, of course, is that the objection was directed at the principle of constitutional privacy itself, which often questioned earlier historical understandings. Presumably, we constitutionally rejected antimiscegenation laws, which abridged the right to intimate life, precisely because the historical understanding of the legitimacy of such laws rested on American cultural racism; we rejected anticontraception and antiabortion laws because the historical understanding of such laws rested on a view of the intrinsic evil of nonprocreational sex that is today unreasonable, indeed quite anachronistic. There is no reason to distinguish interpretive strategies in the way Justice White's opinion suggested, at least if we think there is any good sense in having a right to constitutional privacy at all. To the contrary, the judiciary best performs its mission when it tests all claims to basic human rights by the most reasonable contemporary understanding of what the connotative meaning of those rights is in our circumstances.

Once Justice White dismissed the idea that there could be any right to privacy reasonably enjoyed by gays and lesbians, he accorded antisodomy laws the broadest judicial deference.[15] Common moral opinion would be enough to justify such laws, notwithstanding their failure to conform to any reasonable understanding in contemporary circumstances of John Stuart Mill's harm principle. White concluded his opinion by raising questions about line-drawing: if we protected gay/lesbian consensual adult sex, what about other consensual conduct that takes place in the home? "Victimless crimes, such as possession and use of illegal drugs, do not escape the law where they are committed at home. . . . And if respondent's submission is limited to the voluntary sexual conduct between consenting adults, it would be difficult, except by fiat, to limit the claimed right to homosexual conduct while leaving exposed to prosecution adultery, incest, and other sexual crimes even though they are committed in the home."[16]

There were two concurring opinions; one by Chief Justice Burger repeated the historical claims in Justice White's opinion for the Court, adding little but polemical emphasis. The other, by Justice Powell, agreed with the opinion of the Court that there was no fundamental right of the sort claimed by Hardwick and found constitutional significance in the fact that the case before the Court involved no actual criminal sentence. In fact, the Georgia statute called for a criminal sentence of up to twenty years, and what Powell argued was that "a prison sentence for such conduct—certainly a sentence of long duration—would create a serious Eighth Amendment issue."[17] Powell's constitutional unease with the case reflected what we know about his consideration of the case: he initially believed that the Eighth Amendment rendered the Georgia statute unconstitutional, voting, in a 5–4 majority, for overturning the statute, but after being heavily lobbied by a rather overwrought Chief Justice Burger, he changed his mind and voted to support Justice White's opinion.[18] After he left the Court, Justice Powell, responding to a question posed to him at a public occasion at my law school, effectively confessed error in his change of mind and vote.[19] It is quite clear why: Powell, unlike other justices in the majority, was clearly committed to the principle not only of *Griswold* but of *Roe v. Wade* itself. Once we accept, as Powell evidently did, both the general principle of constitutional privacy and the correctness of its application to contraception and abortion, the failure to apply it to gay/lesbian sex raises questions about how principled a justice's conception of constitutional law is. Powell clearly saw the issue in this way, as he confirmed to a reporter about his recantation: "I do think it was inconsistent in a general way with *Roe*. When I had the opportunity to reread the opinions a few months later, I thought the dissent had the better of the arguments."[20] There can be no more fundamental criticism of any justice, and Powell apparently came remorsefully, as a matter of justice, to accept this criticism of himself.

There is illuminating background that suggests how significant homophobic silencing of voice is in such injustices. When one of Powell's clerks (a gay man, unknown to Powell) urged him to hold the statute unconstitutional, Powell responded to his astonished clerk, "I don't believe I've ever met a homosexual,"[21] a remark he evidently repeated at the conference of the justices on the case. Justice Blackmun later told his clerks that he thought of answering, "Of course you have; You've even had gay clerks," but, like Powell's current clerk, he didn't point this out to Powell.[22] The cultural tradition, underlying homophobia, rests on the unspeakability of homosexuality. In such circumstances, a failure to speak against the silence ratifies the unjust authority of the tradition rather than exposing a person like Powell, striving to do justice, to the voices he most needs to hear.

Justice Blackmun's dissenting opinion (written for himself and Justices Brennan, Marshall, and Stevens) was written by the justice who authored *Roe v. Wade*. In contrast to the majority opinion, Blackmun assumed not only that constitutional privacy is a legitimately inferred and protected constitutional right but that *Roe v. Wade* was a justified application of that right. His concern, like Justice Stevens's in his own dissenting opinion, was almost entirely with the character, substance, and scope of the basic constitutional right that is constitutional privacy rather than with the question of how and why the grounds that rationalized Georgia's sodomy statute failed to meet the standard of compelling secular state purposes that justify abridgment of even basic rights.

What gives Justice Blackmun's dissenting opinion its power was his opening comparison of the Georgia sodomy statute with the way Justice White's opinion for the Court positioned the case: "The Court's almost obsessive focus on homosexual activity is particularly hard to justify in light of the broad language Georgia has used."[23] Georgia's statute was act-centered: it made certain sex acts criminal, irrespective of the gender of the partners. The statute thus criminalized heterosexual and homosexual fellatio, cunnilingus, and anal discourse: "The sex or status of the persons who engage in the act is irrelevant as a matter of state law."[24] Such statutes make sense historically if we understand their origins in the sexual morality of Augustine and Thomas Aquinas: a morality that condemned all nonprocreational sex, heterosexual and homosexual, and that for this reason was not specifically homophobic but rather skeptical of the value of sexuality as such. But what Justice Blackmun's opinion made clear was that it was only the prohibition of homosexual forms of nonprocreational sex that interested Georgia prosecutors, indeed, that even common moral opinion now might reject the criminalization of heterosexual forms of nonprocreational sex, perhaps regarding such sex acts as protected by the constitutional right to privacy (this might have been the view, for example, of a majority of the justices in *Bowers v. Hardwick*, including Justice Powell). Blackmun's analysis clearly showed that Justice White's opinion, by accepting constitutional privacy in the full range of its heterosexual applications and then abruptly, indeed dismissively refusing *any* homosexual applications, was itself the cultural agent of contemporary, modernist homophobia, seeing any evil in nonprocreational sex *only* in its homosexual forms.

Perhaps the closest historical analogy to the Supreme Court's playing such an ugly role in the cultural validation of irrationalist political prejudices was *Plessy v. Ferguson*, in which the Court, interpreting an equal-protection clause that clearly condemned the expression of irrational racial hatred through law, refused to find state-imposed segregation by race to be an expression of such hatred, thus ratifying and supporting a pattern of American apartheid that unconstitutionally dehumanized persons of color, as the Supreme Court was to acknowledge in 1954 when it unanimously overruled *Plessy* in *Brown v. Board of Education. Bowers,* in both its style and its result, gave gay people like me a brutal sense of what African Americans had experienced in *Plessy,* a sense of irrationalist exclusion from human community. I recall that my first response to *Bowers* was an almost physical sense of personal assault not only on myself, as a gay person, but on the subject, constitutional law, that I had, as a teacher and scholar, attempted to impart to my students and readers as one of great humane integrity. I grieved that the Supreme Court could so shamelessly betray its trust. Its holding also set back the case for gay rights in other areas, for, if gay/lesbian sex could legitimately be subject to criminal penalties, the fact of legitimate criminalization could be considered a rational basis for other forms of unjust treatment.

What made Justice Blackmun's dissenting opinion so constitutionally pathbreaking, certainly in terms of the constitutional recognition of the human rights of gays and lesbians, was the obvious sense of humane justice that he brought to the interpretation of the right to constitutional privacy itself. As his remarks about Justice Powell's denial that he knew any homosexuals showed, Justice Blackmun not only knew gay men and lesbians but knew them as persons.[25] Blackmun obviously understood exactly what he said in his dissent in *Bowers v. Hardwick:* "Only the most willful blindness could obscure the fact that sexual intimacy is 'a sensitive, key relationship of human existence, central to family life, community welfare, and the development of personality.' . . . The fact that individuals define themselves in a significant way through their intimate sexual relationships with others suggests, in a Nation as diverse as ours, that there may be many 'right' ways of conducting those relationships, and that much of the richness of a relationship will come from the freedom an individual has to *choose* the form and nature of these intensely personal bonds."[26]

Justice Blackmun, in contrast to Justice White, believed not only in the principle of constitutional privacy but in its applications, including in *Roe v. Wade,* and he thus succeeded in doing what White did not even attempt to do: offering the most plausible normative reading of the earlier constitutional privacy cases as grounded in a basic human right to intimate life when there was no longer a compelling secular basis that could justify the abridgment of such a right. It was because he made much better sense of the existing case law that he could so clearly see that the same right is owed all Americans, including gays and lesbians.

Once a compelling case was made, as Justice Blackmun did, for reading the legitimacy of the principle of constitutional privacy as protecting so basic a human right, owed equally to heterosexuals and homosexuals, it was the force of arguments of principle, as the ground for the legitimacy of judicial review, that justified his argument for extending constitutional privacy to gay/lesbian sex. The Georgia statute, criminalizing such sex, clearly abridged a basic constitutional right, and could not, Blackmun argued, any more present a compelling secular justification than it could to justify the prohibition of the sale and use of contraceptives, in the modern period of overpopulation pressing on scarce resources, "because of demographic considerations or the Bible's command to be fruitful and multiply."[27] Blackmun thus responded to Justice White's worries about line-drawing by drawing reasonable lines: "drugs and weapons are inherently dangerous,"[28] "adultery is likely to injure third persons,"[29] and "the nature of familial relationships renders true consent to incestuous activity sufficiently problematical that a blanket prohibition of such activity is warranted."[30]

The dissenting opinion of Justice Stevens (with whom Justices Brennan and Marshall joined) took as its premise, as did Justice Blackmun's, the authority and meaning of the cases that have protected the constitutional right to privacy. It is from this perspective that Justice Stevens put his constitutional analysis in terms of two questions: First, may a state, like Georgia, prohibit all nonprocreational sex acts, irrespective of the gender of the parties? and second, if not, may a state save the statute by announcing that it will enforce its ban only against partners of the same sex? With respect to the first question, Justice Stevens answered that the principle of the privacy cases so far decided by the Supreme Court clearly protected the right of intimate sexual life of both married and unmarried persons and protected that right whenever the parties "are isolated from observation from others,"[31] grounded in "the right to engage in nonreproductive, sexual conduct that others may consider offensive or immoral."[32] The right, thus recognized by existing case law, clearly forbade the Georgia criminal status targeting nonprocreational sex acts. With respect to the second question, Justice Stevens argued that any selective application of such a statute against homosexuals but not heterosexuals "must be supported by a neutral and legitimate interest— something more substantial than a substantial dislike for, or ignorance about, the disfavored group."[33] But there were two reasons for believing that the state of Georgia itself did not believe there was such an interest:

first, it did not choose to ban only gay/lesbian sex; and second, its prosecutors had chosen not to pursue criminal actions against such conduct.

The dissenting opinions of both Justices Blackmun and Stevens make clear that, once a constitutionally guaranteed right applies, any general argument that appeals to dominant or conventional moral opinion, or majoritarian offense, or long-standing religious tradition cannot suffice to justify serious abridgment of that right unsupported by a compelling secular state purpose. It is at this point that their argument draws upon a form of John Stuart Mill's harm principle: the right of personal autonomy in Mill's liberal political philosophy is instantiated by the right of constitutional privacy, and Mill's point is, of course, that conventional moral opinion cannot suffice to abridge such a basic right in the absence of the conduct in question meeting the requirements of the harm principle (for example, imposing harm on a third party).

But there is a difference between Mill's harm principle and the form of it defended by Justices Blackmun and Stevens. For Mill, the right to personal autonomy was a general right of personal liberty, but in the view of constitutional privacy defended by Blackmun and Stevens, constitutional privacy is specifically a right to sexual liberty in personal, noncommercial relationships, a right that can be abridged if a heavy burden of justification is satisfied (e.g., Blackmun's examples of adultery and incest). There are good reasons, rooted in American constitutional principles, for giving constitutional privacy a broader reading, in line with Mill's pathbreaking argument of liberal political theory. I have defended such a reading, extending privacy as a sexual right to commercial sex and expanding it to include use of "soft" drugs and certain decisions to die.[34] But while the Supreme Court of the United States has given limited recognition to a right to die,[35] it has shown no inclination to expand constitutional recognition of the right in the ways I would endorse consistent with Mill's principle.

I was not neutral about the growing skepticism about the principle of constitutional privacy reflected in *Bowers v. Hardwick,* and I accordingly not only wrote articles and books that were critical of this view (including the theory of John Hart Ely)[36] but became increasingly concerned that appointments to the Supreme Court by then President Reagan were based on the judicial philosophy hostile to the principle of constitutional privacy. In 1987, the year after *Bowers v. Hardwick,* my worries crystallized when President Reagan nominated Judge Robert Bork to the high Court. Judge Bork had written in no uncertain terms about his hostility to the principle of constitutional privacy on grounds that seemed to me to lack any historical and normative understanding of either the text or enduring principles of American constitutionalism bearing on the protection of basic human rights owed all Americans. His appointment to the Supreme Court would politicize an issue of basic constitutional principle in ways that threatened what seemed to me the most important ground of judicial review in the United States, the protection of the basic human rights owed all Americans, including political minorities who could not otherwise secure the hearing and the respect that were their due. A Constitution whose legitimacy rested on majority rule and the protection of minority rights was, I thought, in peril from such ill-advised, ideologically driven appointments. It was for this reason that I testified before the Senate Judiciary Committee,[37] expressing my worries about Judge Bork's insensitivity to such an important constitutional principle of law as constitutional privacy.[38] Other law professors made comparable arguments,[39] and Judge Bork's nomination was defeated. The judge who was nominated and confirmed in his stead was Justice Anthony Kennedy, whose views seemed to me and others altogether more reasonable and judicious. Justice Kennedy was to write the opinion for five justices in *Lawrence v. Texas* that would overrule *Bowers v. Hardwick*.

7

LAWRENCE v. TEXAS

Bowers v. Hardwick, decided in 1986, was overruled by *Lawrence v. Texas,* decided in 2003. It took some sixty years for the Supreme Court of the United States to reconsider and overrule *Plessy v. Ferguson* (1896)[1] in *Brown v. Board of Education* (1954),[2] and some thirty years to overrule *Lochner v. New York* (1905)[3] in *Nebbia v. New York* (1934).[4] By comparison, *Bowers,* as authority, was relatively short-lived. Whereas the periods from *Plessy* to *Brown* and from *Lochner* to *Nebbia* were marked by appointments to the Supreme Court of more liberal justices (reflecting shifts in public opinion), the membership of the Supreme Court from *Bowers* to *Lawrence* became, if anything, more conservative, reflecting a number of appointments by Republican presidents committed to the overruling of *Roe v. Wade.* The conservative majority of our current Supreme Court has decided many cases in ways the majority on the Court in *Bowers* would not have: it has been skeptical of racial classifications to the extent of rarely upholding them, even when ameliorative in otherwise reasonable affirmative action programs,[5] and it has developed doctrines in Commerce Clause and other areas that have limited the powers of Congress in ways the previous members of the Court rejected.[6] But several justices in the conservative majority, in particular Justice Sandra Day O'Connor and Justice Anthony Kennedy, have shown a concern for constitutional principle in the protection of basic rights that has distinguished them from other justices in the majority. Their interpretive work suggests that the principles of constitutional privacy transcend partisan political divisions and touch on deeper matters of constitutional essentials, on which they share common ground with more liberal justices. There were two important cases, decided after *Bowers v. Hardwick,* that suggested that these judges might join with more liberal judges to reconsider *Bowers:*

Planned Parenthood of Southeastern Pa. v. Casey,[7] decided in 1992, and *Romer v. Evans,*[8] decided in 1996.

Bowers v. Hardwick was decided in a period of considerable debate in the nation and on the Supreme Court itself about the legitimacy of *Roe v. Wade,* a debate that clearly showed itself in Justice White's opinion for the Court in *Bowers,* reflecting skepticism not only about *Roe v. Wade* but about the very principle of a constitutional right to privacy. Because of judicial appointments by Republican presidents, by 1992 there was clearly a majority on the Supreme Court that could, if it wished, have overruled *Roe* (including Chief Justice William Rehnquist and Justices Byron White, Antonin Scalia, Clarence Thomas, O'Connor, Kennedy, and David Souter); only two justices clearly committed to *Roe* remained on the high Court (Justices Harry Blackmun and John Stevens). To the surprise of many, three justices in the likely overruling group (namely, O'Connor, Kennedy, and Souter) chose not to overrule *Roe* in *Planned Parenthood of Southeastern Pa. v. Casey,* rather preserving its essential principle (no criminalization before viability), although allowing more regulation before that point than the *Roe* Court had been prepared to accept.

The opinion for the Court of these three justices (joined, on the issue of essential principle, by Justices Blackmun and Stevens), discussed two central points: the legitimacy of constitutional privacy as a principle of American constitutional law and the force stare decisis should have in overruling precedent. What was crucial in their decision to affirm the essential principle of *Roe* was their deliberative coming to judgment that the radical critics of the principle of constitutional privacy (including Justices White, Rehnquist, Scalia, and Thomas) were wrong. They concluded that constitutional privacy was a legitimate principle of American public law in both its dimensions: the identification of a basic human right to intimate life, rooted in conscience and conviction, that grounds the constitutionally protected right; and the requirement that any serious abridgment of such a right can be justified only by a compelling burden of secular justification. *Griswold v. Connecticut* (striking down a criminal ban on use of contraceptives) was a clearly justified application of this principle, and even *Roe v. Wade,* in the view of these justices, implicated the principle. There was no doubt, they argued, that the decision of a woman whether or not to carry a child to term is an aspect of the right to intimate life, both in terms of the sexual relationship that led to the pregnancy and in terms of whether to form a relationship to a child. The question they would have had about *Roe,* were it a case before them of first impression, was whether *Roe* gave appropriate weight to the countervailing state interest in fetal life (which the *Roe* Court acknowledged as a legitimate state interest) in determining the scope and weight of the right to intimate life. What led them to reaffirm the essential principle of *Roe* was that they accepted the principle of constitutional privacy as wholly legitimate, and that the issue of *Roe* was not its principle but the way in which the principle was applied (namely, giving weight to fetal life, for purposes of criminalization, only at viability). Some among these three justices might have drawn this line in a different way (perhaps earlier than viability), but they believed that it was appropriate to overrule an important earlier case, such as *Lochner v. New York* or *Plessy v. Ferguson*, only when its underlying principle was wrong, not when a later Court came to a different view of how the principle should be applied. Overruling *Roe* on its essential point of principle would not rest on compelling arguments of principle, and would indeed subvert public understanding of the legitimacy of judicial review in the United States, which rests on upholding arguments of principle against partisan politics. The three justices, all appointed by Republican presidents hostile to *Roe*, would, if they overruled *Roe*, compromise the legitimacy of the Supreme Court by bending their sense of interpretive responsibility (grounded in arguments of principle) opportunistically to the demands of their political masters.

There was, strikingly, no mention in the opinion for the Court of the three justices, nor in the concurring opinions of Justices Blackmun and Stevens, of *Bowers v. Hardwick* (though Justice O'Connor had concurred in the Court's opinion in that case). The opinion of Justice White for the Court in *Bowers* had expressed a general skepticism about the right of constitutional privacy, only incidentally involved in that case. The three justices writing the opinion for the Court in *Casey* put that skepticism to rest, and indeed reaffirmed the application of the principle in *Roe*, a case crucially involving the weight to be accorded state interests in fetal life. Arguably, there is more of an issue of legitimate state interests in *Roe* than in *Bowers*, which would suggest that the principle of constitutional privacy might reasonably be regarded as even more egregiously violated by a criminal ban on gay/lesbian sex.

Romer v. Evans was not, like *Casey*, only by implication about the continuing authority of *Bowers*. The continuing authority and meaning of *Bowers* were very much at the heart of the interpretive issue in the case, as Justice Scalia made clear in his dissent. In response to political arguments by gay groups in Colorado, laws had been approved by various municipalities in the state that protected gays and lesbians from discrimination on the ground of sexual orientation (on the analogy of the state and federal laws that forbid discrimination on grounds of religion, race, ethnicity, and gender). Sodomy was no longer criminal in Colorado, but groups opposed to gay rights had secured passage of Colorado Amendment Two, an amendment to the state constitution, that not only repealed such antidiscrimination ordinances but forbade any such antidiscrimination laws or policies ever to be effective in Colorado.[9] *Bowers,* which allowed the criminalization of gay/lesbian sex, was implicated in the arguments for Colorado Amendment Two because if the conduct central to a group's identity could be criminal, then it seemed reasonable that a state, which could constitutionally forbid such conduct, might take the less restrictive option of not criminalizing it but discouraging its public acceptability by forbidding any protections of gays and lesbians from people's desire not to associate with them.

Justice Kennedy's opinion for the Court was joined by five justices (Justices O'Connor, Souter, Stevens, Ginsburg, and Breyer); Justice Scalia wrote in dissent for himself, Chief Justice Rehnquist, and Justice Thomas. Kennedy's opinion nowhere mentioned *Bowers,* whereas the authority of *Bowers* was at the center of Justice Scalia's argument in *Romer:* "In holding that homosexuality cannot be singled out for disfavorable treatment, the Court contradicts a decision, unchallenged here, pronounced only 10 years ago, see *Bowers v. Hardwick.*"[10]

What makes *Romer* so important in marking the Court's growing recognition of the constitutional rights of gays and lesbians is its sense, from the very opening of Justice Kennedy's opinion for the Court, that populist support for Colorado Amendment Two is analogous to support for state-endorsed racial segregation in *Plessy v. Ferguson.* I earlier observed that, as Justice Blackmun's dissenting opinion argued in *Bowers,* what made Justice White's opinion for the Court so objectionable in that case was that, analogous to *Plessy,* its endorsement of distinctions that have no basis other than irrational prejudice made the Supreme Court of the United States, in violation of its constitutional responsibilities to treat persons as equals, the unconstitutional agent of the cultural construction of prejudice, whether racism in *Plessy* or homophobia in *Bowers.* Although Justice Kennedy's opinion in *Romer* did not mention *Bowers,* its opening appeal to Justice Harlan's dissent in *Plessy* (the Constitution "neither knows nor tolerates classes among citizens"[11]) strikingly aligned that dissent with Justice Blackmun's dissent in *Bowers.* It was not only the style of Kennedy's opinion that questioned the continuing authority of *Bowers;* it was its substance. Colorado Amendment

Two was unconstitutional, Kennedy argued, because it lacked any rational relationship to legitimate state interests and reflected unconstitutional irrational prejudice. Kennedy did not recognize as legitimate what Justice Scalia, in his dissent, argued *Bowers* established as legitimate: an evil in gay/lesbian sex that justifies criminalization. If such an evil is a legitimate basis for outright banning, it must, Scalia argued, be a rational basis for drawing distinctions. Kennedy's denial of this point suggested *Bowers* is not legitimate.

There was a rather brilliant argument in Justice Kennedy's opinion that clearly attempted to answer Justice Scalia's argument, again without mentioning or discussing *Bowers:* Kennedy's discussion of earlier cases dealing with the Mormons. These cases were of two sorts: those that constitutionally allowed laws that banned Mormon polygamy, although polygamy was then rooted in the right of religious liberty,[12] and those that allowed Mormons to be deprived of the right to vote.[13] Justice Kennedy did not question the authority of the case upholding a ban on polygamy (presumably on the ground that banning a practice rooted in a basic right like religious liberty is allowable if there is a compelling state interest [for example, gender equality] that justifies the ban), but the latter case, he argued, was no longer good law because it rested on the now constitutionally unacceptable view "that persons advocating a certain practice may be denied the right to vote."[14] Just because a religious practice may be constitutionally banned, it does not follow that advocacy of such a practice may be a ground for depriving the advocates of a basic right such as voting. The analogy to gays and lesbians is evident: gays and lesbians now publicly claimed their basic rights on fair terms with other Americans. It might be, if *Bowers v. Hardwick* was good law, that conduct rooted in their conscientious exercise of their right to intimate life might be banned because a compelling state purpose supported such a ban; but it did not follow that their public claims and lives as gays and lesbians could for that reason be the subject of discrimination.

What the analogy showed is how far, in the view of six justices of the Supreme Court, gays and lesbians had come in twenty years, bringing their ethical voices to bear on American politics and constitutional law. Although opposition to gay rights is often grounded in traditional religious views that condemn gay/lesbian sex as an unspeakable crime against nature not to be mentioned among Christians, the growing public presence of gays and lesbians in American intellectual and public life, including arguments by me and others about the justice of their claims, led the six justices to recognize the claims of gays and lesbians as being as much rooted in ethical conviction and argument, at the core of the constitutional protection of religious liberty, as the arguments of their opponents. The analogy of the Mormons was thus striking in giving constitutional recognition to the voices of gays and lesbians as ethical voices, as much entitled to respect as any other voices in America. The argument also suggested that what might have moved the Court in *Romer* was the sense of religious discrimination against gays and lesbians: a sectarian cultural war on the personal and ethical convictions of gays and lesbians analogous to traditional Christian discrimination against Jews and no better justified on constitutional grounds of equal treatment of all forms of conscience, whether traditional religious claims or contemporary ethical voices challenging such claims (I discuss this point further in the next chapter).

Nothing in Justice Kennedy's argument required that *Bowers v. Hardwick* still be considered good law; indeed, his failure even to mention *Bowers* suggested, as Justice Scalia claimed, that the Court now had very real doubts about the authority and weight of *Bowers*. Kennedy's argument showed that *Romer* did not require, though it might permit, the overruling of *Bowers*. It did not require it because that matter would turn, as the Mormon case did, on the weight of the state purpose underlying the criminal bans; it might permit it if the Court found both that a basic right had been violated and that no such compelling purpose could be proven. What plausibly suggested that *Bowers* would be overruled was the premise of Kennedy's argument: that a fundamental right, as basic as the religious liberty rights of the Mormons, was owed to gays and lesbians. Recall that Justice White's argument in *Bowers* denied that any basic right was owed to gays and lesbians. Justice Kennedy took a different view in *Romer,* which suggested that White's dismissal of gay/lesbian rights, as rights, no longer commanded a majority of the Supreme Court—which was to say that the authority of *Bowers* was now in very real doubt.

Two later cases, while unfavorable to the claims made by gays and lesbians, showed the growing seriousness with which the ethical voices of gays and lesbians were taken by American democratic politics, in particular at the state level. The first such case was *Hurley v. Irish-American Gay, Lesbian and Bisexual Group of Boston (GLIB),*[15] decided in 1995, and the second was *Boy Scouts of America v. Dale,*[16] decided in 2000. Both cases involved constitutional issues relating to the application of state laws forbidding discrimination on grounds of sexual orientation. In *Hurley,* a Massachusetts state law forbade discrimination on the basis of sexual orientation in a place of public accommodation, which GLIB had successfully argued in state courts applied to the exclusion of the group from the Boston St. Patrick's Day parade. In *Boy Scouts of America,* a New Jersey law forbade discrimination on the basis of sexual orientation in public accommodations, which the highest court of the state held required admission to the Boy Scouts of a gay man who had publicly advocated gay rights. In *Hurley,* Justice Souter, writing for a unanimous Supreme Court, held that the state statute was unconstitutional as applied to the expressive decisions of a private parade, appealing to the free-speech rights of the organizers of the parade to decide whom they would include in the parade. The Court in *Boy Scouts of America* was more closely divided. Chief Justice Rehnquist, writing for a 5–4 majority that included himself and Justices O'Connor, Kennedy, Scalia, and Thomas, held that the forced inclusion of an unwanted person in a group unconstitutionally infringed the group's freedom of expressive association if the presence of that person affected in a significant way that group's ability to advocate public or private viewpoints, and found this standard unconstitutionally to be violated in the application of the state antidiscrimination law to the gay man in question. In dissent, Justice Stevens, writing for himself and Justices Souter, Ginsburg, and Breyer, denied that the Boy Scouts had proclaimed any antigay philosophy and thus rejected the authority of *Hurley* as governing this case. Unlike GLIB, Dale did not carry a banner or sign, and he expressed no intention of sending any message. It was therefore a mistake for the majority to suppose that *Boy Scouts of America,* like *Hurley,* involved the application of a state statute that violated free-speech rights.[17]

What both cases illustrated was how far the voices of gays and lesbians had come in thirty years in securing some degree of recognition for their claims of justice: in these cases, state laws added sexual orientation to already forbidden grounds of discrimination such as religion, race/ethnicity, and gender. There was, of course, reactionary legislation as well, including not only Colorado Amendment Two but state and federal defense-of-marriage legislation (see Chapter 9) and the like. But robust judicial protection of their free-speech rights had made gay/lesbian protests possible, including the protection of expressive individuality that *Hurley* represented and elaborated. If the Supreme Court would now protect speech that expressed forms of discrimination that are constitutionally forbidden as suspect classes (such as race/ethnicity and gender), it was not surprising that it would protect speech that advocated discrimination on a ground (sexual orientation) not yet fully recognized as a suspect class. It was much less clear, as Justice Stevens argued in his dissent in *Boy Scouts of America,* that there was any comparable free-speech interest involved in that case.

When, however, gays made a constitutional claim to a basic right now robustly accorded other Americans (namely, the constitutional right to privacy), the Supreme Court, in a 6–3 opinion, decisively vindicated their claim in *Lawrence v. Texas*,[18] striking down a Texas sodomy statute, with five justices directly overruling *Bowers v. Hardwick*. Justice Kennedy wrote the opinion of the Court for himself and Justices Stevens, Souter, Ginsburg, and Breyer; Justice O'Connor wrote an opinion concurring in the judgment; Justice Scalia filed a dissenting opinion, joined by Chief Justice Rehnquist and Justice Thomas; and Justice Thomas filed a short dissenting opinion.

The facts of *Lawrence v. Texas* were these. In Houston, Texas, officers of the police department were dispatched to a private residence in response to a reported weapons disturbance. They entered an apartment where Lawrence resided. The officers observed Lawrence and another man engaged in a sexual act, and they were both arrested, held in custody overnight, and charged and convicted before a justice of the peace under a Texas criminal law that forbade sexual relations between parties of the same sex. The petitioners exercised their right to a trial de novo in Harris County Criminal Court, claiming violations of equal-protection guarantees of both the federal and state constitutions. Their claims were rejected, and each was fined and assessed costs. The Court of Appeals for the Texas Fourteenth District considered the petitioners' federal constitutional claims under the Equal Protection and Due Process Clauses of the Fourteenth Amendment. After hearing the case en banc, the court, in a divided opinion, rejected the constitutional claims and affirmed the conviction, appealing, as the basis for its decision, to the authority of *Bowers v. Hardwick*. The Supreme Court granted certiorari to consider, inter alia, whether *Bowers* should be overruled.

Notably, the two justices who wrote opinions holding the Texas statute to be unconstitutional were among the three justices who had in *Casey* reaffirmed the essential principle of *Roe v. Wade*. What their argument there made quite clear was their deliberative conviction that constitutional privacy was a legitimate principle of law and that therefore the essential principle of *Roe*, resting on the reasonable interpretation of a valid principle of law, should not be overruled. Presumably, the overruling of *Bowers* would depend on whether it did justice to this principle of law. Justice Kennedy's opinion for the Court in *Romer v. Evans* had already, as we have seen, cast the continuing authority of *Bowers* in some doubt.

Justice Kennedy's opinion for the Court, in the course of holding the Texas criminal statute unconstitutional, overruled *Bowers v. Hardwick* because, in his view, it did not do justice to the principle of constitutional privacy as it had been developed and elaborated in case law including *Griswold v. Connecticut*, *Roe v. Wade*, and *Planned Parenthood of Southeastern Pa. v. Casey*.

His analysis critically examined *Bowers* on two counts: its understanding of the basic right on which constitutional privacy rests, and its treatment of the purposes that could justify a ban on gay/lesbian sex.

Justice Kennedy questioned the way in which Justice White in *Bowers* described the right in question: "whether the Federal Constitution confers a fundamental right upon homosexuals to engage in sodomy."[19] White's very statement "discloses the Court's own failure to appreciate the extent of the liberty at stake. To say that the issue in *Bowers* was simply the right to engage in certain sexual conduct demeans the claim the individual put forward, just as it would demean a married couple were it to be said marriage is simply about the right to have sexual intercourse."[20] What Kennedy sensitively analyzed was the way Justice White's opinion objectified gay/lesbian sexuality in the same way that anti-Semitism imposed a dehumanized conception of their sexuality on Jews or racism reduced black sexuality to the coupling of cattle. To be sure, criminal statutes that ban gay/lesbian sexuality apply to sex acts, but, consistent with the irrationalist prejudice that motivates such laws, "their penalties and purposes . . . have more far-reaching consequences, touching upon the most private human conduct, sexual behavior, and in the most private of places, the home. The statutes do seek to control a personal relationship that, whether or not entitled to formal recognition in the law, is within the liberty of persons to choose without being punished as criminals."[21]

Justice Kennedy wanted to insist that a fair-minded understanding of the basic right underlying constitutional privacy should take seriously, both in straight and gay sexual relations, the relational integrity of our sexual affections and lives, the connections between sexual expression and companionate friendship and love: "It suffices for us to acknowledge that adults may choose to enter upon this relationship in the confines of their homes and their own private lives and still retain their dignity as free persons. When sexuality finds overt expression in intimate conduct with another person, the conduct can be but one element in a personal bond that is more enduring. The liberty protected by the Constitution allows homosexual persons the right to make this choice."[22]

Justice Kennedy's critical observations about Justice White's characterization of the issue in *Bowers* echoed the same concerns in Justice Blackmun's dissenting opinion in the case, in particular the way in which a right, rooted in conviction, is erased by homophobic sexualization, which treats love as pornography. At the end of his opinion, Justice Kennedy returned to the ugly motives of irrational contempt that motivate such injustice: "The State cannot demean their existence or control their destiny by making their private sexual conduct a crime."[23] Kennedy connected his criticism of White's mischaracterization of the basic right to the unreasonable way he treated the place of history in constitutional interpretation. As I earlier observed, Justice White believed the interpretation of history mattered in constitutional interpretation not in terms of how those who wrote and ratified the Constitution would have applied its terms but in terms of more abstract connotations or intentions that could reasonably be ascribed to the text and then recontextualized in terms of a reasonable understanding of what the text should mean in contemporary circumstances, including our sense of relevant facts and values. But his failure to understand or give weight to the basic right underlying the principle of constitutional privacy led Justice White to a kind of appeal to history that he would have rejected as anachronistic and unreasonable in other interpretive areas. In fact, as Justice Kennedy showed, what history shows is not a specific concern with gay/lesbian sex but a general concern with all forms of nonprocreational sex, heterosexual and homosexual. The constitutional privacy cases up to *Bowers* show a rejection of the historical view of the intrinsic evil of nonprocreational sex as anachronistic and no longer supported by compelling secular arguments in contemporary circumstances. It is for this reason that the Supreme Court found this view of sexual morality an unconstitutional purpose today, and thus no longer sufficient to justify the abridgment of so basic a human and constitutional right as the right to intimate life. What *Bowers* incoherently did was to give the history it had rejected as unreasonable, when interpreting the right to privacy in the context of heterosexuality, controlling weight in the context of homosexuality.

Moreover, Justice Kennedy argued that specific concern with homosexuality did not, as the majority in *Bowers* supposed, have ancient roots: "American laws targeting same-sex couples did not develop until the last third of the 20th century."[24] Kennedy concluded that the uses of history in *Bowers* "are not without doubt and, at the very least, are overstated."[25] In any event, Kennedy argued that "our laws and traditions in the past half century are those of most relevance here," which "show an emerging awareness that liberty gives substantial protection to adult persons in deciding how to conduct their private lives in matters pertaining to sex."[26] These developments "should have been apparent when *Bowers* was decided."[27] Such developments included the recommendation in 1955 of the American Law Institute that criminal laws not impose "criminal penalties for consensual sexual relations conducted in private"[28] and the recommendation in 1957 of the

Wolfenden Report in Great Britain urging the British Parliament to repeal laws punishing homosexual conduct (its recommendations were enacted ten years later).[29] Justice Kennedy put particular weight on the decision of the European Court of Human Rights, which, almost five years before *Bowers*, held that laws criminalizing gay sex were invalid under the European Convention on Human Rights,[30] a decision "authoritative in all countries that are members of the Council of Europe (21 countries then, 45 nations now)" and "at odds with the premise in *Bowers* that the claim put forward was insubstantial in our Western civilization."[31]

But the authorities most decisive on this issue, for Justice Kennedy, were the Court's own precedents, notably *Planned Parenthood of Southeastern Pa. v. Casey* and *Romer v. Evans*. In *Casey*, Justice Kennedy was one of three justices (Justices O'Connor and Souter were the others) who reaffirmed the legitimacy of the principle of constitutional privacy in general and the essential principle of *Roe v. Wade* in particular. The principle of constitutional privacy, thus clarified and reaffirmed, established a basic constitutional right to autonomy in intimate sexual matters, a right that persons seek in both homosexual and heterosexual relationships. And Justice Kennedy wrote for the Court in *Romer v. Evans*, holding that Colorado Amendment Two was "'born of animosity toward the class of persons affected' and further that it had no rational relation to a legitimate governmental purpose."[32] Although the Court had been invited to strike down the Texas statute on equal-protection grounds (because it criminalized only homosexual nonprocreational sex acts), Kennedy declined to adopt that suggestion because it would leave open the possibility that the conduct might be criminal, which would invite unjust discrimination against gays and lesbians and not address the constitutional evil of *Bowers* itself, namely, that "its continuance as precedent demeans the lives of homosexual persons."[33]

In overruling *Bowers*, Justice Kennedy adopted as the Court's rationale the dissent of Justice Stevens in *Bowers*:

> Our prior cases make two propositions abundantly clear. First, the fact that the governing majority in a State has traditionally viewed a particular practice as immoral is not a sufficient reason for upholding a law prohibiting the practice; neither history nor tradition could save a law prohibiting miscegenation from constitutional attack. Second, individual decisions by married persons, concerning the intimacies of their physical relationship, even when not intended to produce offspring, are a form of "liberty" protected by the Due Process Clause of the

Fourteenth Amendment. Moreover, this protection extends to intimate choices by unmarried as well as married persons.[34]

It was because any ban on gay/lesbian sex abridges this basic right, owed all persons on grounds of principle, rationalized by long-standing moral opinions no longer supported by constitutionally compelling justifications, that *Bowers,* which acknowledged neither the right nor the burden of justification, had to be overruled.

On the issue of the required burden of justification, Justice Kennedy discussed various such burdens of justification not met by a total ban on gay/lesbian sex:

> The present case does not involve minors. It does not involve persons who might be injured or coerced or who are situated in relationships where consent might not easily be refused. It does not involve public conduct or prostitution. It does not involve whether the government must give formal recognition to any relationship that homosexual persons seek to enter. The case does involve two adults who, with full and mutual consent from each other, engaged in sexual practices common to a homosexual lifestyle. The petitioners are entitled to respect for their private lives. The State cannot demean their existence or control their destiny by making their private sexual conduct a crime. . . . The Texas statute furthers no legitimate state interest which can justify its intrusion into the personal and private life of the individual.[35]

Kennedy concluded that the basic principles of American constitutional law were intentionally not drafted by the Founders in specific terms, a fact suggesting they did not claim to know "the components of liberty in its manifold possibilities" but were open to new arguments and experience that critically questioned the weight of history on grounds of justice: "They knew times can blind us to certain truths and later generations can see that laws once thought necessary and proper in fact serve only to oppress. As the Constitution endures, persons in every generation can invoke its principles in their own search for greater freedom."[36] The protesting ethical voices of gays and lesbians, building on earlier protest movements, stand foursquare in this tradition.

Justice O'Connor's opinion, concurring in the judgment of the Court, would not have overruled *Bowers v. Hardwick,* in which she had been in the majority. What was constitutionally offensive, for O'Connor, in the Texas statute was not that it banned nonprocreational sex acts but that it banned only homosexual sex acts. In contrast, the Georgia statute, in *Bowers v. Hardwick,* banned nonprocreational sex acts as such. There was no need, on the facts of *Lawrence,* to decide whether a neutral statute, directed at all non-procreational sex acts, "would violate the substantive component of the *Due Process Clause.*" It sufficed that a statute targeting only gays and lesbians violates equal protection, and Justice O'Connor opined that democratic politics can be depended on to eliminate all such statutes: "I am confident, however, that so long as the *Equal Protection Clause* requires a sodomy law to apply equally to the private consensual conduct of homosexuals and heterosexuals alike, such a law would not long stand in our democratic society."[37]

Justice Scalia wrote in dissent for himself, Chief Justice Rehnquist, and Justice Thomas (who also wrote a brief dissent commenting on his own view that such laws are politically unjustified, although constitutional). What was, of course, at work in Scalia's argument was that, like Justice White in *Bowers,* he was skeptical about the principle of constitutional privacy in general and its application to abortion in particular. It was from this perspective that Scalia criticized the opinions of the majority (those of both Kennedy and O'Connor) as politically rather than constitutionally grounded. If his views on the issue of constitutional principle are wrong, as they clearly are, the interest of his dissent is his pressing the issue of the implications of the Court's opinion for the constitutionality of same-sex marriage. On this point, he addressed Justice O'Connor's equal-protection argument:

> This reasoning leaves on pretty shaky grounds state laws limiting marriage to opposite-sex couples. Justice O'Connor seeks to preserve them by the conclusory statement that "preserving the traditional institution of marriage" is a legitimate state interest. . . . But "preserving the traditional institution of marriage" is just a kinder way of describing the State's *moral disapproval* of same-sex couples. Texas's interest . . . [in its sodomy statute] could be recast in similarly euphemistic terms: "preserving the traditional sexual mores of our society." In the jurisprudence Justice O'Connor has seemingly created, judges can validate laws by characterizing them as "preserving the traditions of society" (good); or invalidate them by characterizing them as "expressing moral disapproval" (bad).[38]

We must now investigate the implications of *Lawrence v. Texas* for the future development of American constitutional law.

8

SEXUAL ORIENTATION AS A SUSPECT CLASS

Yuval Merin has argued in his important comparative study of the development and legal recognition of gay/lesbian rights, based on close study of these developments in various constitutional democracies in Europe and North America, that there has been a natural order in this development: first, decriminalization of gay/lesbian sex acts; second, legal developments forbidding discrimination on grounds of sexual orientation on a par with race/ethnicity and gender; and third, legal recognition of same-sex partnerships on terms of equality with opposite-sex partnerships, including, as Merin urges, same-sex marriage, now fully recognized in the Netherlands, Belgium, several provinces of Canada, and the state of Massachusetts. It is a notable feature of the originally Scandinavian development of legal recognition of same-sex partnerships that such recognition was achieved through democratic politics, and later developments in the Netherlands happened in the same way. Judicial review played more of a role in the Canadian developments, which nonetheless enjoy apparently democratic support across Canada.[1]

The United States is in a very different situation, at least on the issue of recognition of same-sex partnerships, as we shall see in the next chapter. After *Lawrence v. Texas*, what next? Decriminalization of gay/lesbian sex acts undercuts the normative premise of other forms of disadvantage directed at gays and lesbians; the criminalization of gay/lesbian sexuality offers a rational ground for employment discrimination that, upon decriminalization, lacks any basis. Comparative law suggests that after decriminalization there will, sooner or later, be further development both of equal-protection principles rendering sexual orientation a suspect ground of discrimination and of legal recognition of same-sex partnerships, including same-sex marriage. I examine in this chapter the case for the suspect nature of sexual orientation and

101

turn in the next chapter to the case for same-sex marriage. As it turns out, they are closely interconnected questions.

As I earlier suggested, in the areas of both race and gender there is a close normative connection between the growing constitutionally suspect quality of these categories and constitutional concern for laws bearing on the right to intimate life, whether antimiscegenation laws or constitutional privacy cases. We can see this as a consequence of the constitutional evil of both racism and sexism, a structural injustice marked by two features: abridgment of basic human rights of conscience, speech, intimate life, and work of a certain class of persons, and rationalization thereof in terms of dehumanizing stereotypes unjustly derived from the culture of such abridgment. As the judiciary came increasingly to understand and condemn the unjust force of such stereotypes in our law, correspondingly, it recognized how the basic right to intimate life had been unjustly abridged on such grounds. We can, I believe, see a similar development in the close connection between the Supreme Court's growing worry about the force of homophobia in American public life in *Romer v. Evans* and its recognition and protection of the basic right of intimate life of gays and lesbians in *Lawrence v. Texas.* Justice Kennedy, who wrote for the Court in both cases, is clearly sensitive to this connection. His argument in *Lawrence v. Texas* crucially acknowledged how the abridgment of the right to intimate life for gays and lesbians plays a larger role in their unjust treatment by the political culture, demeaning their very existence in terms that clearly bespeak dehumanization and cultural erasure. On the other hand, Justice Kennedy, as well as Justice O'Connor, were in the majority in *Boy Scouts of America,* which suggests that they do not regard homophobia as a cultural evil on the same scale as race or gender. But if Yuval Merin is right, and I believe he is, we will see in time a change in view on this question on and off the Supreme Court, and it will show itself in an understanding of sexual orientation as a suspect class on a par with race/ethnicity and gender.

There are, I believe, two compelling reasons for such a development that I would like to explore in this chapter, reasons that draw upon two already suspect classifications under American constitutional law: religion and gender. These considerations are, I believe, already implicit in cases such as *Romer v. Evans* and *Lawrence v. Texas,* so I will further develop the constitutional analysis of those cases. But I will carry the analysis further, suggesting compelling reasons for regarding sexual orientation as a fully suspect classification. This analysis will set the stage for my study in the next chapter of the constitutional arguments for same-sex marriage, for I believe the reaction to these arguments in the United States today shows how problematically homophobic the U.S. political culture is. I turn in the last chapter of the book to an investigation of how we should understand the force of this political psychology in the United States.

The Religion Analogy

There are two dimensions to understanding the constitutional principles that condemn homophobia: first, homophobia's roots in the same structural injustice as that underlying racism and sexism, and second, its direct rationale in the argument for toleration itself. We can see this quite clearly in the way contemporary arguments for gay rights emerged after World War II in the wake of both the antiracist and antisexist movements earlier discussed. For the first time in American history, such arguments were not met with the brick wall of censorship that had been the earlier American response to Walt Whitman's pathbreaking arguments for gay rights.[2] The contrasting European and American responses to Whitman illustrate the point dramatically. Whitman was reasonably interpreted in Great Britain by John Addington Symonds, Oscar Wilde, and Edward Carpenter as a visionary prophet of a new view of sexuality in general and homosexuality in particular.[3] In contrast, blatant U.S. censorship during this period, prominently through obscenity prosecutions, crushed any correlative development in Whitman's own country.[4] The contemporary movement for gay rights emerged in the United States only after World War II, when, in the wake of the antiracist and antisexist movements, broader protections of constitutional guarantees of conscience and speech were extended to dissent in matters of race and gender as well as sexuality. For gays and lesbians, such broader protections of conscience and speech gave rise to the increasingly prominent role in contemporary arguments for gay rights of self-identifying claims to a gay and lesbian identity on terms of justice.[5] The crucial importance of such claims in the contemporary case for gay rights is best understood as an expression of the inalienable right to conscience, and some contemporary forms of political aggression against gay rights should be understood correspondingly as the expression through public law of constitutionally forbidden religious intolerance. Accordingly, I examine here the role the argument for toleration plays in understanding such claims for gay rights and also examine the exclusions of gays and lesbians from the military in this light.

As we earlier saw, the argument for toleration calls for constraints of principle to be placed on the power of the state to enforce sectarian religious views because the enforcement of such views on society at large created entrenched irrationalist intolerance; such intolerance was unjustly rationalized by limiting standards of debate and speakers to the sectarian measure that supported dominant political authority. The rights-based evil of such intolerance was its unjust abridgment of the inalienable right to conscience, the free exercise of the moral powers of rationality and reasonableness in terms of which persons define personal and ethical meaning in living. Although this human right, like others, may be abridged on grounds of secular goods reasonably acknowledged as such by all persons (irrespective of other philosophical or evaluative disagreements), a sectarian view is not sufficient.

The argument for toleration underlies and clarifies the place and weight of the central human rights protected as constitutional rights by the U.S. Constitution, as amended, in particular the rights of conscience and free speech protected by the First Amendment and the right to intimate life protected by the Ninth and Fourteenth Amendments.[6] The American constitutional tradition of the protection of the right to conscience is a particularly robust one, rooted, as it is, in the guarantees of religious liberty by the Free Exercise and Establishment Clauses of the First Amendment. Both these clauses protect different aspects of the exercise of the right to conscience. The Free Exercise Clause addresses the exercise of settled conscientious convictions, condemning as suspect state burdens placed on the exercise of such convictions unsupported by a compelling secular justification;[7] its companion Establishment Clause renders suspect state support of sectarian religious views, again unsupported by an independently compelling secular justification, at stages of acquisition or change in conscientious views, for example, contexts of state action that support or encourage the teaching of and/or conversion to such views.[8] The state may not discriminate either against or in favor of sectarian conscience but must extend equal respect to all forms of conscience.

This constitutional protection of conscientious conviction makes sense against the background of history and political theory that these guarantees reflect. Both Locke and Bayle, who importantly state the argument for toleration as a constitutive principle of legitimate politics, were concerned to protect the free exercise of moral powers of rationality and reasonableness, in terms of which persons define the personal and ethical meaning of their lives, against sectarian impositions on this basic moral freedom; such impositions had, in their views as believing Christians, corrupted the ethical core of Christianity (simple and elevated imperatives of humane mutual respect

and charity) by degrading conscience itself to the measure of sectarian theological dogmas.[9] Both Locke and Bayle, consistent with the dominant
Protestant theological ethics of their age, limited the scope of protected conscience (excluding Catholics and atheists[10]), but they were surely wrong in
linking ethical independence to theism in general or Protestant theism in
particular, as Jefferson and Madison—the central architects of the religion
clauses—acknowledged in extending protected conscience to include
Catholics and atheists.[11] By the twentieth century, consistent with an even
wider understanding of the diverse sources of reasonable ethical conviction,
the scope of conscience included a wide range of religious and irreligious
views protected by both the Free Exercise and Establishment Clauses of the
First Amendment.[12]

No small part of the background of this contemporary interpretive attitude lies in our experience, as a people, with the role of often quite religiously heterodox ethical dissent as the moving force behind some of the
most important and enlightened constitutional reform movements in our
history. I have in mind the abolitionist movement that structured the nation's
normative understanding, in wake of the Civil War, of both the meaning of
that conflict and the Reconstruction Amendments, and the antiracist and
antisexist movements that have cumulatively transformed our understanding
of how constitutional guarantees (including the Reconstruction Amendments) should be interpreted.[13] Such dissent protested the unjust enforcement of the dominant proslavery or racist or sexist orthodoxy as the sectarian
measure of claims and speakers because such enforcement repressed precisely
the claims and speakers who would most reasonably challenge the justice of
its views and practices. To subject the dominant orthodoxy to this kind of
fundamental ethical criticism, such dissent often questioned the unjust role
of established churches in the support of such rights-based evils as slavery or
racism or sexism; dissent was often empowered by conscientious convictions
that were, to say the least, religiously highly unorthodox and sometimes not
conventionally religious at all.[14] The American tradition of religious liberty,
precisely because it made space for ethically independent criticism of politically enforceable religious and moral views, opened the public mind of the
nation to the ethical voices and views that addressed the nation's gravest
injustices, including the role such injustices played in the corruption of basic
constitutional principles and ideals.

It is against this background that we must understand and evaluate what
must be the most striking feature of the kind of protest involved in the contemporary case for gay rights. It protests a structural injustice of the sort also

exemplified by racism and sexism, namely, abridgment of basic human rights of conscience, speech, intimate life, and work, unjustly rationalized in terms of dehumanizing stereotypes resting on such abridgment. The traditional cultural status of homosexuals was not a servile social status thus rationalized, but no space at all. Homosexuals, in this view, were outside any conception of moral community at all, an exile given expression by the striking normative idea of homosexuality as unspeakable. It was, in Blackstone's words, "a crime not fit to be named; *peccatum illud horribile, inter christianos non nominandum*"[15]—not mentionable, let alone discussed or assessed. Such total silencing of any reasonable discussion transformed homosexuality into a kind of cultural death, naturally thus understood and indeed condemned as a kind of ultimate heresy or treason against essential moral values.[16] The English legal scholar Tony Honore captured this point exactly by his observation about the contemporary status of the homosexual: "It is not primarily a matter of breaking rules but of dissenting attitudes. It resembles political or religious dissent, being an atheist in Catholic Ireland or a dissident in Soviet Russia."[17]

The case for gay rights thus centrally challenges the cultural terms of the unspeakability of homosexuality, the claim of its exclusion from the scope of religious and nonreligious conscience that, on grounds of principle, now ostensibly enjoys constitutional protection. It does so in two ways familiar from the similar protests against racism and sexism: it demands basic human rights of conscience, speech, intimate life, and work; and it challenges, in terms of its own moral powers of rationality and reasonableness, the sectarian terms of the moral orthodoxy that have traditionally condemned it. We must shortly assess the merits of both claims, but the important point for present purposes is that the very making of such claims challenges the terms of the peculiar character of the underlying structural injustice. As such, claims of gay and lesbian identity—whether irreligiously, nonreligiously, or religiously grounded—are decidedly among the dissident forms of conscience that should fully enjoy protection under the American tradition of religious liberty. This is shown as much by the nature of the claims made as by the character of the political opposition to them.

The case for gay rights rests, of course, on arguments of justice, which must be assessed by the larger society in such terms. But their empowering significance to homosexuals is that they offer them, perhaps for the first time in human history, the responsible personal and ethical choice of a private and public identity of dignity equal to that of heterosexuals. Such a choice of identity has two compelling features for the homosexuals who increasingly make it. First, it integrates one's authentic sexual passions with a compelling interpretation of the personal and moral good of homosexual friendship and love (grounded in the basic human good of love) as the basis of a life well and ethically lived. Second, it offers and elaborates arguments of public reason about the injustice and ethical wrong of the condemnation and marginalization of homosexuality as a legitimate way of life (centering on the unprincipled failure to respect the self-authenticating right of all persons to the humane and basic good of love); such arguments, properly developed, not only advance understanding of claims of justice for homosexuals but deepen public understanding of the arguments of principle that explain our condemnation of interlinked injustices such as racism, sexism, and homophobia. The identity expresses itself in varied personal and political associations of mutual recognition, support, and respect and in demands for equal justice and for a public culture (including institutional forms) adequate to the reasonable elaboration and cultivation of its ethical vision of humane value in public and private life. Both its constructive and critical arguments are, in their nature, ethical arguments of public reason, appealing to the fundamental and broadly shared ethical imperative of treating persons as equals.[18]

The self-understanding, by homosexuals, of gay rights in these terms corresponds to the political opposition to it. Colorado Amendment Two, which the Supreme Court struck down as unconstitutional,[19] expressly made its reactionary point in terms of banning all laws that recognized antidiscrimination claims of gay and lesbian people; its target was specifically the claims to justice that constitute gay and lesbian identity.[20] Its aim was decisively that advocates of gay and lesbian identity should be compelled to abandon their claims to personal and ethical legitimacy and either convert to the true view or return to the silence of their traditional unspeakability. The political opposition to gay rights agrees with the case for gay rights on one thing: gay and lesbian identity is a choice. Whereas, however, the opposition (on sectarian religious grounds) interprets the choice as moral heresy beyond the pale of acceptable views, its advocates construe the choice as an exercise of legitimate moral freedom long overdue.

Both the advocacy of and opposition to gay rights suggest the distinctively illuminating power of the religious analogy in understanding the case for gay rights, an analogy that Justice Kennedy acknowledged in *Romer v. Evans* when he discussed the analogy between the Mormons and gays and lesbians. The constitutional protection of religion never turned on its putative immutable and salient character (people can and do convert, and can and do conceal religious convictions) but rather on the traditional place of religion in the conscientious reasonable formation of one's moral identity in public and private life and the need for protection, consistent with the inalienable right to conscience, of persons against state impositions of sectarian religious views. In particular, the identifications central to one's self-respect as a person of conscience are not to be subject to sectarian impositions through public law that unreasonably burden the exercise of one's conscientious convictions (the free-exercise principle) or encourage conversions of such convictions to sectarian orthodoxy (the antiestablishment principle). Claims by lesbian and gay persons today have, for both proponents and opponents, exactly the same ethical and constitutional force. For proponents, they are in their nature claims to a self-respecting personal and moral identity in public and private life through which they may reasonably express and realize their ethical convictions of the moral powers of friendship and love in a good, fulfilled, and responsible life protesting against an unjust and now conspicuously sectarian tradition of moral subjugation. For opponents, the political reaction to such claims, reflected in Colorado Amendment Two, is precisely based on sectarian religious objection to the conscientious claims of justice made by and on behalf of lesbian and gay identity as a form of conscience that is entitled to equal respect under fundamental American constitutional guarantees of freedom of conscience. At bottom, for opponents, the point is that the very fact of lesbian and gay identity, precisely in virtue of its conscientious claims to justice, is as unworthy of respect as a traditionally despised religion such as Judaism; the practice of that form of heresy may thus be abridged, and certainly persons may be encouraged to convert from its demands or, at least, be supinely and ashamedly silent.

Of course, to state the opposition to gay rights in this way is constitutionally to condemn it, for nothing can be clearer than the fact that if imposing burdens on gay identity is analogous to anti-Semitism, it is forbidden: "Heresy trials are foreign to our Constitution."[21] There are two ways to resist this conclusion; neither is defensible. First, gay and lesbian identity may be dismissed as not a conscientious view. Second, even assuming it is a conscientious view, there are adequate secular grounds for it to be disfavored and even condemned.

Several ways to limit the scope of protected conscience (excluding gay identity) may be rejected easily. The constitutional protections for liberty of conscience, grounded on equal respect for conscience, have not been and cannot reasonably be limited to established or traditional churches or the dogmas of such churches; the traditional condemnation of homosexuality by traditional American religions cannot be a ground to exclude it from constitutional protection. The American tradition of liberty of conscience has protected, indeed fostered, the many forms of new forms of conscience that arose uniquely in America,[22] including, as we have seen, the claims of conscience expressed through the abolitionist movement that were so sharply critical of established churches.[23] Claims to gay and lesbian identity stand foursquare in this distinguished tradition of new forms of dissenting conscience and are, as such, fully entitled to constitutional protection on terms of principle. Correlatively, the American tradition of religious liberty cannot be and has not been limited to theistic forms of conscience as such but embraces all forms of conscience.[24] Nor has the tradition been limited to protecting only the conscientious identities in which one has been born, for its guarantees are no less for recent converts and include robust guarantees of state neutrality in circumstances that would lend the state's sectarian encouragement to conversion to one form of belief as opposed to another.[25] All forms of conscientious conviction, whether old or new, theistic or nontheistic, are thus guaranteed equal respect in terms of a constitutional principle that renders issues of conscience morally independent of factionalized political incentives.

It would trivialize such guarantees, indeed render them nugatory, not to extend them precisely when they are most constitutionally needed, namely, to antimajoritarian claims of conscience that challenge traditional wisdom on nonsectarian grounds of public reason. Otherwise, the mere congruence of sectarian belief among traditional religions (for example, about the alleged unspeakable evil of homosexuality) would be, as it was in antebellum America on the question of slavery,[26] the measure of religious liberty in particular and human and constitutional rights in general. The traditional orthodoxy, to which any form of dissenting conscience objects on grounds of public reason, would be permitted to silence as unworthy the newly emancipated voice of such progressive claims of justice. In effect, the culture of degradation that sets the terms of a structural injustice such as racism or sexism would, in this view, set the terms of argument. It is, however, such claims to justice of dissenting, antimajoritarian conscience that most require, on grounds of principle, constitutional protection against nescient majorities who would aggressively and uncritically repress such a group on the ground of its daring to make claims to justice critical of the dominant religio-cultural orthodoxy.

The only remaining ground for excluding gay and lesbian identity from the scope of protected conscience must be to dismiss it as not a conscientious view of the requisite sort, presumably because it is concerned with sex. But, there are two difficulties with this view. First, on the assumption that gay and lesbian identity is about sex or sexual life, that fact would, if anything, bring it closer to central concerns of the human conscience in general and religions in particular. Religions organize the terms of sexual life and its place in the mysteries of birth, love, and death under the aspect of eternity, supplying rituals that endow the cycle of living with a sense of enduring personal and ethical values before the terrors of loneliness, loss, decline, and death. Moreover, the experience of one's sexuality is, from its inception, a mysterious, even awful force fraught with a sense of ultimate concern with the other, a longing for communion and transcendence in relationship with a beloved though alien other. It is thus no accident, in the American rights-based constitutional tradition that the right to intimate life is as much a basic human right as the right to conscience; conscience is so personally engaged with the issues of intimate sexual life because both involve the resources of thought, conviction, feeling, and emotion at the heart of the ultimate concerns of moral personality. The claims of gay and lesbian identity address these traditionally religious ultimate concerns and are no less religious for doing so than more traditional approaches to these questions. Indeed, the significance of gay and lesbian identity, for many contemporary homosexuals (including me), is that it enables us, as responsible moral persons and agents, to make redemptive personal and ethical sense of the human depth of our experience of sexuality on equal terms with heterosexuals. We need no longer acquiesce in the unjust stereotypes of our sexuality as inhuman or unnatural or even a diabolic possession but may responsibly engage in rights-based protest of such stereotypes, reclaiming our sexuality and our moral powers of love and transcendence on terms of equal justice.

Second, from the perspective of the case for gay rights, homosexuality is, as Walt Whitman seminally suggested,[27] no more or less exclusively about sex than heterosexuality. We have no difficulty, surely, in understanding the place of heterosexuality in nurturing and sustaining the relationships that, more than any other, are touched with enduring personal and ethical value in living, indeed, that are, if anything is, the personal relationships of mutual transparency, respect, and tender care and concern through which we understand what divine love could mean or reasonably be taken to mean. It does not count against the conscientiousness or even the religiosity of such convictions that opposite-sex intimacies are involved because our traditions—both secular and religious—afford us the moral vocabulary to interpret them as expressions of love (sometimes even as models of divine love) as well as sensual delight. The case for gay rights argues that homosexuals, on grounds of structural injustice, have been denied such moral vocabulary, indeed denied any vocabulary (on the grounds of unspeakability); such repression often sustained and was sustained by unjust stereotypes that crudely sexualized homosexuality in ways structurally similar to the unjust sexualization that supported racism and sexism.[28] The appeal to sexual content (as a ground for excluding gay and lesbian identity from protected conscience) fatally begs the question by indulging such prejudice rather than responsibly facing what must be addressed: whether there is an adequate ground for burdening this form of conscientious conviction. Conscientious conviction it certainly is, as much as any other convictions about the ethical meaning of personal love that are the common sense of our romantic age. Justice Kennedy acknowledged and drew upon this insight in *Lawrence v. Texas* when he criticized the homophobic way in which Justice White interpreted the constitutional right to privacy in *Bowers v. Hardwick,* reducing love to pornography.

We need, then, to investigate what acceptable secular grounds, if any, exist to burden gay and lesbian identity as conscientious convictions that are, like any other, entitled to equal respect. The question applies not just to the right to conscience but to the other human rights traditionally denied to gay and lesbian persons, namely, rights to free speech, intimate life, and work. In all these cases, such basic human rights may only be abridged on grounds of compelling secular grounds of public reason. In fact, as we shall see, there are no acceptable secular grounds for such abridgment in any of these areas, which supports the argument that abridgment of these basic rights is rooted in the same structural injustice as racism and sexism (what I call moral slavery).

To be clear on this point, we need to examine critically the grounds traditionally supposed to rationalize the condemnation of homosexuality. Plato in *The Laws* gave influential expression to such moral condemnation in terms of two arguments: homosexuality's nonprocreative character and (in its male homosexual forms) its degradation of the passive male partner to the status of a woman.[29] Neither of these two traditional moral reasons for condemning homosexuality can any longer be legitimately and indeed constitutionally imposed on society at large or any other person or group of persons.

One such moral reason, the condemnation of nonprocreational sex, can, for example, no longer constitutionally justify laws against the sale to and use by married and unmarried heterosexual couples of contraceptives.[30] The mandatory enforcement at large of the procreational model of sexuality is, in circumstances of overpopulation and declining infant and adult mortality, a sectarian ideal lacking adequate secular basis in the general good that can alone reasonably justify an imposition of state power; accordingly, contraceptive-using heterosexuals have the constitutional right to decide when and whether their sexual lives shall be pursued to procreate or as an independent expression of mutual love, affection, and companionship.[31]

The other moral reason for condemning homosexual sex, the degradation of a man to the passive status of a woman, rests on the sexist premise of the degraded nature of women that has been properly rejected as a reasonable basis for laws or policies on grounds of suspect-classification analysis.[32] If we constitutionally accept, as we increasingly do, the suspect classification of gender on a par with that of race, we must in principle condemn, as a basis for law, any use of stereotypes expressive of the unjust enforcement of gender roles through law. That condemnation extends, as authoritative case law makes clear, to gender stereotypes as such whether immediately harmful to women or to men.[33]

Nonetheless, although each moral ground for the condemnation of homosexuality has been independently rejected as a reasonable justification for coercive laws enforceable on society at large (applicable to both men and women), they unreasonably retain their force when brought into specific relationship to the claims of homosexual men and women for equal justice under constitutional law.[34] These claims in their basic nature are arguments of principle made by gay men and lesbians for the same respect for their intimate love life and other basic rights, free of unreasonable procreational and sexist requirements, now rather generously accorded to men and women who are heterosexually coupled (including, as we have seen, even the right to abortion against the alleged weight of fetal life). Empirical issues relating to sexuality and gender are now subjected to more impartial critical assessment than they were previously, and the resulting light of public reason about issues of sexuality and gender should be available to all persons on fair terms. However, the procreational mandate and the unjust gender stereotype, constitutionally condemned for the benefit of heterosexual men and women, are still ferociously applied to homosexual men and women.[35] This reveals the force of homophobia, a political force so powerful that a claim of fair treatment (an argument of basic constitutional principle if any argument is) was contemptuously dismissed by a majority of the Supreme Court of the United States (5–4) in 1986 in *Bowers v. Hardwick*.[36] No skeptical scrutiny whatsoever was accorded to state purposes elsewhere acknowledged as illegitimate. Certainly no such purpose could be offered as the alleged weight of fetal life, which has been rejected as a legitimate ground for criminalization of all forms of abortion; any claim of public health could be addressed, as it would be in comparable cases of heterosexual relations involving the basic constitutional right of intimate life, by constitutionally required alternatives less restrictive and more effective than criminalization (including use of prophylactics by those otherwise at threat from transmission of AIDS).[37]

Traditional moral arguments, now clearly reasonably rejected in their application to heterosexuals, were uncritically applied to a group much more exigently in need of constitutional protection on grounds of principle.[38] Reasonable advances in the public understanding of sexuality and gender, now constitutionally available to all heterosexuals, were suspended in favor of an appeal to the sexual mythology of the Middle Ages.[39] It is an indication of the genre of dehumanizing stereotypes at work in *Bowers v. Hardwick,* stripping a class of persons of moral personality by reducing them to a mythologized sexuality, that the Court focused so obsessively on one sex act (sodomy); as Leo Bersani perceptively observed about the public discourse (reflected in *Bowers*), it resonated in images (inherited from the nineteenth century) of homosexuals as sexually obsessed prostitutes.[40] The transparently unprincipled character of *Bowers*[41] in such terms thus suggests a larger problem, which connects such treatment of homosexuals with the now familiar structural injustice underlying racism and sexism. It is this unprincipled character that justified the overruling of *Bowers* in *Lawrence v. Texas,* and my argument clarifies why it was that Justice Kennedy could find no compelling secular purpose to sustain such bans on gay/lesbian sex and how and why his argument offered an implicit critique of the unjust force homophobia played in *Bowers v. Hardwick.*

The Gender Analogy

We need better to understand the forces, adverted to in Justice Kennedy's opinion in *Lawrence,* that rationalized such injustice. To begin with, however, we may and should, on grounds of principle, extend the analysis of moral slavery to the traditional reprobation of homosexuality. Homophobia reflects a cultural tradition of rights-denying moral slavery similar to and indeed overlapping with the American tradition of sexist degradation; the root of homophobia is, like that of sexism, a rigid conception of gender roles and spheres, only in this case focusing specifically on gender roles in intimate sexual and emotional life.[42] Homophobia may be reasonably understood today as a persisting form of residual and quite unjust gender discrimination both in its object (stigmatizing homosexuality as inconsistent with gender identity as a man or woman) and in its grounds. With respect to the latter, the nonprocreative character of homosexual sexuality may be of relatively little concern, but its cultural symbolism of disordered gender roles excites anxieties in a political culture still quite unjustly sexist in its understanding of gender roles; indeed, the condemnation of homosexuality acts as a reactionary reinforcement of sexism generally. The emergence of the modern conception of homosexual identity as intrinsically effeminate (in gay men) (and later mannish [in lesbians][43]) accompanied the emergence of modern Western culture after 1700 and was associated with the reinforcement of the sexist definition of gender roles in terms of which the supposedly greater equality of men and women was interpreted.[44] Male homosexuals were thus symbolically understood as "effeminate members of a third or intermediate gender, who surrender their rights to be treated as dominant males, and are exposed instead to a merited contempt as a species of male whore"[45] (in the more overtly sexist and homophile ancient Greek world only the passive male partner would have been thus interpreted[46]). Homosexuals—both lesbians and male homosexuals—are, in this persisting modern view, in revolt against what many still suppose to be the "natural" order of gender hierarchy, women or men, as the case may be, undertaking sexual roles improper to their gender (for example, women loving other women [independent of men[47]] and men loving other men, dominance in women, passivity in men). It is plainly unjust to impose such sexist views, no longer publicly justifiable against heterosexual women or men, on a much more culturally marginalized and despised group—symbolic scapegoats of the feeble and cowardly sense of self that seeks self-respect in the unjust degradation of morally innocent people of good will.[48] It should also be clearly constitutionally condemned as a form of unjust gender discrimination, perpetuating unjustly rigid and impermeable stereotypes (whether of women or men) that enforce their claims by indulging the dehumanization of any gender dissident (as degraded or fallen women).[49]

I earlier observed that homophobia today in the United States expresses a sectarian religious discrimination against the new forms of conviction and speech of gays and lesbians, but we can now see what underlies and explains such discrimination: uncritical forms of patriarchal culture and religion that enforce their unjust claims precisely against those men and women who challenge the unjust gender stereotypes that traditionally condemn gays and lesbians as unspeakable. What makes modernist homophobia an unconstitutional political prejudice is its roots in two already suspect forms of classification: religion and gender, only here unjustly targeted against gays and lesbians in the way that I hope I have clarified.

If I am right about this, it suggests why extending the right to marriage to homosexuals plays so central a role in such modernist homophobia: abridging the right to marriage is as constitutive of homophobia as it was of racism. Homosexuals, because they violate traditional gender roles, are traditionally supposed to be outcasts from the human race as well, and thus incapable and indeed unworthy of being accorded what all persons are, on equal terms, owed: respect for their basic human rights to conscience, speech, intimate life, and work. A way of making this point is to observe that homophobic prejudice, like racism and sexism, unjustly distorts the idea of human rights applicable to both public and private life. The political evil of racism expressed itself in a contemptuous interpretation of black family life (enforced by segregation and antimiscegenation laws that confined blacks, as a separate species, to an inferior sphere).[50] The political evil of sexism expressed itself in a morally degraded interpretation of private life (to which women, as morally inferior, were confined as, in effect, a different species[51]). In similar fashion, the evil of homophobic prejudice is its degradation of homosexual love to the unspeakably private and secretive, not only politically and socially but intrapsychically in the person whose sexuality is homosexual. The intellectual reign of terror that once aimed to impose racism and anti-Semitism on the larger society and even on these stigmatized minorities themselves today aims to enforce homophobia at large and self-hating homophobia in particular on homosexuals as well. Its vehicle is the denigration of gay and lesbian identity as a devalued form of conscience with which no one, under pain of ascribed membership in such a devalued species, can or should identify. Gays and lesbians are thus culturally dehumanized as a nonhuman or inhuman species whose moral interests in love and friendship and nurturing care are, in their nature, radically discontinuous with anything recognizably human. The culture of such degradation is pervasive and deep, legitimating, as we shall shortly see, the uncritically irrationalist outrage at the very idea of gay and lesbian marriage,[52] which unjustly constructs the inhumanity of homosexual identity on the basis of exactly the same kind of viciously circular cultural degradation unjustly imposed on African Americans through antimiscegenation laws.[53] Groups thus marked off as ineligible for the central institutions of intimate life and cultural transmission are deemed subculturally nonhuman or inhuman, alien species incapable of the humane forms of culture that express and sustain our inexhaustibly varied search, as free moral persons, for enduring personal and ethical meaning and value in living.

The common ground of our concern with racism, sexism, and homophobia is the radical political evil of a political culture, ostensibly committed to toleration on the basis of universal human rights, that unjustly denies a class of persons their inalienable human rights as persons with moral powers on the basis of the structural injustice of moral slavery. Liberal political culture, consistent with respect for this basic right, must extend to all persons the cultural resources that enable them critically to explore, define, express, and revise the identifications central to free moral personality;[54] the constitutional evil, condemned by suspect-classification analysis under the Equal Protection Clause of the Fourteenth Amendment, is the systematic deprivation of this basic right for a group of persons unjustly degraded from their status as persons entitled to respect for the reasonable exercise of their free moral powers in the identifications central to an ethical life based on mutual respect.[55] Sexual orientation is and should be a fully suspect classification because homosexuals are today victimized, in the same way African Americans and women are and have been, by irrationalist political prejudices rooted in this radical political evil, denying them the cultural resources of free moral personality.

In particular, any discrimination against gays and lesbians, on the ground that they identify themselves as such, must be regarded, under the view I propose, as especially constitutionally suspect, since the discrimination is directed against conscientious claims of gender identity that rest on both religion and gender as suspect classes. This argument clarifies, I believe, the basis for *Romer v. Evans* and gives reason for constitutional doubts about the "Don't Ask, Don't Tell" policy of the American military.

Anti-Lesbian/Gay Initiatives

The organized opposition to gay rights recently successfully secured the adoption of Colorado Amendment Two, which not only repealed existing state laws that protected gay people from discrimination but also banned all future laws that would recognize such claims by lesbians and gay men.[56] On May 20, 1996, Justice Kennedy, writing for the Supreme Court of the United States, 6–3, struck down Colorado Amendment Two, but on the ground that the classification in question was "so discontinuous with the reasons offered for it that the amendment seems inexplicable by anything but animus toward the class it affects; it lacks a rational relationship to legitimate state interests."[57] The application of the rational-basis test in *Romer* is reminiscent of the first case in which the Supreme Court announced its skepticism about gender classifications, namely, *Reed v. Reed*.[58] The application of the rational-basis standard with the consequence of invalidating such laws was in doctrinal tension with the many cases in which comparable laws with equally overinclusive and underinclusive legislative classifications had been upheld. *Reed* suggested what later cases made clear, that the Court had interpretively come to the view that a heightened level of constitutional scrutiny was owed to gender classifications.[59] The same doctrinal criticism may be made of *Romer* as was earlier made of *Reed v. Reed:* Why was heightened scrutiny owed to this as opposed to other classifications? If the decision is doctrinally problematic as a rational-basis decision, we need to ask how it might be better understood, in particular, what analogies might make this state law, in the words of Justice Scalia's bitter dissent, "as reprehensible as racial or religious bias."[60] In particular, Scalia questioned the elaboration of suspect classifications to include sexual preference when the group in question is, in proportion to its numbers, quite politically powerful.[61]

The strongest constitutional argument for constitutional limits on anti-lesbian/gay rights initiatives is the one suggested by Justice Kennedy's argument in *Romer* about the Mormons: namely, the initiatives in question express constitutionally forbidden sectarian religious intolerance through public law against fundamental rights of conscience, speech, and association of lesbian and gay persons protected by America's first and premier civil liberty, liberty of conscience.[62] The ground for discrimination against gay and lesbian conscience, thus understood, is sectarian religious convictions—sectarian in the sense that they rest on perceptions internal to religious convictions, not on public arguments reasonably available in contemporary terms to all persons.[63] This ground is confirmed, as I earlier argued, by the failure to extend to gay and lesbian persons public arguments (about the acceptability of nonprocreational sex and unacceptability of sexism) otherwise available to all persons on fair terms. The expression through public law of one form of sectarian conscience against another form of conscience, without compelling justification in public arguments available to all, is constitutionally invidious, and therefore constitutionally suspect, religious intolerance. It both unconstitutionally burdens conscience, inconsistent with free-exercise principles, and unconstitutionally advances sectarian conscience, inconsistent with antiestablishment principles. Discrimination specifically directed against the claims of justice made by and on behalf of gay and lesbian conscience expresses such constitutionally forbidden intolerance.

Although the issue has usually been discussed in terms of the cases forbidding constitutional entrenchment of laws forbidding racial discrimination, the more exact analogy would be constitutional entrenchment of prohibitions on claims of religious discrimination made precisely by groups most likely to be victimized in Christian America by such discrimination, for example, Jews. To understand the force of this analogy between political anti-Semitism and homophobia (well supported in both historical and contemporary expressions of such sectarian intolerance[64]), we must remind ourselves about the nature of the constitutional evil of the expression of anti-Semitism through law, in particular, why such political anti-Semitism violates the argument for toleration central to the proper interpretation of American traditions of religious liberty.[65] Political anti-Semitism unjustly abridged basic rights of Jews, in violation of the argument for toleration, precisely because their beliefs and ways of life raised reasonable doubts about the dominant religious orthodoxy. In order not to allow such reasonable doubts to be entertained, the dominant orthodoxy enforced its own status as the measure of tolerable belief and practice by abridging the basic rights by which Jews might reasonably raise doubts on the grounds of irrationalist stereotypes that dehumanized them (including the idea of Jews as the slaves of Christians[66]). I call the mechanism by which such an entrenched orthodoxy unjustly constructed the dehumanized status of dissidents from the dominant orthodoxy "the paradox of intolerance": in effect, precisely the views that dominant orthodoxy most reasonably needs to hear are those paradoxically, savagely repressed on whatever, sometimes quite irrationalist, grounds sustain the embattled legitimacy of the dominant orthodoxy. American constitutional principles, based on the argument for toleration, forbid laws based on such sectarian intolerance.

In light of these reasons, we would and should immediately condemn constitutional entrenchment of political anti-Semitism (in the form of an initiative that forbade all laws protecting Jews as such against discrimination) as an unconstitutional expression of religious intolerance because such laws are in service of precisely the forms of majoritarian religious intolerance that constitutional guarantees of religious toleration condemn as a basis for law. A state that entrenched such initiatives would, in clear violation of free-exercise principles, unconstitutionally burden specifically named conscientious convictions in a blatantly non-neutral way[67] and, in clear contradiction of the principles of our antiestablishment jurisprudence,[68] support a sectarian religious view as the one true church of Americanism to which all dissenters are encouraged to convert. A constitutional jurisprudence that questions the neutrality of unemployment compensation schemes that effectively impose financial burdens on the convictions of Seventh Day Adventists[69] must condemn, a fortiori, laws that specifically target for focused disadvantage the convictions of a religion or form of conscience and must regard as even worse the naming of the group in question in the relevant law.[70] In effect, a state that entrenched such initiatives would itself be the unconstitutional agent of the political evil of intolerance, branding a religious group as heretics and blasphemers against American religious orthodoxy. American constitutionalism, which recognizes neither heresy nor blasphemy as legitimate expressions of state power,[71] must forbid exercises of state power, such as the contemplated initiative, that illegitimately assert such a power, in this case legitimating the dehumanizing evil of political anti-Semitism. The effect of such initiatives would be to enlist the state actively in the unconstitutional construction of a class of persons lacking the status of bearers of human rights, a status so subhuman that they are excluded from the minimal rights and responsibilities of the moral community of persons. Political atrocity thus becomes thinkable and practical.

The case of anti-gay/lesbian initiatives is, as a matter of principle, exactly parallel. A dissenting form of conscience is branded precisely on the grounds of its moral independence and dissenting claims for justice as heresy. The message is clear and clearly intended: persons should convert from this form of conscience, which is wholly unworthy of respect, to the only true religion of Americanism. The initiative is as much motivated by sectarian religion and directed against dissenting conscience as the intolerably anti-Semitic initiative just discussed and draws on tropes and stereotypes familiar in the history of anti-Semitism; one of them, the disproportionate power of the Jews, is indeed echoed in Justice Scalia's dissent in *Romer* (appealing to the disproportionate power of gays as a ground for denying protection of their rights). Homosexuals are to late twentieth-century sectarians what the Jews have traditionally been to sectarians in the Christian West throughout its history: intolerable heretics against dominant religious orthodoxy.[72]

The conception that homosexuality is a form of heresy or treason is both an ancient and a modern ground for its condemnation.[73] In fact, there is no good reason to believe that the legitimacy of such forms of sexual expression destabilizes social cooperation. Homosexual relations are and will foreseeably remain the preference of small minorities of the population[74] who are as committed to principles of social cooperation and contribution as any other group in society at large; the issue, as with all suspect classes, is not one of increasing or decreasing the minority but deciding whether we should treat its members justly with respect as persons or unjustly with contempt as unspeakably heretical outcasts. Indeed, the very accusation of heresy or treason brings out an important feature of the traditional moral condemnation in its contemporary vestments. It no longer rests on generally acceptable arguments of necessary protections of the rights of persons to general goods; on the contrary, both the sexism and condemnation of nonprocreational sex are now inconsistent with the reasonable acceptability as general goods of both gender equality and nonprocreational sex.

Exclusion from the Military

The issue of gay rights came to national attention in President Clinton's initiation of a review of the current policy of exclusion of homosexuals from the military (leading to congressional adoption of Clinton's proposed change in policy, "Don't Ask, Don't Tell"). The pertinent law currently in constitutional dispute is 10 U.S.C. sec. 654, the policy, popularly known as "Don't Ask, Don't Tell," governing the participation of homosexuals in the military service, and the accompanying directives issued by the Department of Defense (DoD) and the secretary of transportation.[75] In the legislation, Congress provided that a service member would be separated from the armed services, pursuant to regulations to be promulgated by the secretary of defense, under terms that generally matched those of the previous policy with the exception of the second ground for separation, which now included a public statement that one was gay except when the person would not engage in gay sex acts.[76] The regulations implementing the new policy stated that its purpose was not aimed at the separation of homosexuals on status grounds alone;[77] the new policy sharply restricted the circumstances under which the military authorities might initiate an investigation of a servicemember (credible evidence of homosexual acts does not include "associational activity such as going to a gay bar, possessing or reading homosexual publications, associating with known homosexuals, or marching in a gay rights rally in civilian clothes").[78] And applicants "shall not be asked or required to reveal whether they are heterosexual, homosexual, or bisexual."[79]

There are a number of constitutional difficulties that could be raised about each of the grounds for exclusion under both the old and new policies: first, the ground of all homosexual sex acts in contrast to sexual relations or untoward sexual exploitation or harassment as such, heterosexual or homosexual, that prejudice legitimate military interests; second, self-identifying speech as a homosexual; and third, same-sex marriage. The exclusion on the basis of gay consensual sex may have been regarded as unproblematic when *Bowers v. Hardwick* was good law. But *Bowers* has now been overruled by *Lawrence v. Texas*. If banning gay sex is now constitutionally unreasonable, the other grounds for this policy can no longer be reasonable, as I shall shortly argue.

Many of the great struggles for inclusion by suspect groups have been over access on equal terms to military service. Perhaps the best evidence of how constitutive participation in the military has been of American nationality and citizenship is the African American experience in the Civil War.[80] Until surprisingly late in the Civil War, President Lincoln was considering various measures that would, after slavery had been decisively ended in the United States, colonize the freedmen and -women abroad, where they could establish their own national forms.[81] Lincoln, though morally opposed to slavery, could, no more than Jefferson (who was also antislavery), contemplate a national community that included African Americans on equal terms.[82] Under the pressure of abolitionist advocacy and military exigency, Lincoln authorized raising African American troops to serve in the war effort,[83] and they played an important role in the Union victory.[84] Under the moral pressure of such participation (albeit in segregated regiments), Lincoln gradually came to the view that African Americans were now morally owed what he had once, like most Americans, assumed to be unthinkable: the radical abolitionist dream of full inclusion of African Americans in the American political and moral community of equal rights and responsibilities.[85] Military service was the moralizing practice of equal responsibilities that gave birth to America's moral growth into at least the serious beginning of a constitutional theory and practice of equal rights.

The later struggle of African Americans to serve in a racially integrated military culminated in President Truman's 1948 executive order calling for desegregation of the armed services, finally embraced by the military after the outbreak of the Korean War in June 1950.[86] That struggle was as central to the antiracist aims of the civil rights movement as integration in public education. If integration in public education would make feasible a new public culture of inclusive educational and cultural opportunity, integration in the military would take the equally important step of forging a practice of the equal responsibilities of all citizens that would institutionalize a more profoundly rooted American sense of the equal rights of all Americans.

Military service has a special character and role under American revolutionary constitutionalism as a public institution concerned with protecting and defending rights-based constitutional institutions (of which the military itself is one). Accordingly, as the African American struggle makes abundantly clear, military service in the United States cannot be cordoned off from the larger struggles of rights-based justice under American constitutionalism. We must, rather, in each case inquire whether a ground for exclusion uncritically enforces a conception of national identity inconsistent with the demands of American constitutionalism.[87]

Issues of this sort are central to ongoing public discussions in the United States about the place and terms of the service of women, if any, in the military. Two issues should be distinguished: first, whether women may serve in the military at all; and second, assuming they may serve, whether they should be excluded from combat. The two issues are related in the following way: if women can reasonably be excluded from combat, the case for exclusion from the military as such may be stronger. For example, in *Rostker v. Goldberg*,[88] the Supreme Court considered the constitutionality of the exclusion of women from the requirement to register for the draft and decided, 6–3, that the exclusion was constitutional. All justices assumed that the combat exclusion was legitimate. On that basis, it was easier for the majority to find the exclusion to be reasonable because considerably lesser numbers of women than men would be needed to serve in combat roles.

Women now serve in the American military; indeed, there are more women in the military in the United States than in any other country.[89] The main issue in dispute has been the legitimacy of the combat exclusion.[90] The 1991 report of a presidential commission on this matter unanimously recommended exclusion of women from ground combat,[91] narrowly (8–7) recommended exclusion of women from service on aircraft in combat missions,[92] and recommended (8-6, 1 abstention) that women be allowed to serve on combatant vessels except submarine and amphibious vessels.[93]

The force of arguments of rights-based feminism in this domain has recently been underscored by the Supreme Court's decision, 7–1, in *United States v. Virginia*.[94] In ruling that the exclusion on the basis of gender from a Virginia public military college was unconstitutional, Justice Ginsburg, writing for the Court, critically examined the college's arguments of alleged gender differences in light of a constitutionally based skepticism about crude gender stereotypes that themselves rest on a history of unjust gender-based discrimination in basic rights and opportunities.[95] Ginsburg conceded, "for purposes of this decision, that most women would not choose VMI's adversative method."[96] But in the same spirit as Justice Brennan's skepticism about giving effect to statistically significant factual differences between men and women rooted in unjust gender stereotypes in *Craig v. Boren,* the Court denied that such differences can "constitutionally deny to women who have the will and capacity, the training and attendant opportunities that VMI uniquely affords."[97] In particular, the Court emphasized that women's integration into both federal military academies and the armed forces abundantly confirmed the equal competence of women as citizen-soldiers once they were afforded an equal opportunity.[98] Accordingly, any exclusion of women from a public military academy, on the grounds of cultural stereotypes of incapacity to be citizen-soldiers, must be held to a high standard of constitutional scrutiny in terms of an exceedingly persuasive justification; only such a level of heightened scrutiny can make sure that the operative generalization rested on compelling grounds independent of the rights-denying cultural stereotype. Such a justification was lacking here, and the exclusion was accordingly ruled unconstitutional.[99]

Justice Ginsburg powerfully brought arguments of rights-based feminism to bear on the military domain, suggesting that gender integration in the military might be as important to the equality of women as racial integration was to African Americans.[100] Our earlier examination of the African American struggle for integration suggests why this should be so. Such defensive rights (to protect one's rights) dignify moral personality as a bearer of rights; it is for this reason that recognition of such rights (for groups previously subjugated) humanizes its members as bearers of human rights (contesting the stereotype of subhumanity that subjugated them).[101] If Justice Ginsburg was correct on the importance to a rights-based constitutional feminism of gender integration in the military domain, then the admission of women to the American volunteer military may now be regarded as constitutionally compelled. If that is so, then Jean Bethke Elshtain may be correct that "there seems little point in maintaining the pretense of combat exclusion for 'their protection.' Nobody can be protected any longer in the old sense of being 'immune from possible destruction.'"[102] In fact, perhaps reflecting the force of such arguments, incremental change in both congressional legislation and Department of Defense rules has substantially eroded the combat exclusion for women.[103] The integration of both African Americans and women into the military supports the analogous case, on grounds of principle, for inclusion of gays and lesbians.[104] The experience of such inclusion both in foreign militaries[105] and in domestic police and fire departments[106] suggests that appropriately articulated and enforced policies of integration are as reasonable and feasible as they have been in the cases of the integration of African Americans and women.[107]

It is certainly striking in this connection that the institutional crucible for the development of the modern American movement for gay rights was the experience, as we earlier saw, of gay men and lesbians in the military during World War II, including their resistance on grounds of justice to discrimination in the military.[108] The practice of gay rights in America, long before it had any publicly articulated theory, was thus formed around a sense of common identity in resisting injustice in the military service they rendered to the United States, as citizens, in perhaps the greatest struggle for human rights in human history. If participation in this struggle energized, as we have seen, already existing claims of justice on behalf of African Americans, it literally forged the practice of making such claims of justice by American gay men and lesbians, who defined their previously unspeakable common identity in terms of making such claims.[109]

The distance gay men and lesbians traveled in this period was, in the terms of my earlier discussion of these issues, the distance from moral slavery to freedom, from submissive unspeakability to morally independent voice on grounds of the central rights-based principles of American constitutionalism. It would take time for such practices to become self-consciously political and to develop a sense of their place in the larger fabric of an emerging rights-based civil rights movement. But they first tested their moral voice in the military context because both its homosocial context, away from traditional ties and communities, and larger rights-based purposes made such a personal and political growth in moral consciousness factually and normatively possible;[110] for this reason, quite unsurprisingly, there might be a higher rate of same-gender sexual behavior in the military than in the general population.[111] Paradoxically, the institution that gave rise to and indeed sustained the practice of gay rights is now the state institution that most vigorously and self-consciously represses those claims, indeed makes the very assertion of such claims the ground for separation from military service.

It is against this background that we must constitutionally assess our current military policy on the exclusion of homosexuals: "Don't Ask, Don't Tell." Certainly, some aspects of the new policy are an advance over the previous policy. It clearly repudiates, for example, using sexual preference as such as a ground for separation, an aspect of the earlier policy that several federal courts have correctly found unconstitutional.[112] It carefully limits the kinds of evidence that may credibly be used to show homosexual acts, excluding, for example, going to gay bars or attending a gay rights parade (thus protecting, to some degree, associational rights). It draws the line, however, at identifying oneself as gay or lesbian and, a fortiori, same-sex marriage, literally making such self-identifying exercises of speech a per se ground for separation. Once having made such a self-identifying statement, it is practically impossible to rebut the inference, which the policy requires one to rebut, namely, that one has a "propensity" to gay sex. As Judge Nickerson made clear in an opinion, later reversed, striking down the policy as unconstitutional, "propensity" here comes to the same thing as having a gay sexual orientation.[113] The central ground for exclusion from the military under the new policy is thus the public assertion of one's identity as a gay and lesbian person.

To rationalize the constitutionality of such a policy, federal circuit courts have implausibly either denied that it significantly restricts speech or claimed that the restriction is in any event a reasonable way of pursuing the clearly justifiable purpose of limiting gay sex.[114] Analogies to support the speech claim, used by two of the circuit courts, have included cases involving the regulation of obscene materials[115] or sexually harassing or provocative fighting words.[116] Neither opinion explains or attempts to explain how a statement of one's homosexuality can reasonably be regarded as obscene or as sexually harassing or fighting words. The statement "I am gay" is not a hardcore pornographic representation of turgid genitals offensive to community values and lacking serious value under current judicial tests for the constitutionally obscene.[117] Nor is the statement in its nature sexually harassing or a provocative epithet such as "damned Fascist."[118]

The second judicial rationalization for the policy of exclusion on the ground of making self-identifying statements as a homosexual (namely, its rational basis in forbidding gay sex) is no more constitutionally reasonable. For one thing, forbidding gay sex is, after *Lawrence,* constitutionally problematic. For another, the focus of the new policy is decidedly on identity, not acts, which is doubly constitutionally unreasonable.

First, public assertion of gay or lesbian identity is not, in its nature, a statement about sex acts any more than a comparable statement of dissenting religious or racial or gender identity is when made against the tradition of moral slavery. As Judge Betty Fletcher observed in her powerful dissent to her circuit court's disposition of this issue, the military's treatment of public statements of gay or lesbian identity ascribes to such statements, in the name of unit cohesion, an interpretation rooted in "biases that cannot be tolerated under the laws."[119] Effectively, the discomfort of heterosexual men with homosexuality, as a kind of irrationalist sense of tribal pollution,[120] is made the measure of unit cohesion. Unit cohesion, as a measure of the performance of groups, is most reasonably understood as a measure of task cohesion, not of generalized social cohesion,[121] a critical understanding central to the integration of both African Americans and women into the military. Social discomfort, based on bias, cannot be a reasonable measure of task cohesion under properly stated and enforced policies of nondiscriminatory treatment in a military that, under such policies, has reasonably integrated African Americans and women.[122] Sexist worries about sexuality, which were not adequate to bar the integration of African Americans or women into the military, cannot, in principle, bar the integration of gays and lesbians on similar terms of justice (including appropriate protections from sexual harassment, heterosexual or homosexual). The experience of foreign militaries and of domestic police and fire departments with such integration of homosexuals supports the common grounds, methods, and success of such policies.[123] In all these cases it has been shown that clearly stated and appropriately enforced policies can enforce a professionally appropriate etiquette so that all persons may attend to their tasks ably and well.[124] Judge Fletcher properly regarded as homophobic the fear of heterosexuals that gays or lesbians could not (contrary to all evidence) appropriately observe such an etiquette in their professional lives (as they have done and continue to do in all professions); such bias, for bias it is, cannot be the constitutionally reasonable measure of service in the American military.

Second, if the policy had been concerned with gay sex acts, it would not reasonably have gone about its business in the way that it did. Many of the courses of conduct expressly ruled out as probative of such sex acts (attending a gay bar or a gay rights rally or having homosexual friends) surely are in fact probative. The structure of the new policy is hospitable to gay sex acts as long as they are clandestine and, of course, discreet. The real concern of the policy is to eliminate assertions of gay identity, a viewpoint-based discrimination against conscience and speech that should have been subjected to much more demanding judicial scrutiny than it was, and struck down on this basis.

All the circuit courts put weight, perhaps decisively, on one last consideration: the deference the judiciary owes the expertise of the legislative and executive branches in running an orderly and effective military service.[125] *Rostker v. Goldberg*[126] is one direct example: the Supreme Court there applied the standard of heightened scrutiny[127] deferentially in view of the judgment of Congress that only men should be required to register for the draft. *Rostker,* decided in 1981, crucially rested on the acceptance by all justices of the legitimacy of the gender-based combat exclusion and may have been superseded both by the erosion of the combat exclusion and by the even higher level of scrutiny that may now be applicable to such gender classifications in light of *United States v. Virginia*.[128] As I earlier suggested, there may now be a compelling constitutional argument why women could not be excluded from the current all-volunteer military.

Whatever may be the appropriate level of judicial scrutiny for constitutional issues involving military service in other contexts, there are, I believe, compelling arguments of principle why a higher level of scrutiny should be accorded exclusions that express and reinforce dehumanizing stereotypes that deprive whole classes of citizens of their equal rights of citizenship. The issue at stake is nothing less than the constitutional conception of national citizenship, including the equal rights and responsibilities central to rights-based, republican citizenship. That is not a conception on which the judgments of military leaders can be regarded as decisive in the way that they might reasonably be regarded in areas relating to issues of military discipline, organization, and readiness. Such judgments of national citizenship may uncritically reflect not impartial judgments of competence and merit in military service but the traditional military's sense of its servicemembers as men, unjustly constructed, as racism and sexism surely are, on the unjust dehumanization of African Americans and women through long-standing traditions of racial or gender segregation. We cannot reasonably put such a strong conception of rights-based moral community at hazard by allowing uncritical conceptions of true manhood, which may have no more basis than Aryan brotherhood, to be the defining measure of American national identity. The analogy to Aryan brotherhood is, I believe, exact if, as I have argued, the exclusion of conscientiously identified homosexuals from the military is, in principle, the same as excluding from such service a religious identity (Judaism) on that sectarian basis. We would reject such a constitutional outrage on grounds of constitutional principle that apply, in contemporary circumstances, to gays and lesbians as well.[129]

9

SAME-SEX MARRIAGE

The question of same-sex marriage, as a constitutional issue, has come very much to the forefront of national attention in light of the decisions under state constitutions of the Hawaii Supreme Court in *Baehr v. Lewin*[1] (later overruled by state constitutional amendment banning same-sex marriage but extending some benefits to gay partnerships); of the Vermont Supreme Court in *Baker v. State of Vermont*[2] (leading to civil-union legislation short of same-sex marriage); and, most recently, by the decision of the Supreme Judicial Court of Massachusetts in *Goodridge v. Department of Public Health*[3] (under which gays and lesbians resident in Massachusetts now can marry). *Baehr* led to legislation approved by Congress and signed by President Clinton to limit the force of the decision, namely, the Defense of Marriage Act (DOMA) of 1996.[4] *Goodridge* has led to serious proposals, endorsed by President George W. Bush, to amend the Constitution of the United States to limit marriage, as an institution, exclusively to one man and one woman.[5] Until these cases, almost all American courts have held, under both state and federal constitutional law, that failure to recognize same-sex marriage is not unconstitutional[6] and have, correlatively, failed to accord same-sex couples benefits such as employee insurance coverage[7] or spousal rights under the law of wills,[8] the immigration laws,[9] or the law of veteran benefits.[10] These cases suggest, especially in light of *Lawrence v. Texas,* that it may be timely to rethink this question fundamentally.

Two important studies, one by William Eskridge[11] and the other by Mark Strasser,[12] have to my mind argued cogently that the denial of same-sex marriage is presumptively unconstitutional, not only on the suspect ground urged in *Baehr* but also on the independent ground of abridging the basic human right to intimate life, a ground in the decisions in *Baker* and *Goodridge;* an important recent book by Evan Gerstmann has powerfully made a

128

case on the latter ground alone.[13] If such statutes are subject to heightened scrutiny, whether on the ground of their suspect quality or their abridgment of a fundamental right, these scholars make clear that no compelling justification could constitutionally legitimate such invidious treatment.[14] I hope to complement their arguments by placing them in the context of the larger argument for gay rights that I offer here.

I begin, as any discussion of this issue must in the United States, with *Lawrence v. Texas,* a decision prominently mentioned at the opening of the opinion of Chief Justice Margaret Marshall for the Supreme Judicial Court of Massachusetts in *Goodridge*.[15] The opinion of Chief Justice Marshall is, of course, based on the guarantees of the state constitution of Massachusetts, not on the federal constitution. But *Goodridge*'s arguments, clearly influenced by the earlier decision in *Lawrence,* could reasonably be transposed into the terms of federal constitutional law. It is certainly true that Justice Kennedy's opinion for five justices in *Lawrence* as well as Justice O'Connor's concurring opinion expressly reserve the question of whether their opinions require any legal recognition of same-sex marriage. But, as we earlier saw, Justice Scalia's dissent for three justices sharply questioned Justice O'Connor's equal-protection opinion, in particular, on this point: "This reasoning leaves on pretty shaky grounds state laws limiting marriage to opposite-sex couples."[16] Justice Kennedy's opinion might also raise questions along these lines, as I hope now to show.

There are three crucial features in Justice Kennedy's normative argument for why the basic right to intimate law, already protected by the constitutional right to privacy in a wide range of heterosexual applications, applies to criminal bans on gay/lesbian sex: (1) such bans seriously abridge the right to autonomy in sexual matters, (2) such sexual decisions are the basis for important personal relationships, and (3) such bans demean the very existence of gay/lesbian persons. As I earlier observed, Justice Kennedy importantly started his analysis and critique of Justice White's opinion in *Bowers v. Hardwick* by taking objection to the way White chose to characterize the claimed right in the case (namely, as a right to sodomy). Bans on gay/lesbian sex certainly bear on sex acts, but Justice Kennedy's point, like the similar point of Justice Blackmun in his dissent in *Bowers,* is that all the earlier constitutional privacy cases did so as well but were never characterized in a dehumanizing way that stripped them of their personal or relational significance. The Georgia statute in *Bowers v. Hardwick* applied its prohibitions equally to heterosexual and homosexual nonprocreational sex acts, but Justice White's opinion homophobically focused only on its homosexual

applications, indulging unjust stereotypes of a sexuality without any relational depth or significance that he would never have indulged in the case of
the heterosexual applications of the statute. Justice Kennedy's opinion went
a step further when he explained why the majority of the Court did not find
acceptable Justice O'Connor's narrower equal-protection rationale for the
result in *Lawrence* (namely, the statute unconstitutionally discriminated
against homosexual sex acts in favor of heterosexual sex acts). Justice
Kennedy argued that such statutes do not bear only on acts or the significance of acts but on the very humanity of gays and lesbians as persons—the
"continuance [of *Bowers*] as precedent demeans the lives of homosexual persons."[17] As he remarked at the conclusion of his opinion, "The State cannot demean their existence or control their destiny by making their private
sexual conduct a crime."[18] What makes such statutes so objectionable is that
they have political life today only when aggressively targeted against gays
and lesbians, and it is their agency in such unconstitutional dehumanization
that leads a majority of the Supreme Court to strike them down.

There is thus in Justice Kennedy's opinion for the Court, as there is in all
constitutional privacy cases, two dimensions: an identification and protection of the basic human right of intimate life and a questioning of traditional
reasons, whether racism or sexism or homophobia, for abridging such a
right. It is, of course, analytically possible that, consistent with these two
dimensions, the holding of *Lawrence v. Texas* will be narrowed solely to the
criminalization of gay/lesbian sex, as the force of criminal law may be
regarded as much more devastating than mere failures to extend legal recognition to gay/lesbian relationships. But, it also seems reasonable that,
depending in particular on the weight given homophobia as a constitutional
evil, constitutional principles would question failures to extend legal recognition to same-sex partnerships. There are two forms such analysis would
take, the first suggested in *Baker v. State of Vermont*, the second by *Goodridge v. Department of Public Health*.

The first such analysis would be that the lack of any legal recognition for
same-sex partnerships would be unconstitutional on two grounds. First,
such a lack fails to accord respect to gays and lesbians for their right to intimate life in such grievous ways, in comparison to straight couples, that it
unconstitutionally abridges their rights. Second, the grounds for such
abridgment are unconstitutionally rooted in irrationalist prejudice that
dehumanizes the interests in companionate love that gays have equally with
straights, as if gays could no more love than animals. It is such concerns that
might lead a court, like that in *Baker v. State of Vermont*, to strike down the

failure to accord any legal recognition of gay/lesbian relationships. But it would be consistent with this view that the same court would regard a legislative response, such as the Vermont civil-union bill, as meeting an acceptable constitutional standard.

The second such analysis shares with the first the view that the lack of any legal recognition for same-sex partnerships unconstitutionally burdens a right to intimate life that, on Justice Kennedy's own description of it in *Lawrence v. Texas,* includes companionate loving relationships over time that must be extended a protection like that already accorded heterosexual couples. But this analysis would regard, as the court in *Goodridge v. Department of Public Health* did, anything short of equal rights to marry under the law as unacceptable, since such a distinction would lack a compelling secular justification and itself enforce a homophobic view of gay/lesbian relationships. Yuval Merin has put the point in terms of an unacceptable separate but equal treatment of gays and lesbians that has no more justification than legal apartheid had earlier.[19] My own view is that the correct analysis of this matter requires one to take quite seriously how constitutionally evil homophobia is and how much the abridgment of the right to intimate life plays in perpetuating this evil, analogous to the evils of racism and sexism.

The right to intimate life has played a central role in each of these interpretive developments both because of the morally fundamental nature of the right itself and because its abridgment has been so historically central to the cultural formation and support of rights-denying dehumanizing prejudices and the political expression they have uncritically been permitted to enjoy through public law and policies. Antimiscegenation laws thus continued, long after the Civil War, the dehumanizing attitudes toward African Americans that had, under slavery, deprived them of the basic rights to intimate life (including marriage and control of family relations) and thus dehumanized their treatment to the level of cattle, reduced to their utility (including reproductive fertility in producing further slaves) to the master class. As Lydia Maria Child first pointed out[20] and Harriet Jacobs explored from the perspective of a former slave woman,[21] antimiscegenation laws abridged the basic human right of intimate life in a way that sustained the sectarian sexual mythology of the subhuman image of African Americans. As James Baldwin, a gay black man, observed of his own sexual exploitation at the hands of a white man, such a mythology could certainly easily sexualize and exploit African Americans, meeting their "enormous need to debase other men."[22] What they could not do was to dignify the lives of African Americans as persons capable of the free exercise of the moral powers central to intimate life, including the right to marriage on whatever terms rationally and reasonably give expression to these powers for them in conferring enduring meaning on personal and ethical life. Abridgment of the right to intimate life played so central a role in this unjust dehumanization because the free exercise of this right centrally frames enduring moral interests in loving and being loved, caring and being cared for, intimately giving value to the lives of others and having value given to one's own life; to be denied respect for such powers is, literally, to be deemed subhuman, incapable of the moral interests that give enduring value to living and sustain that value in others, often over generations.

In the case of women, as we have seen, the abridgment of all their basic rights was rationalized in terms of a sectarian mythology of mandatory gender roles central to their moral slavery. To the extent that such a mythology was uncritically sustained by suffrage feminism, it wreaked havoc on women's rights to intimate life in what I have elsewhere called the "Wollstonecraft repudiation."[23] Indeed, suffrage feminists and their allies censored reasonable public argument not only about the right to free love, properly so called, but about more concrete interpretations of that right, including the right to contraception, abortion, and consensual homosexuality.[24] These rights have been central to the emergence and constitutionalization of rights-based feminism since World War II both because of their intrinsic fundamentality to moral sovereignty and also because their recognition reflects constitutional skepticism about the political force that the traditional grounds for their abridgment had been uncritically allowed to enjoy. No robust constitutional understanding of women's human right to intimate life was possible as long as the political orthodoxy of mandatory gender roles was the measure of such rights. Nothing is, in my judgment, more central to the emancipatory meaning and promise of rights-based feminism (building on and elaborating abolitionist feminism) than its skepticism about the political enforcement at large of such mandatory gender roles, its insistence that women and men be accorded respect for their freedom and rationality in taking responsibility for how and on what terms gender may or should play a role in framing their private and public lives. Growing constitutional skepticism about the legitimate enforcement through public law of such sectarian conceptions of mandatory gender roles has cleared normative space to acknowledge and respect not only women's rights to intimate life but all their basic human rights (both public and private).

Rights-based feminism grounds as well, as I have argued, not only respect for the basic human rights of homosexuals (to conscience, speech, intimate life, and work) but skepticism about the traditional grounds for the abridgment of such rights (including compulsory heterosexuality). Against the background of the distinctive moral slavery of homosexuals (their degraded unspeakability), the claim of any human rights at all must be regarded as an outrageous heresy against traditional values, as it was by the majority of Coloradans who approved Colorado Amendment Two. But the outrage is most polemically overwrought against self-respecting claims to gay and lesbian identity in contemplation of the recognition of the human right of homosexuals, on equal terms with heterosexuals, to intimate life and its reasonable corollary, the right to marriage. Such a right has the force it has, both for its proponents and opponents, because its acknowledgment, like the comparable right to marry of African Americans, so critically addresses the grounds of dehumanization that had excluded the stigmatized group from the moral community of equal rights. The claim to the right to marriage thus takes on a public significance, which the right to consensual sex does not, as a heightened expression of gay and lesbian identity protesting the terms of its unjust treatment. In the case of homosexuals, such dehumanization stigmatized them as fallen women, sexualized prostitutes incapable of exercising the powers of moral personality protected by basic human rights. The consequence of the unjust enforcement of this political epistemology is the common uncritical populist assumption that homosexuality, unlike heterosexuality, is exclusively about sex.[25] This assumption, I believe, is the basis for the wounded sense of outrage surrounding even the suggestion of the legitimacy of extending to homosexuals the humane values of the institutions central to protecting the dignity of heterosexual intimate life. Homosexuals, in this view, can no more marry than animals.

There are two dimensions to any reasonable discussion of this matter: the nature and force of the constitutional right, and the appropriate constitutional burden of justification for any abridgment or regulation of such a right. On the first point, there can be no doubt at all that precedents of the Supreme Court, including *Loving v. Virginia*,[26] *Zablocki v. Redhail*,[27] and *Turner v. Safley*,[28] now regard the right to marriage, grounded in the right to intimate life, as a basic constitutional right. It is part of the moral logic of the principles protecting such basic rights that they extend even to forms that may be highly objectionable: for example, the principle of free speech extends to subversive, racist, or sexist speech, or pornography; the principle of religious liberty extends to all forms of conviction, good and bad. The logic of the principle of marriage as a basic right should be similar: it extends to all persons, including, as *Loving* makes clear, to interracial couples and, as

Turner shows, to criminals. The same logic would extend the right to marriage, as a matter of principle, to same-sex couples, irrespective of the unpopularity of or distaste for such relationships.

Of course, I look at this issue through the prism of a thirty-year partnership with another man, loving and being loved in ways that seem to me indistinguishable from the long-term heterosexual relationships—some unmarried; most married; some married, divorced, and remarried—that I have observed over this time. My partner and I have, of course, lived without the benefit of marriage, but I am speaking about the relational interests that have bound us to one another as a loving couple through the good and the bad, holding securely to the bond of love that has held us together against, I might say, some considerable odds in terms of American cultural homophobia and certainly with no political or legal support whatsoever, indeed with every incentive of social and professional acceptability to pull us apart. If this isn't love, I would like to know what is. Persons in such situations learn to fall back on their own resources, valuing a truth they discover about the depth of love in our human natures. I have always known, as truly as I know anything about what gives life personal and ethical meaning, that our love was based on as deep a human right as persons have, a right as deep as the right of conscience or the right of speech. Indeed, I can understand people who take no interest in religion and even less in reading, writing, and speaking, but I can barely understand people who take no interest in matters of love, however they understand love. Love is a human right if anything is a human right, and it seems to me that what makes respect for human rights so valuable as a constitutional tradition is that it extends, on terms of principle, such respect to all persons equally, irrespective of popular prejudices.

It seems clear that this basic right underlies the reasoning of Justice Kennedy in *Lawrence v. Texas,* and that the most reasonable understanding of this right is that it is the same right as that protected by the constitutional right to marry. What marriage involves is legal recognition, and it seems to me compelling that once American culture comes reasonably to understand what gay/lesbian relationships really are, that understanding will require such recognition. American cultural homophobia means that gays and lesbians are barely *seen,* as persons, which explains why our current understanding of these issues is what it is. I speak at this point only of the right itself, leaving to discussion, as the second point, whether there might be a constitutionally reasonable basis for a distinction between heterosexuals and homosexuals. What makes Justice Kennedy's opinion in *Lawrence* so important, following the dissenting opinions of Justices Blackmun and Stevens in *Bowers*, is the way he understands the basic right in question, a right equally abridged by laws criminalizing heterosexual and homosexual nonprocreational sex acts. But, as Justice Kennedy's opinion makes clear, the right is understood to extend to gay/lesbian sex because of the relational significance of sexual intimacy and the way a homophobic tradition has stripped sexually active gays and lesbians of their humanity, as persons who love and love deeply. It is difficult to see, at the level of discussion of the basic human right involved, how this right could not extend to gay/lesbian couples who want the benefit of marriage as an institution.

Chief Justice Marshall's opinion in *Goodridge v. Department of Public Health* prominently invoked the analogy on this point of antimiscegenation cases, both the 1948 opinion of the Supreme Court of California in *Perez* striking down a legislative ban on interracial marriages[29] and the opinion of the U.S. Supreme Court in *Loving*, nineteen years later, striking down such laws.[30] The facts of *Goodridge* are, Marshall argues, analogous: "A statute deprives individuals of access to an institution of fundamental legal, personal, and social significance—the institution of marriage—because of a single trait: skin color in *Perez* and *Loving*, sexual orientation here. As it did in *Perez* and *Loving*, history must yield to a more fully developed understanding of the invidious quality of the discrimination."[31] The analogy may be reasonably understood in terms of comparable struggles against a dehumanizing moral slavery. The case for such a right for gays and lesbians is connected, as was the similar right for people of color, to the very making of rights-based protest against the terms of the moral slavery of homosexuals, that is, appealing to basic human rights (of conscience, speech, intimate life, and work) to bring to bear on public and private life one's ethical convictions about the good of homosexual love and care and to live a life centered in such convictions and the relationships to which they give rise. At the level of the basic rights, basic human rights apply to all persons, including heterosexuals and homosexuals.

On the second point, any basic human right (such as the right to intimate life) can be abridged, consistent with the argument for toleration, only on compelling grounds of public reason not themselves hostage to a sectarian view that can no longer be regarded as justifiable to the public reason of all persons in the community. On this ground, the Supreme Court, as we have seen, correctly struck down both anticontraception and antiabortion laws. Anticontraception laws rested on what was, in contemporary circumstances, an unjustly sectarian view of mandatory procreational sexuality that many reasonable people no longer accepted as the measure of sexual love; antiabortion laws rest on a conception of fetal life in early pregnancy that cannot be legitimately enforced to abridge the reproductive autonomy of the many women who do not regard that conception of fetal life as a reasonable conception of moral personality. For the same reason, no compelling argument of public reason exists in contemporary circumstances that could justify the abridgment of the right to love of homosexuals. Neither of the two arguments traditionally regarded as justifying such abridgment (the evil of nonprocreational sex and the conception of homosexual love as lowering one party to the status of a woman, a degraded status) can be regarded as publicly reasonable today. The first argument was justly repudiated by the contraception cases; the second by the many cases repudiating the force of sexist stereotypes in public law. *Lawrence v. Texas* implicitly repudiates both rationales.

The Catholic moral conservative John Finnis has argued that even if *Bowers* were properly overruled (as he suggests it should be), it would still be appropriate to make the exclusively procreational model of sexuality the measure of the right to marriage.[32] On this view, as another moral conservative put the point, the right to marriage is determined not solely by commitments arising from love as such, but by "the natural teleology of the body."[33] There is, however, no difference of principle between the sectarian character of such arguments in the one context (*Bowers*) as opposed to another (the right to marriage). Heterosexual couples who are childless, whether by design or by force of circumstances, are not for that reason disqualified from the right to marry, nor could they reasonably be.[34] It is not in fact our law or practice that marriage must be for procreation or that its value is only procreational. When courts have insisted on the point as a ground for refusing same-sex marriage they have "frankly, made up this standard out of thin air, and have applied it only to same-sex couples."[35]

If the natural teleology of the body made any sense as a basis for public law, childlessness violates the natural teleology of the body as much as the relationship of a homosexual couple. But the natural teleology of the body, whatever its legitimate force within sectarian moral and religious traditions, is not a publicly reasonable basis for law. It (like the teleology of nature more generally) cannot reasonably be a basis for public law in a morally and religiously pluralistic society that lacks any reasonable common ground to ascribe to such natural facts a politically enforceable normative purpose.[36] We can reasonably impose such a normative conception on homosexual no more than on heterosexual intimate relations. In both cases, as free and rational persons, we may "employ our powers of mind and body to produce some innovation in the course of nature,"[37] including taking pleasure in one another's bodies in whatever forms one gives or receives mutual pleasure in expressing and sustaining companionate sexual love as an end in itself. Pace Finnis, the illegitimacy of imposing such a sectarian view to forbid same-sex marriage may, if anything, be more unjustified than its imposition on same-sex relations *simpliciter* since abridgment of the right to marriage may play a more pivotally unjust role in the dehumanization of homosexuals and is thus even more unjustified. Both are, of course, unjustified in principle.

The imposition on either heterosexual or homosexual love of the model of mandatory procreational sex is surely, in contemporary circumstances, constitutionally unjust because it politically remakes reality in its own anachronistic sectarian image. In particular, it conspicuously fails to acknowledge what any reasonable understanding of modern life, not hostage to such a sectarian conception, must acknowledge: the force in human life of sexual love as an end in itself that sustains intimate relations of loving and being loved central to giving meaning to personal and ethical life.[38] From this perspective, the political demand that human love, to be maritally legitimate, must conform to the natural teleology of the body usurps the moral sovereignty of the person over the transformative moral powers of love in intimate relations and the identifications central to sustaining personal and ethical value in living, in effect, dehumanizing human sexuality to its purely biological, reproductive aspect. As a Catholic critic of his church's condemnation of homosexuality recently put this point (against, among others, Finnis), "it is extraordinary that so many branches of Christianity should have now degenerated into fertility cults."[39] Such a view, dubious even today on internal religious grounds, can hardly reasonably be the measure of rights and responsibilities in a secular society.[40] The role of human sexuality in the plastic imaginative life and transformative moral passions and identifications of free personality would, by force of law, be unreasonably degraded to the procrustean sectarian measure of a purely animal sexuality.[41]

At bottom, the insistence on opposite sexes, as the legitimate measure of the right to marriage, indulges, as the *Baehr* court saw, constitutionally illegitimate gender stereotypes. Andrew Koppelman has persuasively explored, in this connection, the analogy of the antimiscegenation laws.[42] The prohibition of racial intermarriage was to the cultural construction of racism what the prohibition of same-sex marriage is to sexism and homophobia: "Just as miscegenation was threatening because it called into question the distinctive and superior status of being white, homosexuality is threatening because it calls into question the distinctive and superior status of being male."[43]

In this connection, there is a striking analogy between the form of the argument Finnis offered and the arguments earlier made for antimiscegenation laws. Finnis's argument appealed, as authority on this point, to the work of the Catholic moral theologian Germain Grisez. Grisez appealed to animal biology as a reason for believing that "one-flesh union" (procreative sex in marriage) is the ultimate good of marital union. Grisez argued: "Each animal is incomplete, for a male or a female individual is only a potential part of the mated pair, which is the complete organism that is capable of reproducing sexually. This is true also of men and women: as mates who engage in sexual intercourse suited to initiate new life, they complete each other and become an organic unit. In doing so, it is literally true that 'they become one flesh.'"[44]

Even as a description of animal reproductive biology, this description gets the facts wrong. It fails to distinguish between the activities of animals and the functioning of their organs and other parts. When an animal walks, it acts, and we ascribe to it voluntary acts. But the beating of an animal's heart, an important body organ, is not a voluntary act; the heart functions, but it is not an agent. Organs are parts of animals, but animals are not parts of organisms. To make his case, Grisez irrationally depended on a fact that does not exist. Grisez's mating couple is not an organism but two people who engage in a joint activity for a certain purpose, but they might reasonably engage in that activity for other purposes as well—as an expression of sexual love and intimacy, for example—without wanting to propagate.[45] Why, exactly, is that not a reasonable instantiation of the good of friendship or love?

This mythology of biology as the measure for same-sex marriage plays the same role that a mythology of biological race played in the support of antimiscegenation laws. A pseudoscience of race differences rationalized a view of blacks as racially inferior. In the case of same-sex marriage, a comparable pseudoscience ascribes to the facts of procreative sexuality a mythological organic unity that any other forms of sexual relations must lack. Nothing more is being said than that nonprocreative sex is not procreative, which may be a good or a bad thing, depending on the persons and their circumstances. There is certainly no basis in the biological facts to deny value to nonprocreative sexual relations, as Finnis and Grisez dogmatically suppose, let alone to posit that such relations are evil, let alone immoral, as they also suppose. The role their mythological biology plays here is no better than the role a mythology of race differences plays in dehumanizing people of color.

A revealing historical analogy has been drawn upon in the resistance to contemporary same-sex marriage, namely, arguments taken from the earlier-discussed antipolygamy movement of the nineteenth century. Conservative commentators such as George Will[46] and William Bennett[47] have thus questioned the allegedly conservative advocacy of same-sex marriage, by Andrew Sullivan among others,[48] as affording no limiting principle that would not extend the right to polygamy as well. Arguments against polygamy had two crucial features: a defense of monogamy as central to the values of Western civilization, and a critique of polygamy as reinforcing the unjust subjection of women. But the contemporary gay defense of same-sex marriage does not question monogamy; it insists on it,[49] and it does so, as I have argued here, on the basis of a forceful repudiation of sexist gender roles in the name of the principles of rights-based feminism.[50] Polygamy, as traditionally understood, reinforced such unjust gender roles and thus cannot be regarded as a constitutionally reasonable form of intimate life consistent with these principles. As Nancy Rosenblum recently observed:

> Despite rare exceptions, patriarchy has been the dominant form of polygamy. It has never had its basis in reciprocity or friendship, not even ideally. Its justification has never been the expansiveness of affection or cooperation. It has rested on ideological or spiritual accounts of male authority and female subjection, on status associated with numbers of wives, and of course on beliefs about male sexual power (or the need to temper women's sexual power) and male entitlements. It is doubtful that the known doctrinal supports for polygamy could be rehabilitated and made congruent with democratic sex.[51]

The antipolygamy appeal is not then a reasonable analogy: the arguments for same-sex marriage do not support such an extension any more than they would justify spouse abuse or adultery or, for that matter, no-fault divorce.[52] Compelling secular arguments of gender equality support the limitation of the right to marriage to monogamous couples.[53] But the spirit of the antipolygamy movement is, I believe, very much in play in such appeals: an attempt to insist on an uncritical conception of gender hierarchy in marriage, thus further immunizing the conventional theory of gender roles from much needed rights-based feminist critique (it was, on this ground, that John Stuart Mill, an advocate of feminist equality,[54] condemned the hypocrisy of the American persecution of the Mormons[55]). The antipolygamy movement, like suffrage feminism and the temperance and purity movements, thus importantly censored important arguments of rights-based feminism from public debate and discussion, rationalizing the shrunken and decrepit thing that suffrage feminism became. The ferocity of the populist attack on gay marriage has a similarly reactionary character and basis polemically to insist on a symbolism of marriage as an immovable rock (impermeable to reasonable doubt about gender roles) that is factually unreal and normatively unfair, using homosexuals as the scapegoat politically to reify gender hierarchy in marriage.

Same-sex marriage is not a threat to marriage but a recognition of the deeper moral values in marriage and the principled elaboration of those values to all persons; the case for the legitimacy of gay marriage crucially rests on the value (real and symbolic) reasonably placed in our culture on marriage and family life and argues, as a matter of principle, for fair extension of that value to all persons on fair terms. Richard Epstein has recently put the point cogently:

> When President Bush, for example, talks about the need to "protect" the sanctity of marriage, his plea is a giant non sequitur because he does not explain what, precisely, he is protecting marriage against. No proponent of gay marriage wants to ban traditional marriage, or to burden couples who want to marry with endless texts, taxes, and delays. All gay-marriage advocates want to do is to enjoy the same rights of association that are held by other people. Let the state argue that gay marriages are a health risk, and the answer is that anything that encourages monogamy has the opposite effect. Any principled burden of justification is not met.[56]

Homosexuality is no more exclusively about sex than is heterosexuality. The culturally marked difference between them is the product of a culture of moral slavery constructed, in part, by the unthinkability of extending the right to marriage (as an aspect of the basic human right to intimate life) to homosexuals (because they are assumed to be subhuman, if not animalistic, in their intimate lives). Homosexuals thus justly resist the traditional terms of their dehumanization by insisting on their constitutional right to marriage as an aspect of the basic human right to respect for the dignity of intimate life, the transformative moral passion of mutual love and care in personal and ethical life. Their argument gives, if you will, a distinctly liberal interpretation to the moral appeal of the argument for family values. The idea that gay marriage is a threat to marriage as such can barely be credited, as an argument, when an ethical wrong such as adultery goes quite unmentioned in ostensibly promarriage discourse. The difference, of course, is that adultery is a reasonably popular heterosexual vice,[57] and there is no interest in tackling in a responsible way such serious ethical issues that require a challenge to uncritical public opinion. Rather, same-sex marriage is demonized as a threat to marriage from within an embattled sectarian perspective on gender orthodoxy that still has a hold on uncritical public opinion. Arguments for same-sex marriage, which in fact depend on respect for the dignity of marriage, are thus irresponsibly but conveniently inverted into an attack on marriage, yet another instance of the paradox of forging irrationalist intolerance precisely when public opinion most needs reasonable discussion and debate of real, not unreal, ethical issues.

Such populist uncritical scapegoating is, I believe, quite clearly in play in congressional and presidential approval of the DOMA of 1996.[58] The act's purpose is to exercise federal power to limit the force of the possible legality of same-sex marriage in Hawaii in two ways. First, it expressly excludes same-sex marriage from any of the benefits that accrue to married couples under federal law (thus discouraging even Hawaiian gay and lesbian couples from exercising their rights to marry). Second, it ordains that no other state shall be required to give effect to such same-sex marriage.[59] The purpose of the second provision is to limit any extraterritorial effect of the Hawaii legitimation of same-sex marriage under the Full Faith and Credit Clause of Article IV, section 1, of the U.S. Constitution.[60] Even assuming same-sex marriage were not a constitutional right, this provision would be constitutionally problematic since it claims for Congress a power over the substantive law of marriage that, under the federal system, it does not have; the recognition of Massachusetts same-sex marriages in other states is decisively a matter for state, not federal, law.[61] Since same-sex marriage is, however, a constitutional right, the first provision is unconstitutional as well, illegitimately exercising viewpoint discrimination with respect to a fundamental right.

Arguments for a constitutional amendment to forbid same-sex marriage anywhere in the Union do not rest on sound arguments of constitutional principle but show how politicians in the United States can powerfully mobilize populist prejudice against claims of justice in ways that bespeak the racist demagogues who disgraced American politics for much too long. I believe I have shown why these arguments are not reasonable but rather rest on and appeal to irrational prejudice. My last question is this: How are we to understand the reactionary political psychology to which such arguments so powerfully appeal?

PART III
PSYCHOLOGY

10

PSYCHOLOGY

I have framed the argument of this book in terms of a mapping of my own struggle for voice, as a gay man, onto a larger political and constitutional struggle in which my voice, among other voices, played some part. My argument has shown how, in finding my voice as a gay man and law professor concerned with making the case for gay rights, I drew upon and developed a number of voices (philosophical, personal, historical, legal), all of which were integrated into my sense of how to speak truthfully and be heard justly. As my argument draws to its close, I want to review my story and explain the more recent development in my work of yet other voices (feminist, psychological, literary) and the role they play in understanding the overall structure of both my argument and my life. As I try to show, the voices through which my argument has been made move in a kind of cycle as I end with a better understanding of where and why I began.

Voice, Resistance, Reaction, and Psychology

What makes this story so interesting, comparable to the similar struggles for voice in the struggles against religious intolerance, racism, and sexism, is that the struggle to find one's own personal and ethical voice, as a person in relationship to another, was what motivated the larger struggle for political and constitutional voice. At the center of my story was my coming into loving relationship with another man, a relationship made possible by my ethical struggle for voice but one that also gave a resonance to new experiments in voice. What began for me in the most radically individualistic of intellectual disciplines, Socratic moral and political philosophy, grew through love with another philosopher into a need for forging a larger resonance for our voices and lives. Our relationship could not have survived, let alone flourished, without resistance to the injustice sustained by the lies that I saw all about me, as a boy and now as a man, because such a system of uncontested lies kills the sense of truthful voice in relationship—indeed psychologically requires the death of protesting voice. I sought such resonance in the historical study of protest movements that had already achieved so much in the ethical and constitutional transformation of American life and law. I found through political philosophy, history, and constitutional law the resonance I was seeking and saw the U.S. Supreme Court move during my lifetime from summarily dismissing such arguments[1] to taking them seriously[2] and finally to accepting them.[3]

It is important to see that work like mine depended on an important feature of the legitimacy of judicial review in the United States, namely, that it justify its powers in terms of arguments of principle. This requirement insures that any basic human right protected by constitutional principles be extended on equal terms to all persons.[4] It is because the Supreme Court must justify its powers in this way that it insures, overall, that American institutions better conform to a respect for human rights that alone renders democratic political power legitimate. What made the judiciary the appropriate forum for my arguments is that they aimed to show that a basic human right to intimate life, already robustly extended to the heterosexual majority in the United States, extended to the small homosexual minority as well. It is because the normative, historical, and factual arguments I developed bore on that point that, analogous to comparable arguments successfully made in the struggle against racism and sexism, the judiciary gave them the hearing it did, and ultimately accepted them. It is hard for me to believe that over time the arguments earlier developed with respect to sexual orientation as fully constitutionally suspect will not have, in one way or another, the same impact on same-sex marriage, since the two issues are equally grounded in compelling arguments of principle.

But *Lawrence v. Texas* has only recently been decided, and the comparable developments in other nations (condemning discrimination on grounds of sexual orientation and extending legal recognition to same-sex couples) took place over a fair amount of time.[5] If past is prologue, it is fair to expect that some amount of time will be required before such developments occur in the United States (in Canada, for example, there was a forty-year gap between decriminalization of gay sex and a court opinion recognizing same-sex marriage).[6] Meanwhile, in the wake of *Lawrence v. Texas* and *Goodridge v. Department of Public Health,* we are in a period that I would call politically reactionary on the issue of gay/lesbian rights, as shown in the political support for federal legislation such as the Defense of Marriage Act of 1996, for President Bush's proposed constitutional amendment to ban same-sex marriage, and for recent state constitutional amendments banning same-sex marriage. Americans in 2004 are evidently reactionary on issues of sexual orientation in ways analogous to reactionary attitudes to race in 1967, when *Loving v. Virginia* was decided. Arguably, they are even more reactionary today: a constitutional amendment to limit marriage to same-race couples would not have enjoyed the kind of support that President Bush's proposal clearly does or that state constitutional amendments have, which confirm my general earlier observation that America is, for reasons earlier discussed (the total ban on gay/lesbian protest before World War II), culturally much more homophobic than other liberal democratic nations. My own view is that the proposed constitutional amendment and comparable state amendments are morally shameful and will in time bring shame on their authors and supporters in the same way that the once popular American politics of race now shames and embarrasses us in our own eyes and before the eyes of the world. Some otherwise liberal constitutional scholars have, because of worry about this reactionary politics, urged that no federal constitutional argument for same-sex marriage be pursued at this time, leaving the issue to democratic politics for the time being.[7] I very much doubt they would have made such an argument in 1967 against *Loving,* though at that time Americans clearly opposed marriages between partners of different races. At such a time, we need grounds for resistance from liberal scholars. We needed it then; we need it now. Why is resistance on this issue so psychologically difficult for otherwise good men?

My interest in this last chapter is in putting my legal story in a larger psychological perspective, an investigation that may cast further light both on my journey and on that of American culture, clarifying how and why we have come so far, and why there are reactionary forces that conspicuously resist further progress. Why resist at all? What are the links in the human psyche between resisting voice in relationship and in politics and law? Why does such resistance elicit repressive reactionary fundamentalist politics? These are the questions that I want now to investigate, offering a psychology of resistance to gender stereotypes in which the personal is political.

My inspiration is my recent collaborative relationship with the developmental psychologist Carol Gilligan in teaching a seminar on gender and democracy for the past five years at the New York University School of Law.[8] This collaboration led me to understand and investigate two themes implicit in the argument of the earlier chapters of this book: first, why the contemporary argument for gay rights arose from and elaborated arguments of rights-based feminism; and second, the personal and political psychology that underlay the need to resist injustices such as sexism and homophobia, yet also explained why such resistance gave rise to reactionary political movements.

The subject of psychological investigation was what I saw in the protest movements I had studied for so long and, more introspectively, what I came to see in my own personal and professional life as the psychology underlying my own voice as one, among others, in a protest movement. The new vehicle of such psychological investigation was close reading of literature, in particular the novels of Leo Tolstoy, Virginia Woolf, Arundhati Roy, James Baldwin, and Joseph Conrad. All these novelists explored gender-inflected voices and undervoices in highly patriarchal cultures, and the close study of them (in particular Tolstoy) enabled me better to understand the unjust impact of unjust gender stereotypes on voice, not only on women but on men (straight and gay) as well. I had long been absorbed in the New York culture of performing arts, in particular opera and theater, but had not read and closely studied literature since my youth, and had certainly not used it in my professional work until quite recently. What I found in literature was a new kind of voice that I could use to deepen my understanding of the struggle for voice I had been studying for so long. The psychological sensitivity of this new voice opened my psyche to the connections of my own mature voice to my voice as a boy brought up in a loving family, with parents who were in (for the period) a remarkably egalitarian, loving, and sexually fulfilled marriage. I saw something I had not seen before, which I draw upon in my argument here, namely, the roots of my own mature ethical voice in the voice of my parents—my mother, a feminist in practice though not in theory, and my father, who loved and respected the intelligence and moral agency of his wife and daughter and whose remarkable operatic voice opened his son to a complex world of feeling and aspiration in men more truthful than the patriarchal pieties of the surrounding culture.[9] The movement of my thought through various voices (philosophical, personal, historical, legal) thus moves in a cycle, through psychological investigation aided by literature to understanding and facing what it was difficult for me, as a man, to face: the roots of my voice in my relationship to my mother. I end where I began in relationship to those I have loved and who have loved me, and see my resisting struggle as one to hold on to the values of loving egalitarian relationship that I early learned were the measure of a life worth living.

Through such work I was led to raise questions about what developmental psychology sustains the hold of patriarchy on men and why some men, often through relationships to women, come to resist it. I discovered that the developmental pattern of the voices of five leaders of ethical resistance to injustice (Garrison, Tolstoy, Gandhi, King, and Churchill) arose from a struggle for their distinctively creative ethical voices (voices that resisted the violence of patriarchal manhood) sustained by their relationships to their mothers or maternal caretakers and was often later developed in relationship to other women, their wives or followers.[10] I also discovered the complexity of such men's relationships to maternal caretakers and how important was the quality of these relationships, in particular, how idealized or nonidealized these relationships were. I want to draw on that work at this point in my argument, explaining its view of resistance and then bringing it to bear on a better understanding of gay/lesbian voice as a protest movement grounded in rights-based feminism, and the reactionary politics in the United States that now wars on that movement's further progress.

Men, Honor, and Obligatory Violence

If gender (as traditionally understood in terms of the binary, man and woman) were a rigid and impermeable aspect of our psychological identities as men or women, there would be, contrary to fact, no psychological basis for the resistance of a person such as Garrison to structural injustices such as racism and sexism, since so much of such resistance requires resistance to conventional gender stereotypes (embodied in codes of honor). Yet Garrison did resist in ways that challenged dominant codes of male honor. I begin with the force of such codes and then turn to developing a hypothesis about the psychology of the resistance of men such as Garrison and others to them.

Honor codes exemplify the unjust demands of patriarchy on the psychology of men, with sons and daughters placed under the hierarchical authority of fathers.[11] These demands take the form of an obligatory violence directed against any voice that challenges, in particular, the strict social controls over women's sexuality (including arranged marriages) that are required to advance patriarchal dynastic ends: virginity before marriage and monogamous fidelity after marriage. A father's or brother's or lover's or husband's sense of honor, as a man, is defined in terms of his control over the chastity or fidelity of women, irrespective of personal feeling or desire. Any challenge to this control was an insult that triggered violence, as a condition of manhood under patriarchy. Such control was, in dominantly face-to-face and largely illiterate Mediterranean societies, understood in terms of how matters publicly appeared, so that men were vulnerable to dishonor because women (often in fact quite innocent of sexual relations) merely appeared less strictly modest and reticent than was expected in their relations to men.[12] Such dishonor, sometimes arising only from gossip,[13] required a violent reaction, extending even to killing wives or daughters. A man's most intimate feelings and relations were, under the code of honor, subject to rules that rested as much on repressing his personal feeling and voice as on repressing those of women.

Codes of honor, thus understood, are aspects of patriarchal institutions (resting on precisely the mythological idealization of gender stereotypes) that sustain forms of structural injustice through violence directed against any challenge to the terms of gender stereotypes, which often idealize good women as asexual and denigrate sexual women as bad women.[14] Within its framework, women do not exist as persons with moral individuality, let alone sexual agency and subjectivity, independent of the roles assigned them by patriarchy. The patriarchal culture of nineteenth-century Italy illuminated the kind of tragic losses and repressed voices that such objectifying gender stereotypes, as a general matter, both inflicted and covered over, namely, the sacrifice of children born out of wedlock.[15] The honor code condemned both sexual relations out of wedlock and the illegitimate children often born of such relations as intrinsically shameful.[16] The code, enforced by local Catholic priests and the police, rationalized bullying unwed mothers into abandoning children to public institutions and sometimes effectively imprisoned the women in such institutions as compulsory wet nurses. The consequence for the babies was usually death.[17] Families sometimes protested such separations in terms of their "infinite grief," robbing a mother "of the dearest object of her heart,"[18] suggesting traumatizing emotional losses that must have been widespread. But such losses, consistent with the political psychology of patriarchy, were often not acknowledged but instead were covered over with gender-stereotypical idealizations, as of the foundlings in Naples as "children of the Madonna,"[19] most of whom in fact died. Meanwhile, their real mothers, if they were wet nurses in the foundling homes, were "treated as livestock."[20]

The developmental psychology that makes possible a conception of manhood that can sustain such patriarchal demands requires traumatic separation of young boys from their mothers in contrast to the developmental continuity allowed to girls until early adolescence.[21] The marks of such trauma are not only loss of intimate voice and memory but the disassociation from intimate relationship and voice that patriarchal manhood requires. Idealizing stereotypes are, in their nature, objectifying, supported by a psychology that lends itself to the forms of violence required to hold such stereotypes in place in patterns of structural injustice. The gender stereotypes include idealization (the asexual good woman) and denigration (the sexual bad woman).

The honor code, thus understood, is held in place by a system of physical and psychological violence triggered by deviance from its demands, which enter into the psyches of men and women through their loss of protesting voice and their consequent vulnerability to shaming by any appearance of deviation from the code and the expression of such shaming in violence, whether physical or psychological. The psychology of shaming is in conflict with a democratic ethics of reciprocity based on the free and equal voice of all persons, an ethics that expresses itself in ideals of equal respect as the foundation of friendship and love expressive of free and equal voice. This ethics enters into our psyches through the experience of love and respect consistent with its demands and shows itself in guilt and remorse when one culpably violates the demands of equal respect and the forms of love it makes possible.[22]

Democratic Manhood

This alternative in developmental psychology may underlie the turn to resistance that I discovered first in Garrison and then in each of the other men I studied. The story is by no means always the same in each case, and some of these men certainly lived in some degree of contradiction between their overall protest against structural injustice and the forms of patriarchy they still allowed to dominate parts of their lives. But there is a remarkably similar alternative developmental psychology in their lives, one that made psychologically possible for them a more democratic conception of manhood much more sensitive to issues of suppressed voice (including the voices of women) than patriarchal manhood.

What is remarkably discernible in the case of each of the men I studied (Garrison, Tolstoy, Gandhi, King, and Churchill) is, instead of the developmental trauma of early boyhood separation from mothers, a staying in significant intimate relationship with the loving moral voice, care, and concern of maternal persons (biological mothers or an aunt, in the case of Tolstoy) and placing continuing value and weight on these women's voices and insights as a significant counterweight to traditional patriarchal demands. How should we understand this common experience and its links, if any, to their turn to resistance?

Certainly, Virginia Woolf in *Three Guineas* suggested links between women's claims to voice and resistance to political violence: "[We are] fighting the tyranny of the patriarchal state as you are fighting the tyranny of the Fascist state."[23] Sara Ruddick recently refined Woolf's insight in her pathbreaking inquiry into the voices of mothers that have been traditionally patriarchally silenced.[24] Ruddick was well aware that the loving care of children is, has been, and should be done by men as well but chose, for reasons of exposition, to call all such care "maternal work."[25] Such work includes, for Ruddick, three tasks: preservation, growth, and acceptability, all of which require a loving care that she, drawing on Iris Murdoch and Simone Weil, called "attentive love."[26] Ruddick certainly saw the complex strands in such work, some of which may be distorted by narcissism and others guided by patriarchal aims. But she insisted that we take seriously at least those strands of maternal practice of intimate voice and responsiveness in which mother and child can read one another's human world well after the mother-child attunement of infancy.[27] Ruddick's brilliant insight was to identify in such maternal care practices of resistance required to maintain connection in the right developmental way, including sustaining life and growth,[28] renouncing one's lethal powers to nurture the vulnerably powerless,[29] limiting aggression to maintain connection,[30] and even willingness to suffer as a developmental strategy of moral education.[31] Such practice has implicit in it four ideals: renunciation, nonviolent resistance (where feasible), reconciliation, and peacekeeping.[32]

My hypothesis about the alternative developmental psychology here under examination is that the five men I studied shared a common developmental psychology that, in contrast to the traumatic break with mothers required by the Oedipal patriarchal story in early boyhood, prominently included staying in significant relationship to the loving voice and care of maternal caretakers, understood as displaying the features of attentive love and implicit ideals of resistance that Ruddick described so well. Many women, though living under patriarchy, are not the subjects of close patriarchal regulation and thus enjoy some freedom of voice, especially within the domain marked as that of women, giving expression to an ethical voice, based on their experience, in the form of a personal religion or way of life exemplifying the hidden transcripts through which subordinated groups nourish a voice of ethical resistance to their subordination. When men such as Garrison, Tolstoy, Gandhi, King, and Churchill, as boys and sometimes later, give ethical significance and weight to the voices of such women, not suppressing them as patriarchy requires, they develop in themselves as men an ethical voice (given a public expression to perceptions rooted in maternal hidden transcripts) that raises questions of justice about gender itself, because the voices of the women with whom they identify express an ethical voice independent and often critical of patriarchy (which accords authority only to the voice of hierarchical fathers). This is a psychologically and ethically liberating position because the ethical voice of such men questions the role of manhood in rationalizing forms of political violence and thus raises questions about the many forms of structural injustice that depend on such violence. Such men find themselves not in violence but in new forms of artistic and ethical voice that resist it. This story may be much more common than Freud supposed even in his own period, let alone today, when, as Ruddick's work showed, feminist women are bringing their convictions to bear on both their private lives as mothers and their public lives as citizens. The unjust political demands of patriarchy would, to the extent that patriarchy is hegemonic or at least still very powerful, show themselves by the attempt to suppress or marginalize the developmental experiences that would psychologically threaten the stability of patriarchy.[33]

But, of course, not all persons with this background will make of it what the men here under examination did. The demands of patriarchy can lead people to repudiate or deny or marginalize psychological propensities that do not appear to have any legitimacy or ethical appeal. To make sense of why some men rather unusually (for men) acted on their sense of psychological truth, we need to address how and why they held on to their sense of lived truth in relationship, as one among life's most enduring and sustaining humane values, and were motivated for this reason to resist unjust patterns of structural injustice.

The stability of structural injustice requires the violent repression of any voice that would reasonably question its authority or legitimacy, which includes not only the voices of women but those of men as well. The vehicle of this psychology for men takes the form of a sense of manhood defined by codes of honor. Such codes vary. They do not, for example, always take the precise form of the Mediterranean honor code earlier discussed; under Icelandic honor codes, for example, "virginity was a non-issue," as men, not women, were placed on a pedestal.[34] But apparently, such codes pervasively enforce gender idealizations in the form of "the widespread presence of something recognizable as the heroic ethic from the cold North Atlantic to the Arabian desert."[35] Their force rests, as we have seen, on trauma and disassociation, a psychology prone to violence against any threat to the gender idealizations that sustain structural injustice.[36] Response to such threats includes, as in the early republican period in the United States[37] and in the American antebellum South,[38] practices of dueling triggered by insults to masculine honor. James Gilligan's important study of violent criminals shows us how alive this culture remains today,[39] and Chris Hedges, Mark Juergensmeyer, and others show how powerful it remains as the trigger to ethnic violence and genocide in the former Yugoslavia and elsewhere, including the resorting to violence by Islamic and other fundamentalists.[40] Forms of these codes clearly existed in antebellum America, imperial Russia, Gandhi's India, King's America, and Churchill's Britain.

My hypothesis is that these men resisted such disassociation by holding on to the psychological truth of loving association experienced in their relationships of loving care to maternal caretakers. If patriarchal manhood armors itself through disassociation from the voices and feelings that reasonably contest gender idealizations, democratic manhood self-consciously disarms itself from the role violence plays in traditional manhood, remaining truthful to personal voice, relationships, and experiences. The consequence is a freeing of a personal and ethical voice that questions the violence that sustains the structural injustices supported by patriarchal manhood. Whereas patriarchal manhood is tied to hierarchy and a rigid gender binary, democratic masculinities work "within a paradigm of connectedness (mind in body, body in mind; self in relationship, relationship in self; thought in feelings, feelings in thought) and reflecting the perception that men and women are inseparably connected (man in woman, woman in man). Freed from hierarchy and from loss, gender becomes more variable, more improvisational, and the shaming of manhood less explosive."[41] What this marks in the psychology of men such as Garrison, Tolstoy, Gandhi, King, and Churchill is their cultivation of a free ethical voice, developed in relationships to the voices of antipatriarchal women, that questions patriarchal violence.

Gay/Lesbian Resistance

This hypothesis certainly clarifies my own experience: a boy's voice nurtured in close relationship to a beloved mother and father whose own relationship was remarkably egalitarian and antipatriarchal. As I struggled to come to terms with my sexual orientation, I determined to live in a manner consistent with that voice from which I had learned so much about truth in relationship based on free and equal voice.[42] It was because I had been attuned to free voice in egalitarian relationship, in particular the voice of my mother, that my struggle for ethical and truthful voice in a gay relationship increasingly found resonance in the ethical voice of second-wave feminism, building on antebellum abolitionist feminism.[43]

It is not my view that gay men are, by virtue of their sexual orientation, less drawn to patriarchy than straight men. But one of the range of ethical and personal choices faced by gay men is the extent to which they will insist on their identity as gay men against the terms of the homophobia that afflicts them. If they make the choice to protest such homophobic disadvantage, as I have,[44] then they may make the choice as a way of pursuing what I have here called democratic manhood, something they have come to value in their personal relationships, and their choice reflects, in my view, the ethics and psychology of men such as the five I have named. We can, I believe, see this ethics and psychology in the resistance of gay men such as Walt Whitman and Edward Carpenter, both of whom closely linked their own struggles for ethical voice, as gay men, to a feminism that called for a new ethical voice for women.[45] There is nothing inevitable or necessary in this choice. It may involve costs, both external and internal, that a more silent, assimilationist identity would not impose. But choices of this sort are never made in terms of such costs, which, from the perspective of a psyche rooted in what I have called free ethical voice, are not worthy considerations.

A kind of courage is, no doubt, required, but it is not the courage of conventional patriarchal manhood. In my case, though I think of both my mother and father as maternal caretakers whose loving voices gave resonance to my sense of antipatriarchal voice, I know that whatever courage was involved in my choice was learned not from my father but from the free ethical voice of my Italian American mother, who had an informed and intelligent view on everything and let you know it. Her religion was a very personal form of Roman Catholicism in which the sacred heart of Jesus was the voice of ethics, a voice I, otherwise quite unreligious, carry in my psyche. Her ultimate criticism of an evil such as anti-Semitism, or, closer to hand, homophobia, was its heartlessness. When I was considering how public a role I should take in protesting homophobia, a conversation with my mother was decisive. It was not that she supported my choice; she was much too protective of me to easily sacrifice her son for what seemed to her a crackpot liberal ideology. But when I confronted her with the question of whether she wanted me to lead a life that seemed to me a cowardly failure to stand by my convictions, she responded forcefully that she did not want *that*. She knew by then that my life with my companion was very like the life of loving care, passion, and egalitarian voice she had had with my father, and she could see, because she had lived with us for long periods during her desolate loneliness after my father's death, how much our love meant to each of us and how it showed itself in our love and care of her when she most needed this kind of care and support. My mind was made up, then, not by what she wanted me to do but by my sense of what the ethical voice she had imparted to me required. My mother has since died, but her voice is always with me, testing relationships in the way she did for their truth. It is the voice of this book.

When men come to question a manhood that endorses violence against any threat, they must question, as I did, the violence of homophobia both in others and in themselves. I saw early on that patriarchy, which corrupted so many heterosexual relationships, corrupted homosexual relationships as well, and that I could not reliably depend on the patriarchal cultural assumptions that were widely accepted in the America of my youth. I would have to find an ethical voice that would enable me to hold on to my sense of truthful voice in relationship, which was where I began the narrative of this book in its opening chapter. What inspired that narrative was coming into loving relationship with a man and wanting that relationship to flourish. But truthful voice in relationship could not be sustained in a homophobic political culture based on violence and lies, and I increasingly saw that voice as a feminist one, joining with women in protesting the degree to which the power of patriarchy depended on crushing any voice, in particular a free sexual voice, that resisted its authority. Resistance was therefore psychologically imperative, and resisting voice was thus the basis of both my personal and professional life. My work has been a series of experiments in such voice, seeking personal and political resonance.

Historically, gay men have responded to homophobic political cultures in different ways, and the emergence of overt political and constitutional resistance to such cultures has been for some traumatic. Take Tennessee Williams, a gay man who, during a very homophobic period of American life, produced several world-class masterpieces of the stage, including *A Streetcar Named Desire* and *Cat on a Hot Tin Roof*. By comparison, the plays of his later career, during which a movement for gay rights was gathering momentum, are embarrassingly bad, suggesting a loss of imagination when he faced a less homophobic environment. My point is not limited to great artists such as Williams. It applies to many gays of his period, men who found gay rights quite threatening, indeed traumatic.[46]

My point is that such consequences, though real, are themselves very much a result of living a life under a hegemonic regime of deep injustice, and therefore are irrelevant to the justice of claims of rights, whether the claims are those of people of color, of women, or of gays. Human beings are incredibly resourceful, finding under circumstances of often terrible injustice ways of living that endow their lives with meaning and happiness. Think of African American culture, which, under conditions of terrible racism, produced jazz and the blues, music now universally honored as distinctively, brilliantly American. Gay men and lesbians living under homophobic regimes have been among the most extraordinary examples of such human creativity, finding in imagination, intelligence, and wit a place in which they could endow themselves and their often creative place in culture with great dignity and humanity as well as a sense of fun and zest for living.[47] But these features of human creativity do not make injustice any less unjust or any less worthy of criticism and change.

My point applies equally to antidiscrimination laws and to laws extending a measure of legal recognition to same-sex couples. I have no doubt that some gays, including those in long-term relationships, do not themselves want legal recognition. A long-term partner might regard any such proposal as a sign of loss of faith in loving relationship as a responsive relationship of mutual care, emotional transparency, and passionate attachment. No one forms a gay relationship against the background of long-standing cultural homophobia, let alone stays in such a relationship, unless the love between the partners is about as strong as a romantic personal attachment between two complex, often ambitious individuals can be. Gay relationships are, from this perspective, among the most deeply committed to highly personal romantic love, feeling, and devotion. It is the very romanticism of such attachments that may make legal recognition, let alone marriage, uncongenial to some partners. But that is, I submit, no reason why such legal recognition should not be available to gays on terms of equality with opposite-sex partnerships, especially since lack of recognition is so culturally significant in the homophobic construction of gays as subhuman, incapable of the intimate associations that make us human.[48]

I make these remarks as cautions against inappropriate generalization from any gay man's experience, including mine, during a period when people (including me) made arguments for gay rights and over time persuaded courts and even politicians to give some legal recognition to their human rights. My story may be highly individual, arising at a particular historical moment and in special circumstances of background and psychology. Perhaps the experience of gays and lesbians now and later may be quite different, not insisting on connections between homophobia and other forms of structural injustice that were central to my life and thought, beginning, as they did, in the 1960s in the United States. On the other hand, I want to be truthful to my experience, which reasonably connects my personal life to constitutional and other developments in ways that have not been sufficiently noticed and analyzed. Psychologically, these questions were for me inseparable. Finding a resisting voice in loving relationship was, for reasons I now must explore, as necessary for the relationship as it was for the philosophical and constitutional arguments made as an expression of such voice. This aspect of our experience has, I believe, a larger resonance for many younger gay men and lesbians living today in increasingly public ways, demanding the respect that is their due. They are finding, as we found earlier, that the personal is political. Love is as deep a human imperative as any in our psyche, and it is this universal imperative of the heart that underlies the emergence of the most important civil rights movement in the United States since the 1960s, a civil disobedience to unjust laws that deprive gays and lesbians of their rights to love and to marry.

It puts my experience on this point in illuminating perspective to compare it to that of one of my teachers, H. L. A. Hart, who famously wrote in Great Britain in defense of the Wolfenden Committee's 1957 recommendation to decriminalize consensual homosexuality.[49] Many gay men of my generation found in Hart's arguments the first recognition anywhere of our unjust suffering and saw that resistance was possible, and could even be successful. I wanted to study with Hart, after my undergraduate work at Harvard with John Rawls, in order to develop the kind of moral independence and ethical integrity that I had read in Hart's work. In the year that I studied with him, I found him to be a brilliant teacher, wildly exuberant, humane, generous, and demanding in precisely the ways I needed. I lost touch with him, although I know he followed my work, and was shocked to learn later of a terrible depression in later life that incapacitated him for long periods, albeit with productive intervals, until his death. It was only quite recently that Nicola Lacey, while visiting at New York University School of Law from London University, shared with me her brilliant psychobiography of Hart, later published by Oxford University Press as *A Life of H. L. A. Hart*.[50] I learned of Hart's own suffering, as a gay man; his decision to marry and have children with a remarkable woman who knew his orientation; their marital unhappiness, including the wife's many open affairs with other men (some close friends of Hart); Hart's own apparent sexual inactivity outside the marriage; and his growing sense of a crisis of creative voice that led to vocational crisis and personal despair.[51] Hart's terrible depression finally made sense to me. His recognition of my own unjust suffering (and that of other gay men) evidently arose from recognizing his own, and he had certainly resisted in ways that no other man, straight or gay, of his period had. But I was moved by a sense of horror that his efforts had had so little effect on his own life, a failure he must have come to experience as catastrophic as he watched the new toleration he had made possible extend to gay men and lesbians a happiness in relationship that he had been unable or unwilling to pursue.

I was also moved by Hart's even deeper struggle for emancipated ethical voice within his Judaism, his resistance to British anti-Semitism as well as homophobia. This struggle explained his passion for justice, which was, I now understood, what had so moved me when I studied with him, more even than his intellectual brilliance and his relentless demands for better writing and more clarity in argument. My partner is Jewish, and no doubt my own passion for gay rights is closely connected with my searing personal sense, knowing and loving him as I do, of the atrocity of anti-Semitism. Reflecting on what Hart had meant for me clarified my psychological development that had increasingly seen the case for gay rights as based on a resistance to religious intolerance such as anti-Semitism.

Learning about Hart helped me put my own narrative in perspective, in particular the ways in which it was rooted in an ongoing gay relationship that gave rise to a voice of resistance and gave me a loving resonance for that voice. The relationship flourished through resistance. In consequence, I don't regard such resistance as calling for the heroic sacrifice of self that Hart imposed on himself, for it was such resistance that made my life in truthful relationship worth living. The relationship was, for me, through resistance more real, because more reasonable, than the homophobic culture of my youth, which, as I came to see, rested on violence and lies. The French gay poet Rimbaud wrote, "Love has to be reinvented."[52] If homophobia sometimes inflicts on gay people a shutting down of loving voice, that voice's emergence in relationship, based on resistance, is not so much reinvention as it is a rebirth, a gap in experience that I believe heterosexuals (whose loves enjoy such strong cultural support) may barely understand or even imagine. It is desolating to come to believe, once one has moved on from the love of one's family of origin, that there can be nothing else, that life must be lived untouched by love. My story shows, like the stories of so many other gay and lesbian persons who lived through this period with me, how powerfully rooted resistance must be to make a rebirth of love possible. Resistance was the condition of a reasonable trust of one's feelings and emotions and con-

victions, and trust a condition of love.[53] Hart's resistance reminds me of
the tragic voice and heroic courage of men such as Tolstoy, Gandhi, and
King, for whom the struggle for voice against patriarchal violence came at
a terrifying cost of personal marital happiness because their protests of
injustice did not extend to the force of patriarchy in their personal lives.[54]
The struggle for democratic voice in these men against patriarchal violence
moves me deeply, touching something alive in my psyche, and I trust in
yours. These men, with all their internal conflicts and contradictions, lived
more worthily than other men because they confronted and challenged the
injustices sustained by patriarchal manhood. But good men should not be
required to be tragic heroes to speak truth to injustice; we should, if we
can, find a route, as men, to ethical voice that is less demanding and more
humane. My own path to resistance maps such an alternative route, for it
shows how resistance to patriarchy, in both its public and its intimately private forms, makes possible what makes life worth living. It is with the quo-
tidian yet rewarding character of this conflict that I want to end this book.
Democratic manhood will have a larger appeal to the extent that its
demands are in line with what men reasonably want in a good life. To the
extent that one can show that its demands are bearable by the most ordi-
nary of men as well as rewarding, one will have made a better case for its
ethical and personal appeal.

This psychology clarifies my and my partner's resistance and why, as academics, we lived and wrote as we did, committed to free voice, whatever the
repressive forces or insults directed against us. One of the most powerful
motivations to the resistance of African Americans against racism and of
women against sexism was the need for some measure of truth about the
character of intimate relationships, otherwise burdened by racist and sexist
stereotypes of gender and race that unjustly sexualize and objectify. Homophobia burdens gays and lesbians with a comparable system of lies that cannot and will not do justice to gay/lesbian love. Think of what it would be
like to be brought up and to live in a hegemonic culture that told you from
the earliest years of your nascent erotic feelings that those feelings were
unspeakable and could not reasonably connect to one's ethical intelligence,
let alone to a way of life centered in passionate erotic love and all that such
love makes creatively possible in a human life, personally and ethically. Think
of also being subjected not just to lies but to every form of pressure—social
as well as legal—to live a lie, tearing one apart from loving relationships that
make life worth living. Resistance in such an environment is a psychological
necessity to see clearly and feel precisely love, if one has the grace to experi-

ence love, and to understand and value its place in what makes a life human. If resistance is for this reason the condition of loving relationship, such resistance had a much broader resonance, as others found in such resistance the route to some measure of fulfillment.

This psychology clarifies as well the roots of reaction against such increasingly public resisting voices, that is, the psychology of patriarchal manhood under threat. The key, I believe, is that unjust gender stereotypes about men bear heavily on the voices of men in order to hold them in their patriarchal roles and on women only to the extent required to enable men to maintain such roles. It is because gender stereotypes bear so heavily on the voices of men that it is so psychologically difficult for men to question the role that patriarchy unjustly plays in our political and social lives. Patriarchy enters into the psyche of men through a traumatic disassociation from relationship that men take to be in the nature of things.[55] In consequence, men are vulnerable to a shaming of their manhood, depending on gender stereotypes, that renders it difficult for them to question those stereotypes. There may for this reason be particular psychological difficulties for men, gay and straight, in resisting homophobia, difficulties not experienced by women, straight and lesbian, whose developmental history may be more free of patriarchal control of voice.

We can see this issue clearly posed in Colm Toibin's insightful discussion of the art of the black gay writer James Baldwin.[56] In Toibin's persuasive analysis, Baldwin the black artist eloquently questioned the degree to which Richard Wright's protest of American racial injustice had led him, as an artist, to write the novel *Native Son,* which indulged rather than questioned racist stereotypes of the sexuality and violence of black men. In contrast, Baldwin's novel *Go Tell It on the Mountain* showed how an artistic and protesting voice might produce a work better as art and protest because it gave a rounded portrait of the sexuality and violence of a black man, modeled on his foster father, a portrait that explored, through his relationships to the women in his life, the complex war in the psyche of such a man between real and idealized sexual desire, religious belief, love, and hatred. What Baldwin was able to do with black masculinity, he was not, however, Toibin argued, able to do with his own homosexuality in *Giovanni's Room:* "Placing a murder . . . at the center of his gay plot was to do to homosexuals what he had attacked Wright for doing to black people—adding impetus to the popular notion that they were alarming."[57] This analysis suggests that, in the psychology of men's resistance to injustice, the most psychologically difficult place is one that requires resistance to dominant gender stereotypes, for such resistance exposes men to the shaming of their manhood. It is here that even an ethical and artistic voice as free and intelligent as Baldwin's was crippled, in treating homosexuality, by the vulnerability to shame that kills understanding and even love. What he could do as a black man he could not do as a gay man. Yet the challenge to such gender stereotypes remains the most important task of basic justice of our time, one that should absorb all persons of good will, men and women, straight and gay. There is every reason to believe that the point is today as urgent and important as it has ever been, as we are poised between patriarchal and democratic manhood, at home and abroad.

The great historical lesson of the totalitarianisms of the twentieth century, which almost brought civilization as we know it to cataclysmic destruction on several occasions, is the terrifying price we pay when our technology is so much in advance of our ethics and politics. But we know that the political violence of fascism, for example, with its genocidal murder of six million innocent Jews, was motivated fundamentally by an aggressively political anti-Semitism, and that it fed upon and cultivated a sense of manhood based on codes of honor at least as old as those described in *The Iliad*. As we earlier saw, unjust gender stereotypes were quite central to a Nazi manhood hardened even to genocidal murder of millions.[58] And the bloodily totalitarianism of Stalin's communism (including the starvation of at least five million peasants[59]) was crucially driven by an indoctrination of an ideal of the soldier constantly on duty,[60] which, like Hitler's fascism, bizarrely justified state-imposed mass killing as self-defense.[61] It is no accident that there are close links in totalitarian political method between fascism and Soviet communism,[62] based, as they are, on conceptions of a hardened manhood rooted in violence against any dissent to or doubt about the terms of state-enforced structural injustice.[63]

There is every reason to believe that this political psychology remains very much in place since the end of the Cold War as we find similar patterns of violence, rooted in a sense of manhood whose honor rests on violence in support of forms of structural injustice—for example, extreme religious intolerance, racism, and ethnic hatred in Bosnia, Yugoslavia, and Rwanda—and various forms of secular and religious terrorism and other forms of state-sponsored violence.[64] Mark Juergensmeyer has persuasively analyzed the global rise of fundamentalist violence, at home and abroad, in terms of a highly gendered armoring of humiliated men in a cosmic war. What triggers such violence is perceived threats to manhood: "Nothing is more intimate than sexuality, and no greater humiliation can be experienced than failure over what one perceives to be one's sexual role. Such failures are often the basis of domestic violence; and when these failures are linked with the social roles of masculinity and femininity, they can lead to public violence. Terrorist acts, then, can be forms of symbolic empowerment for men whose traditional sexual roles—their very manhood—is perceived to be at stake."[65]

Such violence, when successful, challenges our manhood, now self-consciously in transition between patriarchal and democratic manhood. The worry is that our response will be inconsistent with our considered values, which include traditions of nonviolent dissent that we rightly honor. Arundhati Roy recently put the worry in the following terms: "Any government's condemnation of terrorism is only credible if it shows itself to be responsive to persistent, reasonable, closely argued, nonviolent dissent. And yet, what's happening is just the opposite. The world over, nonviolent resistance movements are being crushed and broken. If we do not respect and honor them, by default we privilege those who turn to violent means."[66]

We need now, more than ever, to remind ourselves of the traditions that Roy worries we may forget, traditions of nonviolence that, as in the American civil rights movement of the 1960s, were brilliantly successful at a cost in human life that, though deplorable, was small compared with "a single day of battle in the Civil War or World War II."[67] Nonviolence, in comparison to violence, may better advance and secure justice at less cost. We need now, more than ever, to keep such nonviolent alternatives lucidly in mind. In contrast, Roy points acidly to the rise of religious fascism in Gandhi's democratic India, as politicians manipulatively encourage and fail to punish pogroms that use political violence to sustain religious and ethnic intolerance.[68] What Roy sees in her native India (resort to violence rather than nonviolent protest), she claims to see in democratic America's comparable betrayal of the politics of Martin Luther King, Jr., in its response to terrorism, the wars in Afghanistan and in Iraq: wounded manhood turning without compelling reason to violence.[69] Roy, a feminist, is asking the right questions, as she does when she insists that we face Churchill's contradictions[70] and our own. In particular, she sees in American wars in Afghanistan and Iraq a patriarchally grounded corruption of judgment about the aims and means of the just use of force, made possible by overwhelming feelings of shame and humiliation at the unjust use of violence against ourselves. A nation so patriarchally corrupted in its judgments confuses its justice and power with legitimacy in the use of force, resorting to violence unnecessarily and in ways that fuel violence rather than voice and dialogue.

Our traditions include nonviolent and violent forms of ethical resistance, both based on speaking in a voice, empowered by relationships to the voices of antipatriarchal women, that resists the injustices supported by the violence of patriarchal manhood. These traditions include the resistance to fascism, led by Churchill, which was surely a reasoned last resort, one that should, as he urged, have been undertaken earlier when aggression was clearly threatened. But they include as well the remarkably effective forms of nonviolent resistance shown by Garrison, Tolstoy, Gandhi, and King (all inspired by Jesus of Nazareth).

What marks the psychology of all these forms of ethical resistance is a disarming of manhood that frees ethical voice, not only in speakers but in audiences as well. This psychology is distinguished not only by the justice of the claims made in these men's incomparable voices but by their willingness to speak truthfully in resistance to injustice and to endure unjust treatment for thus speaking, exposing themselves to bullying condemnation, violence, and even death (Gandhi and King were murdered), thus making clear the roots of such injustice in violence against ethical voice. The values of such men are shown by the primacy they accord to voice in ethical resistance, exposing their own voices to free testing before impartial arbiters, seeking always reasonable consensus through dialogue in preference to the violence of wounded manhood that humiliates, provoking a cycle of violence that feeds on itself. When such voices ethically persuade in a way that patriarchal violence does not, it is because their very willingness to speak in these ways enables them to address a voice in their audiences that is still alive and responsive under the armor of patriarchal manhood. Roy asks us: Are we keeping faith with such traditions, or are we allowing an enemy to remake us in his violently repressive patriarchal image (undertaking preemptive wars, unsupported by imminent and proportional threat, and conducting such wars in ways that contradict the values of democratic equal dignity we claim to uphold)? We need to understand ourselves and our traditions and to ask, as Roy does, the right questions, which interrogate our own psyches, including our vulnerability to shame and violence. We will not be able to ask and answer such questions, addressed to our domestic as well as foreign policies, responsibly until we speak in a voice as free as that of a Garrison or a King or a Churchill, finding in ourselves a courage that understands and is not bullied into silence by our fears as men in transition, as we are, between patriarchal and democratic manhood. We need to find a courage that allows us to speak from an ethical voice rooted firmly in our democratic values. To do so, we must deliberatively map for ourselves the complex normative and psychological terrain we are negotiating.[71]

The contemporary challenge of manhood in the United States is not the same as that faced by Garrison, Tolstoy, Gandhi, King, and Churchill because our circumstances are different. However, what is central to their achievement (the liberating ethical powers of a free voice in men inspired by their relationships to the antipatriarchal voices of women) is very much our continuing challenge and opportunity. We face, much more self-consciously than they, the one issue that so threatened their manhood, namely, relations to women on just terms, which includes, for us, relations to gays and lesbians on just terms. If the issue so threatened such remarkable men, we can perhaps see why it still so threatens us as we face forms of reactionary fundamentalist political violence, at home and abroad, driven by a sense of patriarchal honor in part outraged by our values, including our liberalism and its corollary, feminism.

One form of this fundamentalist political violence at home is directed at feminism in general, and the form of feminism in particular that underlies the contemporary case for gay rights. That case thus has available to it a normative resource only incompletely available, at best, to the first generation of advocates of gay rights, namely, rights-based feminism. A case for gay rights drawing on rights-based feminism has certainly been made before, notably by Walt Whitman[72] and developed by Emma Goldman[73] and Edward Carpenter,[74] in ways seeking common ground between arguments for rights-based feminism and gay rights. But the case for rights-based feminism was morally compromised by its strategic alliances (with the temperance and purity movements) based on reinforcing gender stereotypes as part of the development of suffrage feminism;[75] Goldman, for example, was notably marginalized by most American feminists of her day.[76] Even Carpenter's remarkably prophetic attempt to unite rights-based feminism with arguments for gay rights was flawed by the ways in which his arguments indulged and sometimes reinforced the unjust gender stereotypes of both women and homosexuals;[77] other advocates of gay rights were aggressively misogynistic.[78] Contemporary rights-based feminism has, however, carried its analysis of the role of gender stereotypes in rationalizing injustice to women far enough reasonably to acknowledge lesbianism as a legitimate feminist alternative,[79] and the case for gay rights deepens this analysis to criticize, on feminist grounds of principle, the role that gender stereotyping uncritically continues to play in the oppression of both gay men and lesbians.[80]

From this perspective, the struggle for gay rights may reasonably be regarded as at the cutting edge of an important criticism of the sexist terms in which family life continues largely to be understood. The dehumanization of homosexuals retains popular appeal when brought into relation to claims for same-sex marriage because, consistent with Freud's observation of the narcissism of small differences,[81] it enables a culture with a long history of uncritical moral slavery of women and homosexuals not to take seriously, let alone think reasonably about, the growing convergences of heterosexual and homosexual human love in the modern world. These include shared economic contributions to the household and convergent styles of nonprocreational sex and elaboration of erotic play as an end in itself. They also include an interest in sex as an expressive bond in companionate relationships of friendship and love as ends in themselves; several partners over a lifetime; when there is interest in children, only in a few of them; and insistence on the romantic love of tender and equal companions as the democratized core of sharing intimate daily life.[82] Indeed, some studies suggest that, if anything, homosexual relationships more fully develop features of egalitarian sharing that are more often the theory than the practice of heterosexual relations.[83] Could it even be, as I earlier suggested, because long-standing gay and lesbian relationships so clearly illustrate the powers of romantic love in the modern world that homophobic denial wars so aggressively on them, not only denying their existence, but determined to make them as tragically miserable as possible? If love, then a tragically flawed love?[84] The uncritical ferocity of contemporary political homophobia draws its populist power from the compulsive need to construct Manichean differences where none reasonably exist, thus reinforcing institutions of gender hierarchy perceived now to be threatened. In particular, as Whitman argued,[85] democratic equality in homosexual intimate life threatens the core of traditional gender roles and hierarchy. Consistent with the paradox of intolerance, the embattled sectarian orthodoxy does not explore such reasonable doubts but polemically represses them by remaking reality in its own sectarian image of marriage, powerfully deploying the uncritical traditional stereotype of the homosexual as the scapegoat of suppressed doubts (excluding the homosexual from the moral community of human rights, including the basic human right to intimate life). Homosexuals are the natural scapegoat for this uncritical backlash against feminism[86] because they, unlike women, remain a largely marginalized and despised minority. Proponents of traditional sectarian orthodoxy still object strongly to many of the achievements of the feminist movement (some to the decriminalization of contraception, others to that of abortion, still others to now mainstream feminist issues such as the Equal Rights Amendment[87]), but they have lost many of these battles, and the sectarian hard core, hostile to feminism and civil rights measures in general,[88] takes its strategic stand where it still can against members of a traditionally stigmatized and silenced minority who are, like the Jews in Europe, easily demonized.[89] We can see the force of this politically reactionary fundamentalism in the role the attack on same-sex marriage plays in mobilizing the religious right in the United States, a force carefully cultivated and encouraged by the Bush administration in proposing a constitutional amendment banning same-sex marriage.[90]

What is objectionable here is fundamentalism as a basis for public laws and policies in a constitutional democracy, for, as John Rawls observed, "fundamentalist religious doctrines and autocratic and dictatorial rulers will reject the ideas of public reason and deliberative democracy."[91] I understand fundamentalism as the appeal to the certainty of a certain specific understanding of authority, rooted in the past, a certainty that is to guide thought and conduct irrespective of reasonable contemporary argument and experience to the contrary. I distinguish two kinds of objectionable religious fundamentalism: source-based and norm-based. A source-based fundamentalism is rooted in certain texts or interpretations of such texts, ascribing to them an apodictic meaning and truth value that does not and cannot be squared with reasonable arguments available to and accessible to nonbelievers. Protestant fundamentalism is usually of this form, placing an interpretive weight on certain texts that is not open to other, often more reasonable interpretations, let alone to reasonable views of nonbelievers who don't regard such texts as authoritative.[92]

Another form of source-based fundamentalism, not specifically religious but still objectionable, is historical originalism in American constitutional interpretation. The only consistent originalist in the United States has been Raoul Berger, who argued that no interpretation of a constitutional text can be correct that does not track the things in the world to which the text was or would have been applied by the founding generation that enacted the provision in question (whether the Constitutional Convention of 1787 and ratifying states, or the Congress and ratifying states for the Bill of Rights of 1791, or the Reconstruction Congress and ratifying states for the Reconstruction Amendments, including the Fourteenth Amendment of 1868).[93] Berger thus argued that most of the modern judiciary's interpretation of the Fourteenth Amendment, including the striking down of state-sponsored racial segregation as unconstitutional in *Brown v. Board of Education*,[94] was wrong because the Reconstruction Congress, which enacted the Fourteenth Amendment, clearly regarded racial segregation as not violative of equal protection. A somewhat less consistent originalist was Judge Robert Bork, abortively proposed by President Reagan for appointment to the Supreme Court of the United States, who accepted the current judicial understanding that racial classifications, including those underlying racial segregation, were forbidden but thought it was wrong to extend constitutional interpretation any further; in particular, Judge Bork sharply objected to the principle of constitutional privacy because, he argued, it did not correspond to any reasonably specific originalist understanding.[95]

I regard originalism as a source-based fundamentalism because it ascribes decisive normative weight not to the text of the Constitution or to its interpretation over time but solely to a certain view of the authority of Founders, in particular, the ways in which the Founders applied or would have applied the constitutional text in their enactment circumstances, what may be called Founders' denotations. This approach is unreasonable, as I have argued at length elsewhere,[96] not only because it fails to fit with the text and interpretive traditions over time of authoritative institutions such as the Supreme Court but because it corresponds to no defensible political theory of the values of constitutionalism, and certainly not to the view taken of those values' authority by leading Founders such as James Madison.[97] For all these reasons, originalism is an objectionable source-based fundamentalism, as objectionable as Protestant fundamentalism, because it appeals, as a decisive source in constitutional interpretation, to a form of historical understanding that is not sensitive to reason and deliberation in contemporary circumstances, indeed expressly refuses to accept such reasonable argument as relevant in legitimate constitutional interpretation.

New natural law, another form of fundamentalism that advocates traditional Catholic views of sexual morality (including the wrongness of contraception, masturbation, abortion, and nonprocreational sex acts, gay and straight), is closely tied not to texts (scriptural or constitutional) but to moral arguments allegedly implicit in a tradition of thought developed by and elaborated by Catholic religious authority, including the papacy.[98] Analysis of the arguments of new natural law reveals another essentially originalist style of argument (tied to specific views on sexuality and morality, however anachronistic today, of Augustine and Thomas Aquinas), one that uses such arguments to support another objectionable form of fundamentalism that is norm-based. What characterizes this form of fundamentalism is its rigid moral categories: a list of basic goods and deontological constraints protecting them that are not reasonable to persons outside the tradition of papal religious authority, and indeed that are rooted in a tradition whose authority in certain domains is today based on a conspicuously unreasonable, willful refusal to take account of the voices of those who dissent from the tradition, defending the authority of a highly patriarchal male celibate clergy. Such inflexible moral rigidity suggests psychological roots that mix hatred and fear, in particular the fear of embattled patriarchal manhood of desires now all too attractive because the lives of men and women, straight and gay, show how well life may be lived through a more democratic manhood and womanhood.

All these forms of fundamentalism are, of course, quite doctrinally different. But they share certain striking features: an appeal to a certainty ascribed to some authority, often in the past, about matters of gender and sexuality, a claim of certainty or self-evidence that doggedly refuses to acknowledge the broad range of contemporary arguments and experiences that reasonably cast in doubt such claims, in particular the arguments and experiences of the recently emancipated ethical voices of women and gays and lesbians bearing on the injustice of traditional views of gender and sexuality.

The lack of reasonable argument underlying contemporary fundamentalisms suggests, finally, that what they share, in addition to a common structure of unreasonable beliefs, is a common personal and political psychology, what I call the political psychology of reactionary fundamentalism. Such fundamentalisms make sense only against the background of contemporary reasonable arguments, many of them found to be constitutionally compelling in the United States and elsewhere, that question traditional views of sexuality and gender. What unites all fundamentalisms, irrespective of other differences, is a common reactionary psychology that reacts violently to any suggestion of the nonabsolutism of traditional patriarchal authority, which in the United States currently targets same-sex marriage. The appeal of this psychology is to a patriarchal manhood threatened by gender equality.

From this perspective, the choice of gay and lesbian identity may elaborate the terms of gender equality on deeper grounds of principle. I earlier observed that because of a different developmental history, men, straight and gay, may be more vulnerable to homophobia than women. For this reason, facing and overcoming the problem of patriarchy in gay relationships may be more important than many suppose. If two men can love in a relationship, based on free and equal voice, that very fact challenges the psychology of disassociation from relationship of patriarchal manhood, which depends on hierarchical relations of sons to fathers. If men can relate to one another on the very different basis of responsive emotional intelligence between equals, they show how men can release the psyche from hierarchy, making possible a more improvisatory, experimental, reasonable, indeed democratic way of living and being that rests on honest voice, skeptically intelligent questioning, listening, and responsiveness. Of course, men and women in straight relationships are often struggling to develop a similar kind of relationship, but it may be precisely because straight women are more willing to accommodate men's difficulties in sustaining such relationships that men are not challenged to overcome residual patriarchal assumptions they carry in their psyches. In contrast, gay men in relationship may, as men, find it imperative to resist patriarchy as the only way they can sustain a relationship acceptable to both partners.[99] For this reason, such experiments in living are of interest not only to gays but to the larger culture increasingly concerned, as it is and should be, with forging a conception of both public and private life more consistent with principles of gender equality. A choice of gay and lesbian identity is, in its nature, an empowering ethical protest of conventional gender stereotyping that enables homosexuals, like heterosexuals, to live as individuals with hearts and minds authentically open to the grace of love. To this extent, the stakes of the struggle for gay rights, both for gays and for straights, are not only public and private justice but a human psyche more capable of what makes love possible and valuable in a human life: emotional presence in relationship.

But such an identity is, of course, a threat to forms of manhood founded on its repression. The case for gay rights thus invites closer attention to yet another pervasive feature of all the forms of structural injustice studied here, namely, the fact that the injuries inflicted on identity are very much supported by a reactionary sense of identity (for example, in racism, of whites as superior or, in sexism, of conventional heterosexual men as superior). The political power of structural injustice importantly depends on its constitutive power in the formation of such identity in intimate life. Identity thus formed in intimate relations (as sexism clearly is) has a personal intimacy that, when under attack, construes the attack as a direct threat to self, in particular invoking the protection of family values. Study of the case for gay rights confirms the political power of this dynamic. Gender identity (patriarchal manhood and womanhood) has been formed in intimate relations on terms that enforce gender hierarchy as the measure of intimate life in ostensibly egalitarian America (thus ideologically compelling the unspeakability of homosexual love); in consequence, the populist reactionary response to the case for gay rights takes the form of resisting alleged unjust aggression against a threatened sense of self, appealing, paradoxically, to family values. There is senting voice but the way any internal voice of doubt in patriarchal men has itself been silenced, a vulnerability to the shaming of one's manhood to which even otherwise good men are subject in this sensitive psychological domain.

Freud observed of anti-Semitism that its irrationalism was its heightening of small, morally irrelevant differences into Manichean stereotypical truths.[101] The homophobically motivated reaction to same-sex marriage reflects the same irrationalism, rooted in the quashing of the voice of reasonable doubt in men and women required to sustain patriarchy uncritically in intimate life. The United States has undoubtedly made enormous strides in recognizing the just claims of protest movements of people of color and of women, and even, recently, some claims of gays and lesbians. We can question patriarchy in many areas of our lives, but not in our intimate lives, which sets the stage, I believe, for the reactionary political psychology that wars on same-sex marriage.

What motivates this psychology is its mythological idealization of gender: marriage must be between a man and a woman. Catharine R. Stimpson, who has been in a long-term lesbian relationship (including bringing up four children) for as long as I have been in a gay relationship, writes, as I do, from her experience of how indistinguishable gay/lesbian relationships are from straight long-term relationships (marriages, if you will). From this perspective, the slogan ("marriage is between a man and a woman") does not arise from experience because it clearly falsifies experience (straight and gay) of companionate love in the modern world and promotes lies, but it indulges, as a kind of ideologically driven political, wishful thinking, an extraordinary mythology of gender: "Those who have proposed the flagrantly anti–gay marriage constitutional amendment, in part out of political cynicism and in part out of real hatred and fear, would assassinate the Constitution—and justify themselves by proclaiming the sanctity of a gilded portrait of marriage that is breathtakingly calculated and ahistorical, as if all marriages in all times and all places resembled that of an idealized upright Dad and an idealized loving Mom, who bear and rear virtuous children who do well on standardized tests."[102]

James Baldwin wrote acutely in 1985 of the underlying American idea of masculinity: "This ideal had created cowboys and Indians, good guys and bad guys, punks and studs, tough guys and softies, butch and faggot, black and white. It is an ideal so paralytically infantile that it is virtually forbidden—as an unpatriotic act—that the American boy evolve into the complexity of manhood."[103] Such idealization bespeaks underlying traumatic

no factual basis for this argument; indeed, there are decisive obje
irrationalism (ideologically transforming, consistent with the
intolerance, victims into aggressors). But the populist appeal
requires explanation. The explanation is the continuing politic
homophobia as a structural injustice—the tangled sexist ideology
alizes this injustice as an ideological support for gender hiera
temporary circumstances.

The absorbing interest of the case for gay rights, in conte
cumstances, is that it confronts a form of structural injustice
other forms, remains very largely intact. The constitutional pr
now liberally condemn conspicuous forms of racism, sexisr
Semitism have enjoyed only limited, quite recent application to
homophobia.[100] What makes this so striking is that, as we hav
constitutional principles of conscience, of intimate life, and of
nation fully apply to the laws that continue to disadvantage ga
people. In particular, the constitutional principles that now cor
gender stereotypes disadvantageous to both men and women
a matter of principle, the important role of gender stereotypes
homophobia. That these issues are barely seen, let alone acted
the continuing power of the structural injustice of homophobi
were, exempts—without an explanation or any sense of a need
and lesbians from the principles now aggressively extended t
basic rights of all other Americans. The political reaction to s
riage clearly illustrates this point.

The political reaction to judicial recognition of same-sex m
the continuing psychological power of a patriarchal manhood
uously under threat in the United States, in transition, as we
patriarchal and democratic manhood. Thus a patriarchal manh
hegemonic; its codes of honor mythologically divided women
bad, traumatically separated men from real relationships to
invested the energy of manhood in violence as a response to
the extent that this psychology remains alive, it arises from t
ration from women, which shows itself in idealization rather
ship. As my earlier analysis of homophobia shows, such irrati
like racism and sexism, often most powerfully reveals itself ir
targeting of the right to intimate life. Racist fury over misceg
analogous to homophobic rage at same-sex marriage, patri
repressing democratic voice. What holds patriarchal manho
cally in place is not only the way political coercion is directed

breaking of real relationships of boys with their mothers and of men with women, a sense of loss covered by the idealization of good asexual women and the denigration of bad sexual women. Gay men play a role in this script, as they have since the emergence of modernist homophobia in the eighteenth century: they are as outlaws to their gender, fallen women, or prostitutes. Same-sex marriage is an affront to this ideology because it speaks a truth about men and women in loving relationship that breaks the disassociation on which this psychology depends: it insists that such men and women be seen as the persons they are rather than as sexist tropes. The injustice of patriarchy rests on the violent suppression of such truthful voice, and this violence thus takes as its repressive object the very idea of same-sex marriage.

What the reactionary political power of this psychology in the United States must show is the degree to which patriarchy is the heart of darkness at the intimate center of heterosexual marriage in America. Our law and our life remain obdurately insensitive to a reasonable social democratic restructuring of rights and responsibilities of men and women in public and private life, and our lives are thus framed by an injustice so unspeakable that we have come to regard it as in the nature of things.[104] Such injustice rests on the suppression of voice, including sexual voice. Heterosexual love and marriage in America are, for this reason, framed by an idealization that shadows loss.

I have traced in this work a personal struggle for voice that arose out of the sense of truthful voice in loving relationship to a man, my partner now for some thirty years. What I earlier grounded in moral philosophy, in history, and in constitutional law, I have now grounded in a personal and political psychology that arose from relationship and that required resistance to the lies that erased and denigrated the very possibility of such relationship, based on free and equal voice in love. Living in the truth of loving relationship is, I have come to believe, one of the deepest needs of the human psyche, which clarifies why we resist injustice and why injustice often targets intimate life. The story I have told from *Bowers* to *Lawrence* and beyond is our early twenty-first-century retelling of this struggle for voice. We are so much in the midst of it that we lack the perspective we have on the comparable struggles for justice of religious minorities, people of color, and women. I have tried to put the beginning of this story in a perspective that does justice, I believe, to its ethical, constitutional, and psychological significance.

My story began with coming into real loving relationship and unfolded as stages in the struggle for ethical and personal voice in relationship. I end where I began, only now framing my struggle, as a gay man, for voice as an aspect of the larger struggle for a more democratic manhood, a struggle that includes equality in the garden of love. I have told my secrets; they are the secrets all men know and yet many refuse to know—how much the psyche is alive only in relationship. The resisting ethical voice of gay men, because it confronts the homophobia on which patriarchal manhood is built, exposes the lie that hierarchy, not equality, is the only basis of love. This voice, among other feminist voices, can help men in general confront the prison of manhood that destroys love. It may thus be one of the voices that fosters democracy itself. Walt Whitman, America's prophet of gay rights and American democracy, sang of these secrets in his poetry:

> I proceed for all who are or have been young men,
> To tell the secret of my nights and days,
> To celebrate the need of comrades.[105]

NOTES

Chapter 1

1. *Lawrence v. Texas*, 539 U.S. 558, 123 S. Ct. 2472 (2003).

2. *Bowers v. Hardwick*, 478 U.S. 186 (1986).

3. David A. J. Richards, "Constitutional Legitimacy and Constitutional Privacy," *New York University Law Review* 61 (1986): 800.

4. See David A. J. Richards, "Unnatural Acts and the Constitutional Right to Privacy: A Moral Theory," *Fordham Law Review* 45 (1977): 1282; *The Moral Criticism of Law* (Encino, Calif.: Dickenson-Wadsworth, 1977); "Homosexuality and the Constitutional Right to Privacy," *New York University Review of Law and Social Change* 8 (1978–1979): 311; "Sexual Autonomy and the Constitutional Right to Privacy: A Case Study in Human Rights and the Unwritten Constitution," *Hastings Law Journal* 30 (1979): 957; *Sex, Drugs, Death and the Law: An Essay on Human Rights and Overcriminalization* (Totowa, N.J.: Rowman and Littlefield, 1982); *Toleration and the Constitution* (New York: Oxford University Press, 1986); *Foundations of American Constitutionalism* (New York: Oxford University Press, 1989); *Conscience and the Constitution: History, Theory, and Law of the Reconstruction Amendments* (Princeton, N.J.: Princeton University Press, 1993); "Sexual Preference as a Suspect Religious Classification: An Alternative Perspective on the Unconstitutionality of Anti-Lesbian/Gay Initiatives," *Ohio Law Review* 55 (1994): 491; *Women, Gays, and the Constitution: The Grounds for Feminism and Gay Rights in Culture and Law* (Chicago: University of Chicago Press, 1998); *Identity and the Case for Gay Rights: Race, Gender, Religion as Analogies* (Chicago: University of Chicago Press, 1999).

5. See works cited in note 4.

6. *The Compact Edition of the Oxford English Dictionary,* vol. 2 (Oxford: Oxford University Press, 1971), p. 1549.

7. For a suggestive account, see Antonio R. Damasio, *Descartes' Error: Emotion, Reason, and the Human Brain* (New York: Avon Books, 1994); Antonio R. Damasio, *The Feeling of What Happens: Body and Emotion in the Making of Consciousness* (San Diego: a Harvest Book, 1999).

8. Damasio, *The Feeling of What Happens,* p. 86.

9. Ibid., p. 191.

10. See, for elaboration of this point, David A. J. Richards, *Tragic Manhood and*

Democracy: Verdi's Voice and the Powers of Musical Art (Brighton, U.K.: Sussex Academic Press, 2004).

11. William Blackstone, *Commentaries on the Laws of England 1765–1769,* vol. 4, facsimile of first edition ed. by Thomas A. Green (Chicago: University of Chicago Press, 1979), p. 215.

12. The greatest influence on my development there was study with John Rawls in various classes, seminars, and individual tutorials.

13. My first year was spent working with H. L. A. Hart, my second with G. J. Warnock.

14. See David A. J. Richards, *A Theory of Reasons for Action* (Oxford: Clarendon Press, 1971).

15. See H. L. A. Hart, *Law, Liberty, and Morality* (Palo Alto, Calif.: Stanford University Press, 1963).

16. See, on this point, Richards, *A Theory of Reasons for Action,* pp. 82, 135, 162–63, 180, 292, 297.

17. See William B. Rubenstein, "My Harvard Law School," *Harvard Civil Rights–Civil Liberties Law Review* 39 (2004): 317–33.

18. See Richards, "Unnatural Acts."

19. *Doe v. Commonwealth's Attorney,* 425 U.S. 901 (1976), aff'g mem. 403 F. Supp. 1199 (E.D. Va. 1975).

20. See Committee on Homosexual Offenses and Prostitution, *The Wolfenden Report* (New York: Stein and Day, 1963).

CHAPTER 2

1. See David A. J. Richards, *A Theory of Reasons for Action* (Oxford: Clarendon Press, 1971).

2. See Carol Gilligan, *In a Different Voice: Psychological Theory and Women's Development* (Cambridge, Mass.: Harvard University Press, 1982).

3. See, for relevant works of my partner, Donald Levy, "The Definition of Love in Plato's *Symposium,*" *Journal of History of Ideas* 40, no. 32 (April–June 1979): 285–91; "Perversion and the Unnatural as Moral Categories," *Ethics* 90 (1980): 191–202; *Freud Among the Philosophers: The Psychoanalytic Unconscious and Its Philosophical Critics* (New Haven: Yale University Press, 1996).

4. "Prejudice apart, the game of push-pin is of equal value with the arts and sciences of music and poetry," Jeremy Bentham, *The Rationale of Reward,* cited at jeromekahn123.tripod.com/utilitarianismtheethicaltheoryforalltimes/id4.html.

5. See, on these and related points, Elie Halevy, *The Growth of Philosophic Radicalism,* trans. by Mary Morris (Boston: Beacon Press, 1960).

6. See Jeremy Bentham, *An Introduction to the Principles of Morals and Legislation* (New York: Hafner Publishing Co., 1963).

7. For Bentham's views, unpublished during his lifetime, on the decriminalization of homosexuality, see Bentham, "Offences Against One's Self: Paederasty" (part 1), *Journal of Homosexuality* 3 (1978): 389; "Jeremy Bentham's Essay on 'Paederasty,'" *Journal of Homosexuality* 4 (1978): 91.

8. John Stuart Mill, *On Liberty,* ed. by Alburey Castell (New York: Appleton-Century-Crofts, 1947 [1859]).

9. See John Stuart Mill, "The Subjection of Women," in John Stuart Mill and Harriet Taylor Mill, *Essays on Sex Equality,* ed. by Alice S. Rossi (Chicago: University of Chicago Press, 1970), pp. 125–242.

10. See ibid., pp. 125–56.

11. For Mill's fullest defense of higher versus lower pleasures, see John Stuart Mill, *Utilitarianism*, ed. by Oskar Piest (Indianapolis, Ind.: The Library of Liberal Arts, 1957 [1861]), pp. 9–33.

12. Mill, *On Liberty*, pp. 10–11.

13. Ibid., pp. 15–54.

14. Ibid., pp. 55–118.

15. On the value Mill places on individuality, see ibid., pp. 55–74.

16. Ibid., p. 16.

17. Ibid., pp. 55–56.

18. Ibid., pp. 55–74.

19. Ibid., p. 75.

20. Ibid., pp. 75–76, 81–82.

21. Ibid., pp. 82–83.

22. Ibid., pp. 90–91.

23. See, on this point, Richards, *A Theory of Reasons for Action*, pp. 192–95.

24. See, for an important alternative statement and derivation of such principles as fundamental to political liberalism, Joel Feinberg, *The Moral Limits of the Criminal Law*, vol. 1, *Harm to Others* (New York: Oxford University Press, 1984); vol. 2, *Offense to Others* (New York: Oxford University Press, 1985); vol. 3, *Harm to Self* (New York: Oxford University Press, 1986); vol. 4, *Harmless Wrongdoing* (New York: Oxford University Press, 1988).

25. See, on these points, Immanuel Kant, *Foundations of the Metaphysics of Morals*, trans. by Lewis White Beck (New York: Liberal Arts Press, 1959).

26. See John Rawls, *A Theory of Justice* (Cambridge, Mass.: Harvard University Press, 1971); Richards, *A Theory of Reasons for Action*; T. M. Scanlon, *What We Owe to Each Other* (Cambridge, Mass.: Harvard University Press, 1998); Ronald Dworkin, *Sovereign Virtue: The Theory and Practice of Equality* (Cambridge, Mass.: Harvard University Press, 2000).

27. See, for a development of this argument, David A. J. Richards, *Sex, Drugs, Death and the Law: An Essay on Human Rights and Overcriminalization* (Totowa, N.J.: Rowman and Littlefield, 1982), pp. 1–25.

28. See, on this point, David A. J. Richards, *Women, Gays, and the Constitution: The Grounds for Feminism and Gay Rights in Culture and Law* (Chicago: University of Chicago Press, 1998).

29. See H. L. A. Hart, *Law, Liberty, and Morality* (Palo Alto, Calif.: Stanford University Press, 1963).

CHAPTER 3

1. David A. J. Richards, *Toleration and the Constitution* (New York: Oxford University Press, 1986).

2. David A. J. Richards, *Foundations of American Constitutionalism* (New York: Oxford University Press, 1989).

3. David A. J. Richards, *Conscience and the Constitution: History, Theory, and Law of the Reconstruction Amendments* (Princeton, N.J.: Princeton University Press, 1993).

4. David A. J. Richards, *Women, Gays, and the Constitution: The Grounds for Feminism and Gay Rights in Culture and Law* (Chicago: University of Chicago Press, 1998).

5. See, on these points, Richards, *Conscience and the Constitution.*

6. See, for discussion of all these points, Richards, *Women, Gays, and the Constitution,* pp. 288–337.

7. See, on these points, ibid., pp. 155–81.

8. See George Chauncey, *Gay New York: Gender, Urban Culture, and the Making of the Gay Male World, 1890–1940* (New York, Basic Books, 1994).

9. See, on these and related points, David A. J. Richards, *Women, Gays, and the Constitution,* pp. 311–27.

10. See Stephen Jefery-Poulter, *Peers, Queers, and Commons: The Struggle for Gay Law Reform from 1950 to the Present* (London: Routledge, 1991); Jeffrey Weeks, *Coming Out: Homosexual Politics in Britain from the Nineteenth Century to the Present* (London: Quartet, 1990); Jeffrey Weeks, *Against Nature: Essays on History, Sexuality and Identity* (London: Rivers Oran, 1991); Graham Robb, *Strangers: Homosexual Love in the Nineteenth Century* (New York: W. W. Norton, 2003).

11. See, on this point, Jefery-Poulter, *Peers, Queers, and Commons.*

12. Nicholas Bamforth, *Sexuality, Morals and Justice: A Theory of Lesbian and Gay Rights Law* (London: Cassell, 1997), p. 22. See also Richard Plant, *The Pink Triangle: The Nazi War Against Homosexuals* (New York: Henry Holt, 1986).

13. I discuss these and related points at length in David A. J. Richards, *Free Speech and the Politics of Identity* (Oxford: Oxford University Press, 1999).

14. See, for fuller discussion, ibid., pp. 182–209.

15. See Richards, *Women, Gays, and the Constitution,* pp. 172–81.

16. See ibid., pp. 179–81.

17. See, in general, Allan Berube, *Coming Out Under Fire: The History of Gay Men and Women in World War Two* (New York: Free Press, 1990). For lesbian community life during this period, see Elizabeth Lapovsky Kennedy and Madeline D. Davis, *Boots of Leather, Slippers of Gold: The History of a Lesbian Community* (New York: Routledge, 1993).

18. See Donald Webster Cory (pseud.), *The Homosexual in America: A Subjective Approach* (New York: Castle Books, 1951), pp. 4–6, 13–14, 38–48, 152.

19. See ibid., pp. 5, 183, 239.

20. See ibid., p. 6.

21. See ibid., at p. 10.

22. See ibid., at p. 14.

23. On Cory's later manifestation as Edward Sagarin, see John D'Emilio, *Sexual Politics, Sexual Communities: The Making of a Homosexual Minority in the United States, 1940–1970* (Chicago: University of Chicago Press, 1983), p. 168.

24. See Cory (pseud.), *The Homosexual in America,* pp. 34–35, 41.

25. See ibid., p. 39.

26. See ibid., pp. 157–66.

27. See ibid., pp. 106, 152, 237.

28. See ibid., pp. 158, 163–65.

29. See ibid., pp. 15–16.

30. See ibid., p. 21. See Gore Vidal, *The City and the Pillar* (London: Andre Deutsch, 1994 [1948]).

31. See Cory (pseud.), *The Homosexual in America,* pp. 30, 87, 107, 165.

32. See, in general, D'Emilio, *Sexual Politics, Sexual Communities,* pp. 57–74.

33. See, in general, Harry Hay, *Radically Gay,* ed. by Will Roscoe (Boston: Beacon Press, 1996); on the berdache (Native American alternative-gender roles), see ibid., pp. 92–119.

34. See, in general, D'Emilio, *Sexual Politics, Sexual Communities.*

35. For an illuminating general discussion of the dynamics of these groups and their interaction with the wider society, see Urvashi Vaid, *Virtual Equality: The Mainstreaming of Gay and Lesbian Liberation* (New York: Anchor, 1995). See also David Mixner, *Stranger Among Friends* (New York: Bantam Books, 1996).

36. See Colm Toibin, *Love in a Dark Time* (New York: Scribner, 2001), p. 205.

37. See ibid., pp. 205-10.

38. See Eldridge Cleaver, *Soul on Ice* (New York: Dell, 1968), pp. 96-107; for a more muted example, see Stanley Crouch, *Notes of a Hanging Judge: Essays and Reviews, 1979-1989* (New York: Oxford University Press, 1990), pp. 37-41, 231-36. For illuminating commentary, see Dennis Altman, *Homosexual Oppression and Liberation* (New York: Avon, 1971), pp. 190-205.

39. See Betty Friedan, *The Feminine Mystique* (London: Penguin, 1982 [1963]), pp. 238-42.

40. See William H. Chafe, *The Paradox of Change: American Women in the 20th Century* (New York: Oxford University Press, 1991), p. 210; but see p. 211.

41. See Marcia Cohen, *The Sisterhood: The True Story of the Women Who Changed the World* (New York: Simon and Schuster, 1988), pp. 248-51; see also pp. 271-72, 369, 382.

42. For the important challenge of a black lesbian to black sexism and homophobia, see, in general, Audre Lourde, *Sister Outsider: Essays and Speeches* (Freedom, Calif.: Crossing Press, 1983); for the comparable challenge of a black woman to feminism, see bell hooks, *Ain't I a Woman: Black Women and Feminism* (Boston: South End Press, 1981), p. 96; *Feminist Theory: From Margin to Center* (Boston: South End Press, 1984), pp. 23, 150-51; *Killing Rage: Ending Racism* (New York: Henry Holt, 1995), p. 244. For comparable challenges of white lesbians to feminist homophobia, see, in general, Estelle B. Freedman, Barbara C. Gelpi, Susan L. Johnson, and Kathleen M. Weston, eds., *The Lesbian Issue: Essays from* Signs (Chicago: University of Chicago Press, 1982); Marilyn Frye, *The Politics of Reality: Essays in Feminist Theory* (Trumansburg, N.Y.: Crossing Press, 1983); *Willful Virgin: Essays in Feminism, 1976-1992* (Freedom, Calif.: Crossing Press, 1992); Claudia Card, *Lesbian Choices* (New York: Columbia University Press, 1995); Naomi Scheman, *Engenderings: Constructions of Knowledge, Authority, and Privilege* (London: Routledge, 1993); Celia Kitzinger, *The Social Construction of Lesbianism* (London: SAGE, 1987); Sarah Lucia Hoagland, *Lesbian Ethics: Toward New Value* (Palo Alto, Calif.: Institute of Lesbian Studies, 1988); Boston Lesbian Psychologies Collective, *Lesbian Psychologies: Explorations and Challenges* (Urbana: University of Illinois Press, 1987). For an example of the black response to such criticism, see Cornel West, *Race Matters* (Boston: Beacon Press, 1993), pp. 25-28, 45-46, 89; for an example of the feminist response, see Deborah Rhode, *Justice and Gender* (Cambridge, Mass.: Harvard University Press, 1989), pp. 141-42; Patricia Ireland, *What Women Want* (New York: Dutton, 1996), pp. 226-29, 241 (Ireland, a former president of NOW, publicly acknowledges both a husband and lesbian companion, pp. 220, 239). Though NOW changed its position to one more affirmative of the rights of lesbians and gay men (see Ireland, *What Women Want*, pp. 226-29, 241), the issue remains divisive. See, on these points, Sherrye Henry, *The Deep Divide: Why American Women Resist Equality* (New York: Macmillan, 1994), pp. 259-63, 273-75, 287, 291. For example, the implications of the Equal Rights Amendment for gay rights were prominently used against ratification of the amendment. See Jane J. Mansbridge, *Why We Lost the ERA* (Chicago: University of Chicago Press, 1986),

pp. 109, 128–29, 136–37, 144–45; Andrew Kopkind, *The Thirty Years' War: Dispatches and Diversions of a Radical Journalist, 1965–1994,* ed. by JoAnn Wypijewski (London: Verso, 1995), pp. 298–308.

43. See Kopkind, *The Thirty Years' War,* pp. 117–18. For a good discussion of Stonewall, see Martin Duberman, *Stonewall* (New York: Plume, 1993).

44. See Altman, *Homosexual Oppression and Liberation,* pp. 12, 121.

45. See ibid., p. 125.

46. See ibid., pp. 135–36, 207.

47. See ibid., pp. 128–29, 143–44, 152, 186. See, for a similar argument from a lesbian perspective, Claudia Card, *The Unnatural Lottery: Character and Moral Luck* (Philadelphia: Temple University Press, 1996), pp. 163–82.

48. See Altman, *Homosexual Oppression and Liberation,* pp. 61–62, 64.

49. See ibid., p. 180.

50. See Marcel Proust, *Cities of the Plain,* trans. by C. K. Scott Moncrieff (New York: Vintage, 1970), pp. 13–14; for commentary, see Leo Bersani, *Homos* (Cambridge, Mass.: Harvard University Press, 1995), pp. 129–51.

51. See Dennis Altman, *The Homosexualization of America, the Americanization of the Homosexual* (New York: St. Martin's Press, 1982), p. 146.

52. See ibid., pp. 198–99.

53. See ibid., pp. 146–68; Kopkind, *The Thirty Years' War,* pp. 324–32, 501–10, 514.

54. For an important study of Genet along these lines, see Edmund White, *Genet: A Biography* (New York: Knopf, 1993).

55. See, for example, Gilbert Herdt, *Third Sex, Third Gender: Beyond Sexual Dimorphism in Culture and History* (New York: Zone Books, 1994); Walter L. Williams, *The Spirit and the Flesh: Sexual Diversity in American Indian Culture* (Boston: Beacon Press, 1986); David F. Greenberg, *The Construction of Homosexuality* (Chicago: University of Chicago Press, 1988); Martin Bauml Duberman, Martha Vicinus, and George Chauncey, Jr., eds., *Hidden from History: Reclaiming the Gay and Lesbian Past* (New York: New American Library, 1989); Michael Warner, ed., *Fear of a Queer Planet: Queer Politics and Social Theory* (Minneapolis: University of Minnesota Press, 1993).

56. See, for example, David A. J. Richards, "Unnatural Acts and the Constitutional Right to Privacy: A Moral Theory," *Fordham Law Review* 45 (1977): 1282; "Sexual Autonomy and the Constitutional Right to Privacy: A Case Study in Human Rights and the Unwritten Constitution," *Hastings Law Journal* 30 (1979): 30; *The Moral Criticism of Law* (Encino, Calif.: Dickenson-Wadsworth, 1977); *Sex, Drugs, Death, and the Law: An Essay on Human Rights and Overcriminalization* (Totowa, N.J.: Rowman and Littlefield, 1982); *Toleration and the Constitution;* Richard D. Mohr, *Gays/Justice: A Study of Ethics, Society, and Law* (New York: Columbia University Press, 1988); *Gay Ideas: Outing and Other Controversies* (Boston: Beacon Press, 1992); *A More Perfect Union: Why Straight America Must Stand Up for Gay Rights* (Boston: Beacon Press, 1994); Michael Nava and Robert Dawidoff, *Created Equal: Why Gay Rights Matter to America* (New York: St. Martin's Press, 1994); Lisa Duggan and Nan D. Hunter, *Sex Wars: Sexual Dissent and Political Culture* (New York: Routledge, 1995); Robert Wintemute, *Sexual Orientation and Human Rights: The United States Constitution, the European Convention, and the Canadian Charter* (Oxford: Clarendon Press, 1995); William N. Eskridge, Jr., *Gaylaw: Challenging the Apartheid of the Closet* (Cambridge, Mass.: Harvard University Press, 1999).

57. See Adrienne Rich, *Of Woman Born: Motherhood as Experience and Institution* (New York: W. W. Norton, 1976), p. 69.

58. See ibid., pp. 112, 191, 207, 225, 247.

59. See, on this point, Richards, *Women, Gays, and the Constitution*, pp. 72–78, 141–55.

60. See Rich, *Of Woman Born*, pp. 174 (criticizing Shulamith Firestone), 183.

61. See ibid., p. 210.

62. See ibid., pp. 212–13. See, for an important recent treatment of this issue in law, Joan Williams, "Gender Wars: Selfless Women in the Republic of Choice," *N.Y.U. Law Review* 66 (1991): 1559.

63. See Rich, *Of Woman Born*, p. 285.

64. See ibid., pp. 273–74.

65. See ibid., pp. 211–12, 216–17.

66. See, for variant explorations of this theme, Dorothy Dinnerstein, *The Mermaid and The Minotaur: Sexual Arrangements and Human Malaise* (New York: Harper and Row, 1976); Nancy Chodorow, *The Reproduction of Mothering: Psychoanalysis and the Sociology of Gender* (Berkeley: University of California Press, 1978); *Feminism and Psychoanalytic Theory* (London: Polity, 1989); *Femininities Masculinities Sexualities: Freud and Beyond* (London: Free Association Press, 1994); Jane Flax, *Thinking Fragments: Psychoanalysis, Feminism, and Postmodernism in the Contemporary West* (Berkeley: University of California Press, 1990); Jessica Benjamin, *The Bonds of Love: Psychoanalysis, Feminism, and the Problem of Domination* (London: Virgo, 1988). For the constructive strengths of the maternal role for ethical theory and practice, see Sara Ruddick, *Maternal Thinking: Toward a Politics of Peace* (Boston: Beacon Press, 1989); Nel Noddings, *Caring: A Feminine Approach to Ethics and Moral Education* (Berkeley: University of California Press, 1984); *Women and Evil* (Berkeley: University of California Press, 1989).

67. See Rich, *Of Woman Born*, p. 207; see also pp. 193–95.

68. See Adrienne Rich, *On Lies, Secrets, and Silence: Selected Prose 1966–1978* (New York: W. W. Norton, 1979), p. 261.

69. See ibid., pp. 57, 232, 239–40, 282–83, 294, 286–87.

70. See ibid., pp. 10, 17, 224–25. See also Adrienne Rich, "Compulsory Heterosexuality and Lesbian Existence," in Catharine R. Stimpson and Ethel Spector Person, eds., *Women: Sex and Sexuality* (Chicago: University of Chicago Press, 1980), pp. 62–91.

71. See Rich, "Compulsory Heterosexuality," p. 79.

72. See ibid.

73. For an asexual variant, see Esther D. Rothblum and Kathleen A. Brehony, *Boston Marriages: Romantic but Asexual Relationships Among Contemporary Lesbians* (Amherst: University of Massachusetts Press, 1993).

74. On the impact on the sense of self, see, for example, Naomi Wolf, *The Beauty Myth: How Images of Beauty Are Used Against Women* (New York: Anchor, 1991).

75. See Rich, "Compulsory Heterosexuality," p. 63.

76. For a lesbian encomium to the cultural creativity of gay men, see Camille Paglia, *Sexual Personae: Art and Decadence from Nefertiti to Emily Dickinson* (New York: Vintage, 1991), for example, pp. 14–15, 100, 157–58, 380, 434, 653–54.

77. For some provocative such lesbian challenges, see Paglia, *Sexual Personae; Sex, Art, and American Culture: Essays* (New York: Vintage Books, 1992); *Vamps and Tramps: New Essays* (New York: Vintage Books, 1994). For related challenges from dissident feminists, see Daphne Patai and Noretta Koertge, *Professing Feminism:*

Cautionary Tales from the Strange World of Women's Studies (New York: Basic Books, 1994); Rene Denfeld, *The New Victorians: A Young Woman's Challenge to the Old Feminist Order* (New York: Warner Books, 1995); Katie Roiphe, *The Morning After: Sex, Fear, and Feminism* (Boston: Little, Brown, 1993); Christina Hoff Sommers, *Who Stole Feminism: How Women Have Betrayed Women* (New York: Simon and Schuster, 1994).

78. See, for the discussion of some of these points in the context of a larger discussion of changes in masculine role and identity, Elisabeth Badinter, *On Masculine Identity*, trans. by Lydia Davis (New York: Columbia University Press, 1995). See also Elisabeth Badinter, *Man/Woman: The One Is the Other*, trans. by Barbara Wright (London: Collins Harvill, 1989).

79. On this point, see Susan Moller Okin, "Sexual Orientation and Gender: Dichotomizing Differences," in David M. Estlund and Martha C. Nussbaum, eds., *Sex, Preference, and Family: Essays on Law and Nature* (New York: Oxford University Press, 1997), pp. 44–59.

80. On this point, see Kaja Silverman, *Male Subjectivity at the Margins* (New York: Routledge, 1992), pp. 342–51, 354, 372–73. Of course, some such identifications may be subject to their own special distortions; see, for example, Wayne Koestenbaum, *The Queen's Throat: Opera, Homosexuality, and the Mystery of Desire* (New York: Poseidon Press, 1993).

81. See, on this and related points, Martha Nussbaum, "Objectification," *Philosophy and Public Affairs* 24 (1995): 249.

CHAPTER 4

1. See, for pertinent historical discussion, David A. J. Richards, *Women, Gays, and the Constitution: The Grounds for Feminism and Gay Rights in Culture and Law* (Chicago: University of Chicago Press, 1998).

2. For fuller examination of the argument in Locke and Bayle and its American elaboration, notably by Jefferson and Madison, see David A. J. Richards, *Toleration and the Constitution* (New York: Oxford University Press, 1986), pp. 89–128.

3. See Gavin I. Langmuir, *Toward a Definition of Anti-Semitism* (Berkeley: University of California Press, 1990); *History, Religion, and Anti-Semitism* (Berkeley: University of California Press, 1990).

4. See Richards, *Women, Gays, and the Constitution.*

5. See William H. Chafe, *Women and Equality: Changing Patterns in American Culture* (New York: Oxford University Press, 1977), p. 77; on the similar methods of repression, see pp. 58–59, 75–76.

6. Cited in Langmuir, *History, Religion, and Anti-Semitism, p.* 294.

7. See *Brown v. Board of Education,* 347 U.S. 483 (1954).

8. See *Loving v. Virginia,* 388 U.S. 1 (1967); cf. *McLaughlin v. Florida,* 379 U.S. 184 (1964).

9. For citations and commentary, see David A. J. Richards, *Conscience and the Constitution: History, Theory, and Law of the Reconstruction Amendments* (Princeton, N.J.: Princeton University Press, 1993), pp. 80–89.

10. For citations and commentary, see Richards, *Women, Gays, and the Constitution,* pp. 182–90.

11. For citations and commentary, see ibid., pp. 182–90.

12. See Harriet A. Jacobs, *Incidents in the Life of a Slave Girl,* ed. by Jean Fagan Yellin (Cambridge, Mass.: Harvard University Press, 1987 [1861]). For important

commentaries, see Deborah M. Garfield and Rafia Zafar, eds., *Harriet Jacobs and Incidents in the Life of a Slave Girl* (Cambridge: Cambridge University Press, 1996).

13. See Jacobs, *Incidents in the Life of a Slave Girl*, p. 31.

14. See ibid., p. 31.

15. See ibid., p. 35.

16. See ibid.

17. See C. Vann Woodward and Elisabeth Muhlenfeld, *The Private Mary Chesnut: The Unpublished Civil War Diaries* (New York: Oxford University Press, 1984), p. 42.

18. See, for further analysis of King along these lines, David A. J. Richards, *Disarming Manhood: Roots of Ethical Resistance in Jesus, Garrison, Tolstoy, Gandhi, King, and Churchill* (Athens: Ohio University Press, 2005 [forthcoming]).

19. On the continuing power of this cultural construction today, see Andrew Hacker, *Two Nations: Black and White, Separate, Hostile, Unequal* (New York: Charles Scribner's Sons, 1992).

20. See *Plessy v. Ferguson*, 163 U.S. 537 (1896).

21. See *Pace v. Alabama*, 106 U.S. 583 (1883).

22. See Charles A. Lofgren, *The Plessy Case* (New York: Oxford University Press, 1987).

23. See, in general, William Stanton, *The Leopard's Spots: Scientific Attitudes Toward Race in America, 1815–59* (Chicago: University of Chicago Press, 1960).

24. For good general treatments, see Stephen Jay Gould, *The Mismeasure of Man* (New York: W. W. Norton, 1981); Thomas F. Gossett, *Race: The History of an Idea in America* (New York: Schocken Books, 1965); George M. Fredrickson, *The Black Image in the White Mind: The Debate on Afro-American Character and Destiny, 1817–1914* (Middletown, Conn.: Wesleyan University Press, 1971); John S. Haller, Jr., *Outcasts from Evolution: Scientific Attitudes of Racial Inferiority, 1859–1900* (New York: McGraw-Hill Book Company, 1971); Reginald Horsman, *Race and Manifest Destiny: The Origins of American Racial Anglo-Saxonism* (Cambridge, Mass.: Harvard University Press, 1981).

25. See Franz Boas, "Human Faculty as Determined by Race" (1894), reprinted in George W. Stocking, Jr., ed., *A Franz Boas Reader: The Shaping of American Anthropology, 1883–1911* (Chicago: University of Chicago Press, 1974), pp. 221–42.

26. See, in general, C. Vann Woodward, *Reunion and Reaction: The Compromise of 1877 and the End of Reconstruction* (New York: Oxford University Press, 1966); *The Strange Career of Jim Crow*, 3d rev. ed. (New York: Oxford University Press, 1974); *Origins of the New South, 1877–1913* (Baton Rouge: Louisiana State University Press, 1971).

27. See, in general, W. J. Cash, *The Mind of the South* (New York: Vintage Books, 1941).

28. See, for a good general treatment, John Higham, *Strangers in the Land: Patterns of American Nativism, 1860–1925* (New Brunswick, N. J.: Rutgers University Press, 1988). See also Ronald Takaki, *Iron Cages: Race and Culture in 19th-Century America* (New York: Oxford University Press, 1990).

29. See *Brown v. Board of Education*.

30. For a good general study of this development, see James M. McPherson, *The Abolitionist Legacy: From Reconstruction to the NAACP* (Princeton, N.J.: Princeton University Press, 1975).

31. See, in general, William S. McFeely, *Frederick Douglass* (New York: W. W. Norton, 1991).

32. See Anna Julia Cooper, *A Voice from the South*, ed. by Mary Helen Washington (New York: Oxford University Press, 1988 [1892]), at 121–22.

33. See ibid., pp. 119–26. For a good anthology including the work of other nineteenth-century black women often arguing to similar effect, see Bert James Loewenberg and Ruth Bogin, eds., *Black Women in Nineteenth-Century American Life: Their Words, Their Thoughts, Their Feelings* (University Park: Pennsylvania State University Press, 1976).

34. See W. E. B. Du Bois, *The Suppression of the African Slave-Trade* (1896), reprinted in *W. E. B. Du Bois*, ed. by Nathan Huggins (New York: Library of America, 1986), pp. 3–356; *Black Reconstruction in America, 1860–1880* (New York: Atheneum, 1969 [1935]).

35. See W. E. B. Du Bois, *The Souls of Black Folk* (1903), reprinted in *W. E. B. Du Bois*, ed. by Huggins, pp. 359–546.

36. See, in general, David Levering Lewis, *W. E. B. Du Bois: Biography of a Race, 1868–1919* (New York: Henry Holt, 1993); Eric J. Sundquist, *To Wake the Nations: Race in the Making of American Literature* (Cambridge, Mass.: Belknap Press of Harvard University Press, 1993), pp. 457–625.

37. Du Bois, *The Souls of Black Folk*, pp. 364–65.

38. See Lewis, *W. E. B. Du Bois*, pp. 394–97.

39. See Mark V. Tushnet, *The NAACP's Legal Strategy Against Segregated Education, 1925–1950* (Chapel Hill: University of North Carolina Press, 1987); *Making Civil Rights Law: Thurgood Marshall and the Supreme Court, 1956–1961* (New York: Oxford University Press, 1994); Genna Rae McNeil, *Groundwork: Charles Hamilton Houston and the Struggle for Civil Rights* (Philadelphia: University of Pennsylvania Press, 1983); Jack Greenberg, *Crusaders in the Courts: How a Dedicated Band of Lawyers Fought for the Civil Rights Revolution* (New York: Basic Books, 1994).

40. See Evelyn Brooks Higginbotham, *Righteous Discontent: The Women's Movement in the Black Baptist Church, 1880–1920* (Cambridge, Mass.: Harvard University Press, 1993). See also Aldon D. Morris, *The Origins of the Civil Rights Movement: Black Communities Organizing for Change* (New York: Free Press, 1984).

41. See *Gitlow v. New York*, 268 U.S. 652 (1925) (First Amendment held applicable to states under Fourteenth Amendment).

42. See, in general, Harry Kalven, Jr., *The Negro and the First Amendment* (Chicago: University of Chicago Press, 1965).

43. For a good general study, see Taylor Branch, *Parting the Waters: Martin Luther King and the Civil Rights Movement, 1954–63* (London: Papermac, 1990).

44. See Martin Luther King, "Letter from Birmingham City Jail" (1963), in *A Testament of Hope: The Essential Writings of Martin Luther King, Jr.*, ed. by James Melvin Washington (New York: Harper and Row, 1986), pp. 289–302.

45. See ibid., p. 291.

46. See ibid., p. 293.

47. Even under the harsh terms of American slavery, black Americans—though brutally cut off from their native cultures as well as from the rights of American public culture—demonstrated remarkable creativity in giving ethical meaning to their plight, laying the foundations of their later interpretations of the religious and constitutional values of emancipatory freedom that they correctly understood to be at the basis of the public culture around them. See, on the black interpretation of Christian freedom under slavery, Eugene D. Genovese, *Roll, Jordan, Roll: The World the Slaves Made* (New York: Vintage Books, 1974), pp. 159–284; on religious and political freedom under emancipation, see Leon F. Litwack, *Been in the Storm So*

Long: The Aftermath of Slavery (New York: Vintage Books, 1979), pp. 450–556; on the ideals of religious and constitutional freedom of Martin Luther King, see, in general, Branch, *Parting the Waters*.

48. See Franz Boas, *The Mind of Primitive Man*, rev. ed. (Westport, Conn.: Greenwood Press, 1983 [1911]); Stocking, ed., *A Franz Boas Reader*. For superb commentary, see George W. Stocking, Jr., *Race, Culture, and Evolution: Essays in the History of Anthropology* (New York: Free Press, 1968); Carl N. Degler, *In Search of Human Nature: The Decline and Revival of Darwinism in American Social Thought* (New York: Oxford University Press, 1991), pp. 61–83. For a useful recent comparative study of comparable developments in the United States and Britain, see Elazar Barkan, *The Retreat of Scientific Racism: Changing Concepts of Race in Britain and the United States Between the World Wars* (Cambridge: Cambridge University Press, 1992).

49. See Franz Boas, "Race," in Edwin R. A. Seligman, ed., *Encyclopaedia of the Social Sciences*, vol. 7 (New York: Macmillan, 1937), pp. 25–36; *The Mind of Primitive Man*, pp. 45–59, 179. For commentary, see Stocking, *Race, Culture, and Evolution*, pp. 192–94.

50. See Franz Boas, "Changes in Immigrant Body Form," in Stocking, ed., *A Franz Boas Reader*, pp. 202–14; *The Mind of Primitive Man*, pp. 94–96. For commentary, see Stocking, *Race, Culture, and Evolution*, pp. 175–80.

51. See Lewis, *W. E. B. Du Bois*, p. 352; see also pp. 414, 462.

52. See, in general, Boas, *The Mind of Primitive Man*. For commentary, see, in general, Stocking, *Race, Culture, and Evolution*.

53. See Otto Klineberg, *Race Differences* (New York: Harper and Brothers, 1935).

54. See Ruth Benedict, *Race: Science and Politics* (New York: The Viking Press, 1945).

55. See, for example, Boas, "Human Faculty as Determined by Race," pp. 231, 234, 242; *The Mind of Primitive Man*, pp. 230–31.

56. See Degler, *In Search of Human Nature*, pp. 73, 133–37.

57. See Gunnar Myrdal, *An American Dilemma: The Negro Problem and Modern Democracy*, 2 vols. (New York: Pantheon Books, 1972 [1944]). For commentary, see David W. Southern, *Gunnar Myrdal and Black-White Relations: The Use and Abuse of an American Dilemma, 1944–1969* (Baton Rouge: Louisiana State University Press, 1987).

58. See Richards, *Conscience and the Constitution*, pp. 156–60.

59. See Houston Stewart Chamberlain, *The Foundations of the Nineteenth Century*, 2 vols., trans. by John Lees (London: John Lane, 1911).

60. See Madison Grant, *The Passing of the Great Race or The Racial Basis of European History* (New York: Charles Scribner's Sons, 1919).

61. For good general studies, see John Hope Franklin and Alfred A. Moss, Jr., *From Slavery to Freedom: A History of Negro Americans*, 6th ed. (New York: A. A. Knopf, 1988); Donald G. Nieman, *Promises to Keep: African-Americans and the Constitutional Order, 1776 to the Present* (New York: Oxford University Press, 1991).

62. See Raul Hilberg, *The Destruction of the European Jews*, vol. 3 (New York: Holmes and Meier, 1985), pp. 1201–20.

63. For related similarities between the United States and South Africa, see George M. Fredrickson, *White Supremacy: A Comparative Study in American and South African History* (Oxford: Oxford University Press, 1981).

64. See Tushnet, *The NAACP's Legal Strategy Against Segregated Education*.

65. See Mary L. Dudziak, "Desegregation as a Cold War Imperative," *Stanford*

Law Review 41 (1988): 61; Fredrickson, *The Black Image in the White Mind*, p. 330.

66. I develop this thought at greater length in Richards, *Conscience and the Constitution*.

67. See, in general, Hannah Arendt, *The Origins of Totalitarianism* (New York: Harcourt Brace Jovanovich, 1973).

68. See Anthony G. Amsterdam, "Thurgood Marshall's Image of the Blue-Eyed Child in *Brown*," *N.Y.U. Law Review* 68 (1993): 226.

69. See *Brown v. Board of Education*.

70. See *Loving v. Virginia*.

71. See *McLaughlin v. Florida*.

72. See Richards, *Women, Gays, and the Constitution*, ch. 4.

73. See, for a good general study, Paula Giddings, *When and Where I Enter...: The Impact of Black Woman on Race and Sex in America* (New York: William Morrow, 1984). See also bell hooks, *Ain't I a Woman: Black Women and Feminism* (Boston: South End Press, 1981); *Feminist Theory: From Margin to Center* (Boston: South End Press, 1984).

74. See Betty Friedan, *The Feminine Mystique* (London: Penguin, 1982 [1963]).

75. For the changes in the 1940s, see William H. Chafe, *The Paradox of Change: American Women in the 20th Century* (New York: Oxford University Press, 1991), pp. 166–72; for the 1950s, see pp. 188–92.

76. On the importance of Friedan's book, see Chafe, *The Paradox of Change*, p. 195; Jo Freeman, *The Politics of Women's Liberation: A Case Study of an Emerging Social Movement and Its Relation to the Policy Process* (New York: Longman, 1975), pp. 27, 53; Judith Hole and Ellen Levine, *Rebirth of Feminism* (New York: Quadrangle, 1971), pp. 17, 82; Nancy E. McGlen and Karen O'Connor, *Women's Rights: The Struggle for Equality in the Nineteenth and Twentieth Centuries* (New York: Praeger, 1983), p. 29; Carl N. Degler, *At Odds: Women and the Family in America from the Revolution to the Present* (New York: Oxford University Press, 1980), p. 443.

77. See Friedan, *The Feminine Mystique*, pp. 81–82.

78. See ibid., p. 10.

79. See ibid., pp. 26, 62–63.

80. See ibid., pp. 37, 107, 139, 169–70.

81. See ibid., pp. 38, 40–41.

82. See ibid., p. 228.

83. See ibid., pp. 38, 44, 111, 173.

84. See ibid., at p. 44.

85. See ibid., p. 53.

86. See ibid., p. 210.

87. On critical versus uncritical uses of social science, see ibid., at p. 149.

88. For social background, see Glenna Matthews, *"Just a Housewife": The Rise and Fall of Domesticity in America* (New York: Oxford University Press, 1987).

89. See, in general, Friedan, *The Feminine Mystique*, pp. 72–90; on Parker, see p. 76; on Stanton, see pp. 81–82; on securing the suffrage and the death of feminism, see p. 88.

90. See ibid., pp. 59, 282–83.

91. See ibid., pp. 155, 158, 211, 223.

92. See, for example, ibid., pp. 148–49.

93. See ibid., pp. 289–91.

94. See ibid., at pp. 244, 251, 264, 265–68.
95. See ibid., pp. 72, 228, 233.
96. See ibid., p. 275.
97. See ibid., pp. 67–68, 289–91.
98. See ibid., pp. 29, 207, 331.
99. See ibid., p. 16.
100. See Simone de Beauvoir, *The Second Sex,* trans. by H. M. Parshley (New York: Vintage, 1974 [first published in English 1953]).
101. See ibid., pp. xvi, xx, xxi, 131, 144 (citing Sartre and Myrdal), 335.
102. See Friedan, *The Feminine Mystique,* p. 158; see also p. 211.
103. See Freeman, *The Politics of Women's Liberation,* p. 27.
104. See Myrdal, *An American Dilemma,* vol. 2, appendix 5, "A Parallel to the Negro Problem," p. 1073.
105. See Rosalind Rosenberg, *Beyond Separate Spheres: Intellectual Roots of Modern Feminism* (New Haven: Yale University Press, 1982), pp. 162–69, 177.
106. See ibid., pp. 213–19, 226–32.
107. See ibid., pp. 223–26.
108. For Jane Addams on physical differences as the ground for women's superiority, see ibid., p. 41; on skepticism about this ideology, see pp. 111, 176–77, 236.
109. See ibid., pp. 108, 195, 245.
110. See ibid., p. 245.
111. See Friedan, *The Feminine Mystique,* pp. 129–131.
112. See Sara Evans, *Personal Politics: The Roots of Women's Liberation in the Civil Rights Movement and the New Left* (New York: Vintage, 1980).
113. See ibid., pp. 24, 25–26, 57, 101, 120.
114. See Chafe, *The Paradox of Change,* p. 197.
115. See ibid., p. 38.
116. See Evans, *Personal Politics,* p. 25.
117. See Cooper, *A Voice from the South,* pp. 121–22.
118. See Evans, *Personal Politics,* p. 43.
119. See ibid., p. 43.
120. See ibid., p. 45.
121. See ibid., p. 44.
122. See ibid.
123. See ibid., p. 57.
124. See ibid., p. 58.
125. See ibid., p. 57.
126. See ibid., pp. 83–101.
127. For the memorandum, see ibid., pp. 233–35.
128. See ibid., p. 87.
129. See ibid., p. 235.
130. See ibid., p. 236.
131. See ibid.
132. See ibid., p. 237.
133. See ibid., pp. 203–4, 214–15.
134. See ibid., pp. 156–232.
135. On this development, see, in general, Giddings, *When and Where I Enter . . .*
136. See, for example, Ruth Frankenberg, *The Social Construction of Whiteness: White Women, Race Matters* (Minneapolis: University of Minnesota Press, 1993).
137. See *Reed v. Reed,* 404 U.S. 71 (1971).

138. See *Goesaert v. Cleary*, 335 U.S. 464 (1948) (prohibiting women from working as bartenders, except when supervised by husband or father, held constitutional).

139. See *Hoyt v. Florida*, 368 U.S. 57 (1961) (exclusion of women from state jury held constitutional).

140. See *Reed v. Reed*, p. 76.

141. See ibid.

142. See *Loving v. Virginia* (antimiscegenation laws, using a racial classification, are subject to strictest scrutiny and held unconstitutional); *Palmore v. Sidoti*, 466 U.S. 429 (1984) (use of race to determine custody held unconstitutional).

143. See *Harper v. Virginia Board of Elections*, 383 U.S. 663 (1966) (use of poll tax for voting, trenching on fundamental right, held unconstitutional); *Reynolds v. Sims*, 377 U.S. 533 (1964) (malapportionment of state legislature, burdening fundamental equal right to vote, held unconstitutional).

144. See, for example, *Railway Express Agency v. New York*, 336 U.S. 106 (1949) (New York City prohibition of advertising on vehicles, except self-advertising, subject to rational-basis scrutiny, and held constitutional); *Williamson v. Lee Optical Co.*, 348 U.S. 483 (1955) (subjecting opticians, but not sellers of ready-to-wear glasses, to requirement that buyer have had eye examination subject to rational basis, and held constitutional).

145. On this mode of analysis of equal-protection questions, see Joseph Tussman and Jacobus tenBroek, "The Equal Protection of the Laws," 37 *California Law Review* 37 (1949): 341.

146. See *Frontiero v. Richardson*, 411 U.S. 677 (1973).

147. See ibid., p. 684.

148. See ibid.

149. See ibid.

150. Cited in *Frontiero v. Richardson*, pp. 684–85.

151. See ibid., p. 685.

152. See ibid., p. 686.

153. See ibid., p. 686, n. 17.

154. See ibid., p. 688.

155. See ibid., pp. 688–91.

156. See ibid., p. 692.

157. See ibid.

158. See *Craig v. Boren*, 429 U.S. 190 (1976).

159. See ibid., p. 197.

160. See, for example, *Stanton v. Stanton*, 421 U.S. 7 (1975) (establishing female adulthood at eighteen and male adulthood at twenty-one for purposes of child support payments held unconstitutional).

161. See *Craig v. Boren*, p. 199.

162. See ibid., p. 201.

163. See ibid., p. 202, n. 13.

164. See ibid., p. 202, n. 14.

165. See ibid., pp. 208–9, n. 22.

166. See *Michael M. v. Superior Court*, 450 U.S. 464 (1981).

167. See *Rostker v. Goldberg*, 453 U.S. 57 (1981).

168. See *United States v. Virginia*, 116 S. Ct. 2264 (1996).

169. See ibid., p. 2274.

170. See ibid., pp. 11, 15.

171. See ibid., at p. 20.

CHAPTER 5

1. See *Hoyt v. Florida*, 368 U.S. 57, 62 (1961).

2. In *Goesaert v. Cleary*, 335 U.S. 464 (1948), the three dissenters (Justice Rutledge, joined by Justices Douglas and Murphy) dissented because the statute drew an arbitrary distinction "between male and female owners of liquor establishments," 335 U.S., p. 468: a female owner might neither work as a barmaid nor employ her daughter in that position (even if a man were there to keep order), whereas a male owner might employ his wife and daughter as barmaids though he was always absent from the bar. The dissent thus questioned not protective legislation as such but whether this legislation (with its inadequate fit between means and ends) was properly protective.

3. See Mary Wollstonecraft, *A Vindication of the Rights of Woman*, in *The Works of Mary Wollstonecraft*, ed. by Janet Todd and Marilyn Butler (New York: New York University Press, 1989 [1790]), vol. 5, pp. 237–60.

4. See Mary D. Pellauer, *Toward a Tradition of Feminist Theology: The Religious Social Thought of Elizabeth Cady Stanton, Susan B. Anthony, and Anna Howard Shaw* (Brooklyn, N.Y.: Carlson Publishing, Inc., 1991).

5. See, in general, Margaret Hope Bacon, *Mothers of Feminism: The Story of Quaker Women in America* (San Francisco: Harper and Row, 1989).

6. See Jacquelyn Grant, *White Women's Christ and Black Women's Jesus: Feminist Christology and Womanist Response* (Atlanta, Ga.: Scholars Press, 1989), pp. 214, 219–20, 222.

7. See, in general, Susan Starr Sered, *Priestess, Mother, Sacred Sister: Religions Dominated by Women* (New York: Oxford University Press, 1994). On spiritualism in particular, see Ann Braude, *Radical Spirits: Spiritualism and Women's Rights in Nineteenth-Century America* (Boston: Beacon Press, 1989); on Shakerism, see Nardi Reeder Campion, *Ann the Word: The Life of Mother Ann Lee, Founder of the Shakers* (Boston: Little, Brown, 1976); Lawrence Foster, *Women, Family, and Utopia: Communal Experiments of the Shakers, the Oneida Community, and the Mormons* (Syracuse, N.Y.: Syracuse University Press, 1991), pp. 17–71; Henri Desroche, *The American Shakers: From Neo-Christianity to Presocialism*, trans. by John K. Savacool (Amherst: University of Massachusetts Press, 1971); Marjorie Procter-Smith, *Women in Shaker Community and Worship: A Feminist Analysis of the Uses of Religious Symbolism* (Lewiston, N.Y.: Edwin Mellen Press, 1985); Stephen J. Stein, *The Shaker Experience in America* (New Haven: Yale University Press, 1992); Jean M. Humez, *Mother's First-Born Daughters: Early Shaker Writings on Women and Religion* (Bloomington: Indiana University Press, 1993); Louis J. Kern, *An Ordered Love: Sex Roles and Sexuality in Victorian Utopias—The Shakers, the Mormons, and the Oneida Community* (Chapel Hill: University of North Carolina Press, 1981), pp. 71–136.

8. See David A. J. Richards, *Women, Gays, and the Constitution: The Grounds for Feminism and Gay Rights in Culture and Law* (Chicago: University of Chicago Press, 1998), ch. 3.

9. See, in general, Betty A. DeBerg, *Ungodly Women: Gender and the First Wave of American Fundamentalism* (Minneapolis, Minn.: Fortress Press, 1990).

10. See William H. Chafe, *The Paradox of Change: American Women in the 20th Century* (New York: Oxford University Press, 1991), pp. 166–72, 188–92.

11. Important antiestablishment cases include *McCollum v. Board of Education*, 333 U.S. 203 (1948) (release time for religious education unconstitutional) (cf. *Zorach v. Clauson*, 343 U.S. 306 [1952] [not unconstitutional if release time is for

religious teaching off site]); *Engel v. Vitale,* 370 U.S. 421 (1962); *Abington School Dist. v. Schempp,* 374 U.S. 203 (1963) (requirements of sectarian prayers unconstitutional); *Epperson v. Arkansas,* 393 U.S. 97 (1968) (banning teaching Darwin unconstitutional). Important free-exercise cases include *United States v. Ballard,* 322 U.S. 78 (1944) (truth or falsity of religious belief not subject to state inquiry); *Torcaso v. Watkins,* 367 U.S. 488 (1960) (requirement that officials must swear belief in God held unconstitutional); *United States v. Seeger,* 380 U.S. 163 (1965) (conscientious exemption for those who object to all wars must extend to all beliefs, religious and nonreligious); *Welsh v. United States,* 398 U.S. 333 (1970) (accord); but cf. *Gillette v. United States,* 401 U.S. 437 (1970) (failure to exempt selective conscientious objectors supported by adequate secular purpose). For commentary on these developments, see, in general, David A. J. Richards, *Toleration and the Constitution* (New York: Oxford University Press, 1986), pp. 67–162.

12. *Meyer v. Nebraska,* 262 U.S. 390 (1923) (unconstitutional to forbid parent to hire a teacher to educate one's child in the German language).

13. *Pierce v. Society of Sisters,* 268 U.S. 510 (1925) (unconstitutional to forbid parent to send child to religious school).

14. *Skinner v. Oklahoma,* 316 U.S. 535 (1942).

15. See *Griswold v. Connecticut,* 381 U.S. 479 (1965).

16. See Ellen Chesler, *Woman of Valor: Margaret Sanger and the Birth Control Movement in America* (New York: Anchor, 1992), pp. 11, 230, 376, 467. For an illuminating discussion of the development of Sanger's argument from the feminist fringe to endorsement as a basic human right of modernity by the Supreme Court of the United States, see John W. Johnson, *Griswold v. Connecticut: Birth Control and the Constitutional Right to Privacy* (Lawrence: University Press of Kansas, 2005).

17. See *Eisenstadt v. Baird,* 405 U.S. 438 (1972) (unconstitutional to criminalize contraception distribution to unmarried persons).

18. See *Carey v. Population Services International,* 431 U.S. 678 (1977) (unconstitutional to prohibit sale or distribution of contraceptives to minors under sixteen).

19. See *Roe v. Wade,* 410 U.S. 113 (1973).

20. See *Planned Parenthood of Southeastern Pennsylvania v. Casey,* 505 U.S., 112 S. Ct. 2791, 120 L. Ed. 2d 674 (1992).

21. See *Bellotti v. Baird,* 443 U.S. 622 (1979) (state can involve parent in a child's abortion decision only if it affords a judicial bypass procedure so that parental consent is not a veto on the choice); but cf. *H. L. v. Mattheson,* 450 U.S. 398 (1981) (sustaining a parental notice, rather than consent, requirement).

22. Cited in Chesler, *Woman of Valor,* p. 127.

23. See Richards, *Women, Gays, and the Constitution,* ch. 4.

24. See, on American revolutionary constitutionalism as framed by these events, David A. J. Richards, *Foundations of American Constitutionalism* (New York: Oxford University Press, 1989); *Conscience and the Constitution: History, Theory, and Law of the Reconstruction Amendments* (Princeton, N.J.: Princeton University Press, 1993).

25. See Francis Hutcheson, *A System of Moral Philosophy,* 2 vols. in 1 (New York: Augustus M. Kelley, 1968 [1755]), p. 299.

26. See John Witherspoon, *Lectures of Moral Philosophy,* ed. by Jack Scott (East Brunswick, N.J.: Associated University Presses, 1982), p. 123. For further development of this point, see Richards, *Toleration and the Constitution,* pp. 232–33.

27. See Jonathan Elliot, *The Debates in the Several State Conventions on the Adop-*

tion of the Federal Constitution, vol. 2 (Washington, D.C.: Printed for the Editor, 1836), p. 269.

28. See ibid., vol. 3, p. 54.

29. See Kenneth M. Stampp, *The Peculiar Institution* (New York: Vintage, 1956), pp. 198, 340–49; Eugene D. Genovese, *Roll, Jordan, Roll: The World the Slaves Made* (New York: Vintage Books, 1974), pp. 32, 52–53, 125, 451–58.

30. See Stampp, *The Peculiar Institution,* pp. 199–207, 204–6, 333, 348–49; Herbert G. Gutman, *The Black Family in Slavery and Freedom, 1750–1925* (New York: Vintage Books, 1976), pp. 146, 318, 349.

31. See Gutman, *The Black Family in Slavery and Freedom,* p. 318.

32. See Theodore Dwight Weld, *American Slavery as It Is* (New York: Arno Press and the New York Times, 1968 [1839]), p. 56.

33. See Ronald G. Walters, *The Antislavery Appeal: American Abolitionism After 1830* (New York: W. W. Norton, 1978), pp. 95–96.

34. See Peggy Cooper Davis, *Neglected Stories: The Constitution and Family Values* (New York: Hill and Wang, 1997).

35. Justice Harlan, in fact, grounded his argument on the Due Process Clause of the Fourteenth Amendment, but the argument is more plausibly understood, as a matter of text, history, and political theory, as based on the Privileges and Immunities Clause of the Fourteenth Amendment for reasons I give in Richards, *Conscience and the Constitution,* ch. 6. For further elaboration of this interpretation of *Griswold,* see Richards, *Toleration and the Constitution,* pp. 256–61.

36. See Werner Sollors, *Beyond Ethnicity: Consent and Descent in American Culture* (New York: Oxford University Press, 1986), p. 112.

37. Thomas R. R. Cobb, *An Inquiry into the Law of Negro Slavery in the United States of America* (New York: Negro Universities Press, 1968 [1858]), p. 39.

38. See ibid., p. 40.

39. See, in general, Gutman, *The Black Family in Slavery and Freedom.*

40. See William Harper, "Memoir on Slavery," reprinted in Drew Gilpin Faust, ed., *The Ideology of Slavery: Proslavery Thought in the Antebellum South, 1830–1860* (Baton Rouge: Louisiana State University Press, 1981), p. 110.

41. See James Henry Hammond, "Letter to an English Abolitionist," reprinted in Faust, ed., *The Ideology of Slavery,* pp. 191–92.

42. See, for example, William Harper, "Memoir on Slavery," pp. 107, 118–19; Hammond, "Letter to an English Abolitionist," pp. 182–84.

43. See, for example, Thomas Roderick Dew, "Abolition of Negro Slavery," reprinted in Faust, ed., *The Ideology of Slavery,* p. 65; William Harper (citing Dew), "Memoir on Slavery," p. 100.

44. For a good general discussion of such inversions, see Kenneth S. Greenberg, *Masters and Statesmen: The Political Culture of American Slavery* (Baltimore, Md.: The Johns Hopkins University Press, 1985).

45. For further defense of this position, see Richards, *Conscience and the Constitution,* ch. 6.

46. See Augustine, *The City of God,* trans. by Henry Bettenson (Harmondsworth, U.K.: Penguin, 1972), pp. 577–94.

47. Thomas Aquinas elaborates Augustine's conception of the exclusive legitimacy of procreative sex in a striking way. Of the emission of semen apart from procreation in marriage, he wrote: "After the sin of homicide whereby a human nature already in existence is destroyed, this type of sin appears to take next place, for by it

the generation of human nature is precluded." Thomas Aquinas, *On the Truth of the Catholic Faith: Summa Contra Gentiles,* trans. by Vernon Bourke (New York: Image, 1956), pt. 2, ch. 122(9), p. 146.

48. On how personal this decision now is, see, in general, Elaine Tyler May, *Barren in the Promised Land: Childless Americans and the Pursuit of Happiness* (New York: Basic Books, 1995).

49. For further discussion of the right to privacy and contraception, see Richards, *Toleration and the Constitution,* pp. 256–61.

50. For further discussion, see ibid., pp. 261–69; Ronald Dworkin, *Life's Dominion: An Argument About Abortion, Euthanasia, and Individual Freedom* (New York: Knopf, 1993), pp. 3–178.

51. See Richards, *Toleration and the Constitution,* pp. 266–67.

52. See Carol Gilligan, *In a Different Voice: Psychological Theory and Women's Development* (Cambridge, Mass.: Harvard University Press, 1982).

CHAPTER 6

1. See Yuval Merin, *Equality for Same-Sex Couples: The Legal Recognition of Gay Partnerships in Europe and the United States* (Chicago: University of Chicago Press, 2002), table 4, pp. 327–28.

2. See *Dudgeon v. United Kingdom,* 45 Eur. Ct. H.R. (1981) P 52.

3. See *People v. Onofre,* 51 N.Y. 2d 476 (1980), *cert. den.,* 451 U.S. 987 (1981).

4. See, on these points, John Hart Ely, *Democracy and Distrust: A Theory of Judicial Review* (Cambridge, Mass.: Harvard University Press, 1983); "The Wages of Crying Wolf: A Comment on *Roe v. Wade,*" *Yale Law Journal* 82 (1974): 920.

5. See Charles Fried, *Order and Law: Arguing the Reagan Revolution—A Firsthand Account* (New York: Simon and Schuster, 1991), pp. 80–84; Kent Greenawalt, *Religious Convictions and Political Choice* (New York: Oxford University Press, 1988), pp. 120, 168.

6. See references in previous note.

7. See, for an extended critique, David A. J. Richards, *Toleration and the Constitution* (New York: Oxford University Press, 1986).

8. Cited in *Bowers v. Hardwick,* 478 U.S. 186, 187 (1986).

9. *Bowers v. Hardwick,* pp. 190–91.

10. Ibid., pp. 191–92.

11. Ibid., p. 194.

12. Ibid.

13. "If slavery is not wrong, nothing can be wrong," cited in Richards, *Conscience and the Constitution: History, Theory, and Law of the Reconstruction Amendments* (Princeton, N.J.: Princeton University Press, 1993), p. 62.

14. See *Williams v. Florida,* 399 U.S. 78 (1970).

15. Ibid., pp. 195–96.

16. Ibid.

17. Ibid., p. 197.

18. See, on these points, John C. Jeffries, Jr., *Justice Lewis F. Powell, Jr.: A Biography* (New York: Fordham University Press, 2001), pp. 511–30.

19. See, on this point, ibid., p. 530; William N. Eskridge, *Gaylaw: Challenging the Apartheid of the Closet* (Cambridge, Mass.: Harvard University Press, 1999), p. 150.

20. Quoted in Jeffries, Jr., *Justice Lewis F. Powell, Jr.*, p. 530.

21. Quoted in ibid., p. 521.

22. See ibid., p. 528.

23. *Bowers v. Hardwick*, p. 200.

24. Ibid.

25. I can attest to this from personal experience. I met Justice Blackmun around 1984 in connection with his leading a seminar on justice and society, with Norval Morris, at the Aspen Institute (I had prepared the course materials) and talked with him often in the seminar about his work. He struck me, as well as my partner (who was with me), as a remarkably open, humane human being, certainly when dealing with a clearly gay couple. We met several years before *Bowers,* but in light of our meeting, the depth of his feelings about this issue, reflected in his dissent in *Bowers,* struck me as in line with the moral character and humanity of the man. Character matters in law as in life.

26. *Bowers v. Hardwick*, p. 205.

27. Ibid.

28. Ibid., p. 209.

29. Ibid., p. 209, n. 4.

30. Ibid.

31. Ibid., p. 217.

32. Ibid., p. 218.

33. Ibid., p. 219.

34. See, on these points, David A. J. Richards, "Commercial Sex and the Rights of the Person: A Moral Argument for the Decriminalization of Prostitution," *University of Pennsylvania Law Review* 127 (1979): 1195; "Drug Use and the Rights of the Person: A Moral Argument for the Decriminalization of Certain Forms of Drug Use," *Rutgers Law Review* 33 (1981): 607; "Constitutional Privacy, the Right to Die, and the Meaning of Life: A Moral Analysis," *William and Mary Law Review* 22 (1981): 327; *Sex, Drugs, Death and the Law: An Essay on Human Rights and Over-criminalization* (Totowa, N.J.: Rowman and Littlefield, 1982).

35. See *Cruzan v. Director, Missouri Dept. of Health*, 497 U.S. 261 (1990) (in absence of living will, Missouri may constitutionally limit a person's protected right to refuse medical service by requiring clear and convincing evidence that person would have wanted discontinuance of life-sustaining procedures). But cf. *Washington v. Glucksberg,* 521 U.S. 702 (1997) (prohibition of physician-assisted suicide does not violate constitutional right to privacy).

36. See, in particular, Richards, *Toleration and the Constitution.*

37. Kathleen Sullivan, then of Harvard Law School and later dean of Stanford Law School, asked me to appear with her before the Senate Judiciary Committee to testify about our worries about Judge Bork's views on constitutional privacy.

38. Testimony before Senate Judiciary Committee on nomination of Robert H. Bork to be associate justice of the Supreme Court of the United States, 1987 (see *Nomination of Robert H. Bork to Be Associate Justice of the Supreme Court of the United States: Hearings Before the Senate Committee on the Judiciary,* 100th Congress, 1st Session (1987), 3047 (statement of David A. J. Richards).

39. For the reflections of another law professor pivotally involved in the Bork hearings on *Lawrence,* see Laurence H. Tribe, "*Lawrence v. Texas*: The 'Fundamental Right' That Dare Not Speak Its Name," *Harvard Law Review* 117 (2004).

CHAPTER 7

1. *Plessy v. Ferguson,* 163 U.S. 537 (1896).

2. *Brown v. Board of Education,* 347 U.S. 483 (1954).

3. *Lochner v. New York,* 198 U.S. 45 (1905).

4. *Nebbia v. New York,* 291 U.S. 502 (1934).

5. See, for example, *Adarand Construction, Inc. v. Pena,* 515 U.S. 200 (1995) (striking down ethnic preference in federal contracting under strict scrutiny). But cf. *Grutter v. Bollinger,* 539 U.S. 306 (2003) (upholding law school admissions for minority students keyed to critical mass).

6. See *United States v. Lopez,* 514 U.S. 549 (1995) (federal statute criminalizing possession of firearm on school property held unconstitutional under Commerce Clause); *United States v. Morrison,* 529 U.S. 598 (2000) (federal statute giving civil remedies for gender-motivated violence unconstitutional under both Commerce Clause and Reconstruction Amendments).

7. *Planned Parenthood of Southeastern Pa. v. Casey,* 505 U.S. 833 (1992).

8. *Romer v. Evans,* 517 U.S. 620 (1996).

9. See Amendment Two to Colorado Constitution, art. 2, sec. 2 (adopted November 3, 1992). The full text of Amendment Two is as follows: "Neither the State of Colorado, through any of its branches or departments, nor any of its agencies, political subdivisions, municipalities or school districts, shall enact, adopt or enforce any statute, regulation, ordinance or policy whereby homosexual, lesbian or bisexual orientation, conduct, practices, or relationships shall constitute or otherwise be the basis of, or entitle any person or class of persons to have or claim any minority status, quota preferences, protected status or claim of discrimination. This Section of the Constitution shall be self-executing."

10. *Romer v. Evans,* p. 636.

11. Quoted in ibid., p. 623.

12. *Reynolds v. United States,* 98 U.S. 145 (1878) (upholding application of a federal law making bigamy a crime in the territories to a Mormon claiming that polygamy was his religious duty).

13. *Davis v. Beason,* 133 U.S. 333 (1890).

14. *Romer v. Evans,* p. 634.

15. *Hurley v. Irish-American Gay, Lesbian, and Bisexual Group of Boston,* 515 U.S. 557 (1995).

16. *Boy Scouts of America v. Dale,* 530 U.S. 640 (2000).

17. Justice Souter filed a separate dissent joined by Justices Ginsburg and Breyer.

18. *Lawrence v. Texas,* 539 U.S. 558, 123 S. Ct. 2472 (2003).

19. Ibid., p. 2478.

20. Ibid.

21. Ibid.

22. Ibid.

23. Ibid., p. 2484.

24. Ibid., p. 2479.

25. Ibid., p. 2480.

26. Ibid.

27. Ibid.

28. Cited at ibid.

29. Cited at ibid., p. 2481.

30. See *Dudgeon v. United Kingdom,* 45 Eur. Ct. H.R. (1981) P 52, discussed in *Lawrence v. Texas,* p. 2481.

31. *Lawrence v. Texas,* p. 2481. See, on the unusual character of Justice Kennedy's appeal to constitutional developments abroad, William N. Eskridge, Jr., "United States: *Lawrence v. Texas* and the Imperative of Comparative Constitutionalism," *International Journal of Constitutional Law* 2, no. 3 (July 2004): 555–60.

32. *Lawrence v. Texas,* p. 2482.

33. Ibid.

34. Quoted in ibid., p. 2483 (footnotes and citations omitted).

35. Ibid., p. 2484.

36. Ibid.

37. Ibid., p. 2487.

38. Ibid., p. 2496 (footnotes and citations omitted).

CHAPTER 8

1. See Yuval Merin, *Equality for Same-Sex Couples: The Legal Recognition of Gay Partnerships in Europe and the United States* (Chicago: University of Chicago Press, 2002).

2. See, for fuller discussion of Whitman from this perspective, David A. J. Richards, *Women, Gays, and the Constitution: The Grounds for Feminism and Gay Rights in Culture and Law* (Chicago: University of Chicago Press, 1998), pp. 297–310.

3. See, for fuller discussion, ibid., pp. 311–27.

4. See ibid., pp. 327–37.

5. See, on this point, Nan D. Hunter, "Identity, Speech, and Equality," *Virginia Law Review* 79 (1993): 1695.

6. See, for an extended statement and defense of this position, David A. J. Richards, *Toleration and the Constitution* (New York: Oxford University Press, 1986).

7. See, in general, ibid., pp. 141–46. Free-exercise analysis was somewhat narrowly interpreted in *Employment Div. Ore. Dept. of Human Res. v. Smith,* 495 U.S. 872 (1990) (religiously inspired peyote use not constitutionally exempt from neutral criminal statute criminalizing such use, and thus state permitted to deny employment benefits to persons dismissed from their jobs because of such use). The case, however, notably acknowledged the continuing authority of leading free-exercise cases such as *Sherbert v. Verner,* 374 U.S. 398 (1963) (denial of state unemployment benefits, unavailable to Seventh Day Adventist because of failure to work on sabbath day, unconstitutionally burdens free-exercise rights), and *Wisconsin v. Yoder,* 406 U.S. 205 (1972) (state compulsory education law unconstitutionally burdens free-exercise rights of Amish parents to remove children from school after eighth grade). In *Church of the Lukumi Babalu Aye, Inc. v. City of Hialeah,* 508 U.S. 520 (1993), the Supreme Court clarified that *Employment Div. v. Smith* in no way limited the availability of free-exercise analysis of a state law that non-neutrally targeted a specific religion (in this case, criminalizing animal sacrifice in Santeria religious rituals). The authority of *Smith* was cast in doubt in light of the Religious Freedom Restoration Act of 1993, S. Rep. 111, 103rd Congress, 1st session, 14 (1993); for commentary, see Douglas Laycock, "Free Exercise and the Religious Freedom Restoration Act," *Fordham Law Review* 62 (1994): 883. The constitutionality of the Religious Free-

dom Restoration Act of 1993 was recently assessed by the Supreme Court in light of whether, on grounds of Section 5 of the Fourteenth Amendment, it constitutionally expands or unconstitutionally contracts the constitutional right judicially defined by the Supreme Court in its free-exercise jurisprudence, including *Smith*. For relevant case law on this question, see *South Carolina v. Katzenbach*, 383 U.S. 301 (1956); *Katzenbach v. Morgan*, 384 U.S. 641 (1966); *Oregon v. Mitchell*, 400 U.S. 112 (1970). The Act was held unconstitutional. See *City of Boerne v. P. F. Flores*, 521 U.S. 507 (1997).

8. See Richards, *Toleration and the Constitution*, pp. 146–62.

9. See, for further argument on this point, ibid., pp. 89–98.

10. See ibid., pp. 95–98.

11. See ibid., pp. 111–13.

12. Under the Free Exercise Clause, the Supreme Court has tended, in the interest of reasonably developing the basic value of equality, to expand the constitutional concept of religion to protect conscience as such from coercion or undue burdens. See, for example, *United States v. Ballard*, 322 U.S. 78 (1944) (forbidding any inquiry into the truth or falsity of beliefs in a mail-fraud action against the bizarre "I am" movement of Guy Ballard [alias "Saint Germain, Jesus, George Washington, and Godfre Ray King"]); *Torcaso v. Watkins*, 367 U.S. 488 (1960) (declaring unconstitutional a state requirement that state officials must swear belief in God); and *United States v. Seeger*, 380 U.S. 163 (1965) and *Welsh v. United States*, 398 U.S. 333 (1970) (congressional statutory exemption from military service—limited to religiously motivated conscientious objectors to all wars—extended to all who conscientiously object to all wars). But see *Employment Div. Ore. Dept. of Human Res. v. Smith*. And under the Establishment Clause, the Supreme Court has notably insisted that the public education curriculum may not privilege sectarian religious rituals and views over others. See, for example, *Engel v. Vitale*, 370 U.S. 421 (1962) (use of state-composed "nondenominational" prayer in public schools held violative of Establishment Clause); *Abington School Dist. v. Schempp*, 374 U.S. 203 (1963) (reading of selections from Bible and Lord's Prayer in public schools violative of Establishment Clause); *Wallace v. Jaffree*, 472 U.S. 38 (1985) (state authorization of one-minute period of silence in public schools "for meditation or voluntary prayer" held violative of Establishment Clause); *Lee v. Weisman*, 504 U.S. (1992) (nondenominational prayer at high school graduation held violative of Establishment Clause); *Epperson v. Arkansas*, 393 U.S. 97 (1968) (state statute forbidding teaching of evolution in public schools violative of Establishment Clause); *Edwards v. Aguillard*, 482 U.S. 578 (1987) (state statute requiring balanced treatment of creationist and evolution science held violative of Establishment Clause).

13. See, in general, David A. J. Richards, *Conscience and the Constitution: History, Theory, and Law of the Reconstruction Amendments* (Princeton, N.J.: Princeton University Press, 1993); *Women, Gays, and the Constitution*.

14. For specific elaboration and defense of this point, see David A. J. Richards, "Public Reason and Abolitionist Dissent," *Chicago-Kent Law Review* 69 (1994): 787; see also, in general, Richards, *Women, Gays, and the Constitution*.

15. William Blackstone, *Commentaries on the Laws of England 1765–1769*, vol. 4, facsimile of first edition ed. by Thomas A. Green (Chicago: University of Chicago Press, 1979), p. 215.

16. See, on this point, Richards, *Toleration and the Constitution*, pp. 278–79.

17. See Tony Honore, *Sex Law* (London: Duckworth, 1978), p. 89.

18. On the pervasiveness of this ideal in Western religious and ethical culture, see Richards, *Toleration and the Constitution,* pp. 69, 71, 78, 93, 123–28, 134, 272–73, 275. For an exploration of the form, content, and force of the critical and constructive aspects of these ethical arguments on behalf of lesbian and gay identity, see ibid., pp. 269–80; David A. J. Richards, *Sex, Drugs, Death, and the Law* (Totowa, N.J.: Rowman and Littlefield, 1982), pp. 29–83; David A. J. Richards, "Unnatural Acts and the Constitutional Right to Privacy: A Moral Theory," *Fordham Law Review* 45 (1977): 1281; Richards, "Sexual Autonomy and the Constitutional Right to Privacy: A Case Study in Human Rights and the Unwritten Constitution," *Hastings Law Journal* 30 (1979): 957.

19. See *Romer v. Evans,* 116 S. Ct. 1650 (1966).

20. For fuller discussion, see Richards, *Women, Gays, and the Constitution,* ch. 7.

21. *United States v. Ballard,* 322 U.S. 78, 86 (1944) (Douglas, J., writing for the Court).

22. See, in general, Sydney E. Ahlstrom, *A Religious History of the American People* (New Haven, Conn.: Yale University Press, 1972), especially pp. 491–509 (Shakers, Society of the Public Universal Friend, New Harmony, Oneida Community, Hopedale, Brook Farm, the Mormons), 1019–33 (Science of Health [Christian Science], New Thought, Positive Thinking), 1059–78 (Black Pentecostalism, Father Divine, Sweet Daddy Grace, Nation of Islam, Booker T. Washington, Martin Luther King).

23. For specific elaboration and defense of this point, see Richards, "Public Reason and Abolitionist Dissent." See also Richards, *Conscience and the Constitution,* pp. 58–107.

24. For further development of this argument, see Richards, *Toleration and the Constitution,* pp. 67–162.

25. For fuller discussion, see ibid., pp. 146–62.

26. For further development of this point, see Richards, "Public Reason and Abolitionist Dissent."

27. For citations and commentary, see Richards, *Women, Gays, and the Constitution,* pp. 307, 366, 434.

28. On this point, see, in general, Elisabeth Young-Bruehl, *The Anatomy of Prejudices* (Cambridge, Mass.: Harvard University Press, 1996).

29. See Plato, *The Laws,* Book 8, 835d–842a, in *The Collected Dialogues of Plato,* ed. by Edith Hamilton and Huntington Cairns (New York: Pantheon, 1961), pp. 1401–2. On the moral condemnation of the passive role in homosexuality in both Greek and early Christian moral thought, see Peter Brown, *The Body and Society: Men, Women, and Sexual Renunciation in Early Christianity* (New York: Columbia University Press, 1988), pp. 30, 382–83. But for evidence of Greco-Roman toleration of long-term homosexual relations even between adults, see John Boswell, *Same-Sex Unions in Premodern Europe* (New York: Villard Books, 1994), pp. 53–107. I am grateful to Stephen Morris for conversations on this point. Whether these relationships were regarded as marriages may be a very different matter. For criticism of Boswell's argument along this latter line, see Brent D. Shaw, "A Groom of One's Own?" *New Republic,* July 18 and 25, 1994, pp. 33–41.

30. See *Griswold v. Connecticut,* 381 U.S. 479 (1965); *Eisenstadt v. Baird,* 405 U.S. 438 (1972).

31. For further discussion, see Richards, *Toleration and the Constitution,* pp. 256–61.

32. See, for example, *Frontiero v. Richardson,* 411 U.S. 677 (1973); *Craig v. Boren,* 429 U.S. 190 (1976). On homophobia as rooted in sexism, see Young-Bruehl, *The Anatomy of Prejudices,* pp. 143, 148–51.

33. For cases that protect women from such harm, see *Reed v. Reed,* 404 U.S. 71 (1971) (right to administer estates); *Frontiero v. Richardson* (dependency allowances to servicewomen); *Stanton v. Stanton,* 421 U.S. 7 (1975) (child support for education). For cases that protect men, see *Wengler v. Druggists Mutual Ins. Co.,* 446 U.S. 142 (1980) (widower's right to death benefits); *Craig v. Boren* (age of drinking for men).

34. On the continuities among heterosexual and homosexual forms of intimacy in the modern era, see, in general, John D'Emilio and Estelle B. Freedman, *Intimate Matters: A History of Sexuality in America* (New York: Harper and Row, 1988), pp. 239–360; Anthony Giddens, *The Transformation of Intimacy: Sexuality, Love, and Eroticism in Modern Societies* (Cambridge: Polity, 1992). See also Barbara Ehrenreich, Elizabeth Hess, and Gloria Jacobs, *Remaking Love: The Feminization of Sex* (New York: Anchor, 1986); Anne Snitow, Christine Stansell, and Sharon Thompson, eds., *Powers of Desire* (New York: Monthly Review Press, 1983); Carole S. Vance, ed., *Pleasure and Danger: Exploring Female Sexuality* (Boston: Routledge and Kegan Paul, 1984).

35. On the unjust gender stereotype uncritically applied to homosexual men and women, see Susan Moller Okin, "Sexual Orientation and Gender: Dichotomizing Differences," in David M. Estlund and Martha C. Nussbaum, eds., *Sex, Preference, and Family: Essays on Law and Nature* (New York: Oxford University Press, 1997), pp. 44–59.

36. *Bowers v. Hardwick,* 478 U.S. 186 (1986).

37. The argument applies, in any event, only to those forms of sex by gay men likely to transmit the disease; it does not reasonably apply to lesbians, nor does it apply to all forms of sex (including anal sex) by gay men. So the argument that sex acts as such can be criminalized on this basis is constitutionally overinclusive, inconsistent with the basic right thus abridged. The regulatory point is that even gay men at threat by virtue of their sexual practices can take preventive measures against this threat (by using condoms). For a recent discussion of what further such reasonable preventive measures the gay men at threat might take, see Gabriel Rotello, *Sexual Ecology: AIDS and the Destiny of Gay Men* (New York: Dutton, 1997).

38. For further criticism, see David A. J. Richards, *Foundations of American Constitutionalism* (New York: Oxford University Press, 1989), pp. 209–47.

39. Justice Blackmun put the point acidly: "Like Justice Holmes, I believe that 'it is revolting to have no better reason for a rule of law than that it was laid down in the time of Henry IV. It is still more revolting if the grounds upon which it was laid down have vanished long since, and the rule simply persists from blind imitation of the past.'" *Bowers* (quoting Oliver Wendell Holmes, "The Path of the Law," *Harvard Law Review* 10 [1897]: 457, 469).

40. See Leo Bersani, "Is the Rectus as a Grave?" in Douglas Crimp, ed., *Cultural Analysis/Cultural Activism* (Cambridge: The MIT Press, 1988), pp. 211–12, 222.

41. I develop this argument at greater length in Richards, *Foundations of American Constitutionalism,* ch. 6; and in David A. J. Richards, "Constitutional Legitimacy and Constitutional Privacy," *N.Y.U. Law Review* 61 (1986): 800. See also Anne B. Goldstein, "History, Homosexuality, and Political Values: Searching for the Hidden Determinants of *Bowers v. Hardwick,*" *Yale Law Journal* 97 (1988): 1073; Nan D. Hunter, "Life After *Hardwick,*" *Harvard Civil Rights–Civil Liberties Law Review* 27

(1992): 531; Janet E. Halley, "Reasoning About Sodomy: Act and Identity in and After *Bowers v. Hardwick,*" *Virginia Law Review* 79 (1993): 1721; Anne B. Goldstein, "Reasoning About Homosexuality: A Commentary on Janet Halley's 'Reasoning About Sodomy: Act and Identity in and After *Bowers v. Hardwick,*'" *Virginia Law Review* 79 (1993): 1781; Kendall Thomas, "The Eclipse of Reason: A Rhetorical Reading of *Bowers v. Hardwick,*" *Virginia Law Review* 79 (1993): 1805.

42. See Suzanne Pharr, *Homophobia: A Weapon of Sexism* (Inverness, Calif.: Chardon Press, 1988); Sylvia A. Law, "Homosexuality and the Social Meaning of Gender," *Wisconsin Law Review* (1988): 187; Young-Bruehl, *The Anatomy of Prejudices,* pp. 35–36, 143–51; Okin, "Sexual Orientation and Gender: Dichotomizing Differences."

43. On the later development of lesbian identity, see Lillian Faderman, *Odd Girls and Twilight Lovers: A History of Lesbian Life in Twentieth-Century America* (New York: Columbia University Press, 1991); Carroll Smith-Rosenberg, *Disorderly Conduct: Visions of Gender in Victorian America* (New York: Knopf, 1985), pp. 245–97.

44. See, in general, Randolph Trumbach, "Gender and the Homosexual Role in Modern Western Culture: The 18th and 19th Centuries Compared," in Dennis Altman, Carole Vance, Martha Vicinus, and Jeffrey Weeks, eds., *Homosexuality, Which Homosexuality? International Conference on Gay and Lesbian Studies* (London: GMP Publishers, 1989), pp. 149–69.

45. See ibid., at p. 153.

46. For a probing recent study, see Eva Cantarella, *Bisexuality in the Ancient World,* trans. by Cormac O Cuilleanain (New Haven, Conn.: Yale University Press, 1992); but see also John Boswell, *Same-Sex Unions in Premodern Europe* (New York: Villard Books, 1994), pp. 53–107.

47. For commentary on the sexism of heterosexism, see Adrienne Rich, "Compulsory Heterosexuality and Lesbian Existence," in Catharine Stimpson and Ethel Spector Person, eds., *Women: Sex and Sexuality* (Chicago: University of Chicago Press, 1980); also reprinted in Henry Abelove, Michele Aina Barale, and David M. Halperin, eds., *The Lesbian and Gay Studies Reader* (New York: Routledge, 1993), pp. 227–54.

48. On the antifeminism of antigay sectarian groups, see Didi Herman, *The Antigay Agenda: Orthodox Vision and the Christian Right* (Chicago: University of Chicago Press, 1997), pp. 103–10; on such groups' opposition, in general, to the agenda of civil rights in all areas, see pp. 111–36, 140.

49. For important recent arguments along these lines, see Katherine M. Franke, "The Central Mistake of Sex Discrimination Law: The Disaggregation of Sex from Gender," *University of Pennsylvania Law Review* 144 (1995): 1; Mary Ann C. Case, "Disaggregating Gender from Sex and Sexual Orientation: The Effeminate Man in the Law and Feminist Jurisprudence," *Yale Law Journal* 105 (1995): 90.

50. See *Loving v. Virginia,* 388 U.S. 1 (1967) (antimiscegenation laws held to be an unconstitutional expression of racial prejudice).

51. See Lillian Faderman, *Surpassing the Love of Men* (New York: William Morrow, 1981), at pp. 85–86, 157–58, 181, 236.

52. For further development of this argument, see Richards, *Women, Gays, and the Constitution,* ch. 8.

53. See, for eloquent development of this point, Andrew Koppelman, "The Miscegenation Analogy: Sodomy Law as Sex Discrimination," *Yale Law Journal* 98 (1988): 145. See also Andrew Koppelman, *Antidiscrimination Law and Social Equality* (New Haven, Conn.: Yale University Press, 1996), pp. 146–76.

54. For development of this theme, see Will Kymlicka, *Liberalism, Community, and Culture* (Oxford: Clarendon Press, 1989), pp. 162–78; Yael Tamir, *Liberal Nationalism* (Princeton, N.J.: Princeton University Press, 1993), pp. 13–56.

55. For further development and defense of this position, see, in general, Richards, *Women, Gays, and the Constitution*.

56. See Amendment Two to Colorado Constitution, art. 2, sec. 2 (adopted November 3, 1992). For full text of Amendment Two, see Chapter 7, note 9. The voters of Colorado approved Amendment Two by a vote of 53 percent to 47 percent. On July 19, 1993, the Colorado Supreme Court affirmed the grant of a preliminary injunction against the amendment. See *Evans v. Romer*, 854 P. 2d 1270 (Colo. 1993), *cert. den.*, U.S., 114 S. Ct. 419, L. Ed. 2d (1993). On December 14, 1993, Judge H. Jeffrey Bayless granted a permanent injunction against the amendment, finding that, under the strict-scrutiny standard applicable to the constitutional assessment of the amendment under *Evans,* the state had failed to justify the amendment in terms of compelling state interests. See *Evans v. Romer*, 1993 WL 518586 (Colo. Dist. Ct.), reprinted in *The Bill of Rights Versus the Ballot Box: Constitutional Implications of Anti-Gay Ballot Initiatives,* Continuing Legal Education Materials, presented by the Gay-Lesbian Bisexual Law Caucus of The Ohio State University, March 12, 1994 (on file with *Ohio State Law Journal*), pp. 23–32.

57. See *Romer v. Evans*, 116 S. Ct. 1620, 1627 (1996).

58. See *Reed v. Reed*, 404 U.S. 71 (1971).

59. For further discussion of the judicial development and its background, see Richards, *Women, Gays, and the Constitution*, ch. 5.

60. See *Romer v. Evans*, p. 1629.

61. Ibid., p. 1637.

62. See, in general, William Lee Miller, *The First Liberty: Religion and the American Republic* (New York: Knopf, 1987); Thomas J. Curry, *The First Freedoms: Church and State in America to the Passage of the First Amendment* (New York: Oxford University Press, 1986); Leonard W. Levy, *The Establishment Clause: Religion and the First Amendment* (New York: Macmillan, 1986).

63. In its position paper, Colorado for Family Values, the sponsor of Colorado Amendment Two, invoked sectarian religious arguments to justify the initiative: "Gay behavior is what the Bible calls 'sin' because sin defines any attempt to solve human problems or meet human needs without regard to God's wisdom and solutions as found in Scripture and in His saving grace and mercy," cited in John F. Niblock, "Anti-Gay Initiatives: A Call for Heightened Judicial Scrutiny," *UCLA Law Review* 41 (1993): 157, n. 17.

64. For historical support of the idea of Satan to condemn Jewish unbelief and the analogy of such scapegoating to homophobia, see Elaine Pagels, *The Origin of Satan* (New York: Random House, 1996), pp. 102–5; on the analogy between anti-Semitism and homophobia in the intolerance of the Christian right, see Herman, *The Antigay Agenda*, pp. 85–86, 125–28.

65. On the argument for toleration, see Richards, *Conscience and the Constitution*, pp. 63–73; see also, in general, Richards, *Toleration and the Constitution*.

66. For citations and commentary, see Richards, *Women, Gays, and the Constitution*, 402–3, 419.

67. See *Church of the Lukumi Babalu Aye, Inc. v. City of Hialeah*, 508 U.S. 520 (1993) (law forbidding animal sacrifice by the Santeria religion held violative of neutrality required in state burdens on religious practices by free-exercise clause).

68. See, in general, Richards, *Toleration and the Constitution*, pp. 146–62.

69. See *Sherbert v. Verner*, 374 U.S. 398 (1963), whose authority was reaffirmed in *Employment Div. Ore. Dept. of Human Res. v. Smith*, 494 U.S. 872 (1990).

70. The imagined case is thus even worse than *Church of the Lukumi Babalu Aye, Inc. v. City of Hialeah*, in which the religion of Santeria was not specifically named in the statute found, on analysis, unconstitutionally to be directed against that religious group.

71. "Heresy trials are foreign to our Constitution" (Douglas, writing for the Court), *United States v. Ballard*, 322 U.S. 78, 86 (1944). On the unconstitutionality of blasphemy prosecutions under current American law of free speech and religious liberty, see Leonard W. Levy, *Blasphemy: Verbal Offense Against the Sacred from Moses to Salman Rushdie* (New York: Knopf, 1993), pp. 522–33, commenting, inter alia, on *Burstyn v. Wilson*, 343 U.S. 495 (1952) (censorship of movie, as sacrilege, held unconstitutional).

72. On the role that anti-Semitic ideology, in fact, implicitly plays in the homophobia of the Christian right, see Herman, *The Antigay Agenda*, pp. 85–86, 116–28. On the historical background of such intolerance in ideas of Satan as the cause of Jewish unbelief and the analogy to contemporary homophobia, see Pagels, *The Origin of Satan*, pp. 102–5.

73. Throughout the Middle Ages, homosexuals were prosecuted as heretics and often burned at the stake on that ground. See Derrick S. Bailey, *Homosexuality and the Western Christian Tradition* (New York: Longmans, Green, 1955), p. 135. "Buggery," one of the names for homosexual acts, derives from a corruption of the name of one heretical group alleged to engage in homosexual practices. See ibid., pp. 141, 148–49. For a modern use of the idea of treason in this context, see Patrick Devlin, *The Enforcement of Morals* (London: Oxford University Press, 1965), pp. 1–25. For rebuttal, see H. L. A. Hart, *Law, Liberty, and Morality* (Palo Alto, Calif.: Stanford University Press, 1963); Hart, "Social Solidarity and the Enforcement of Morals," *University of Chicago Law Review* 35 (1967): 1.

74. The original Kinsey estimate that about 4 percent of males are exclusively homosexual throughout their lives is confirmed by comparable European studies. See Paul H. Gebhard, "Incidence of Overt Homosexuality in the United States and Western Europe," in J. M. Livingood, ed., *National Institute of Mental Health Task Force on Homosexuality* (Washington, D.C.: U.S. Government Printing Office, 1972), pp. 22–29. The incidence figure remains stable, though many European countries do not apply the criminal penalty to consensual sex acts of the kind here under discussion. See Walter Barnett, *Sexual Freedom and the Constitution* (Albuquerque: University of New Mexico Press, 1973), p. 293. Recent surveys indicate that as little as 2.8 percent of the population identify themselves as gay and less than half that number as lesbian. See Robert T. Michael, John H. Gagnon, Edward O. Laumann, and Gina Kolata, *Sex in America: A Definitive Survey* (Boston: Little, Brown, 1994), p. 176.

75. For a good review of the historical background, see Lawrence J. Korb, "The President, the Congress, and the Pentagon: Obstacles to Implementing the 'Don't Ask, Don't Tell' Policy," in Gregory M. Herek, Jared B. Jobe, and Ralph M. Carney, eds., *Out in Force: Sexual Orientation and the Military* (Chicago: University of Chicago Press, 1996), pp. 290–301.

76. The second grounds is now written: "(2) That the member has stated that he or she is a homosexual or bisexual, or words to that effect, unless there is a further finding, made and approved in accordance with procedures set forth in the regulations, that the member has demonstrated that he or she is not a person who

engages in, or attempts to engage in, has a propensity to engage in, or intends to engage in homosexual acts," 10 U.S.C. sec. 654(b).

77. See DoD Directive 1332.14, Encl. 3, pt. 1, at H.1b(2).

78. See Guidelines for Fact-Finding into Homosexual Conduct, Encl. 4 to DoD Directive 1332.14, Enlisted Administrative Separations, and Encl. 8 to DoD Directive 1332.30, Separations of Regular Commissioned Officers, News Release 605-93, Office of Assistant Secretary of Defense (Public Affairs), Washington, D.C. 20231, December 22, 1993, p. 4-4.

79. See DoD Directive 1304.26, Encl. 1, at B.8.a.

80. See James M. McPherson, *The Struggle for Equality: Abolitionists and the Negro in the Civil War and Reconstruction* (Princeton, N.J.: Princeton University Press, 1964), pp. 192–220.

81. See David Herbert Donald, *Lincoln* (New York: Simon and Schuster, 1995), pp. 166–67, 343–44, 346–48, 396–97.

82. For an important recent study of Jefferson and his racist legacy to America, see Paul Finkelman, *Slavery and the Founders: Race and Liberty in the Age of Jefferson* (Armonk, N.Y.: M. E. Sharpe, 1996), pp. 105–67.

83. See McPherson, *The Struggle for Equality,* pp. 193–97.

84. See ibid., pp. 197–220.

85. See Donald, *Lincoln,* pp. 430, 456–57, 526–27, 556.

86. See Donald G. Nieman, *Promises to Keep: African-Americans and the Constitutional Order, 1776 to the Present* (New York: Oxford University Press, 1991), pp. 139–42; Michael R. Kauth and Dan Landis, "Applying Lessons Learned from Minority Integration in the Military," in Gregory M. Herek, Jared B. Jobe, Ralph M. Carney, eds., *Out in Force: Sexual Orientation and the Military* (Chicago: University of Chicago Press, 1996), pp. 86–105.

87. On the relevance of this experience to the integration of gays and lesbians into the military, see Kauth and Landis, "Applying Lessons Learned from Minority Integration in the Military."

88. See *Rostker v. Goldberg,* 453 U.S. 57 (1981).

89. See Jean Bethke Elshtain, *Women and War* (New York: Basic Books, 1987).

90. See, in general, Presidential Commission on the Assignment of Women in the Armed Forces, *Women in Combat: Report to the President* (Washington, D.C.: Brassey's, 1991) (hereafter *Women in Combat*); Nancy Loring Goldman, *Female Soldiers—Combatants or Noncombatants?* (Westport, Conn.: Greenwood Press, 1982). For general skepticism about service of women in the military, see Brian Mitchell, *Weak Link: The Feminization of the American Military* (Washington, D.C.: Regnery Gateway, 1989).

91. *Women in Combat,* pp. 24–27.

92. Ibid., pp. 28–30.

93. Ibid., pp. 31–33.

94. See *United States v. Virginia,* 116 S. Ct. 2264 (1996).

95. Ibid., pp. 2280–84.

96. Ibid., p. 2280.

97. Ibid.

98. Ibid., p. 2281.

99. Ibid., pp. 2281–87.

100. The Court indeed cited *Sweatt v. Painter,* 339 U.S. 629 (1950) (admitting African Americans to University of Texas Law School) as a relevant analogy.

101. For an important exploration of this theme in terms of a normative argument

for rights of resistance, by battered women, to violence from their spouses, see Jane Maslow Cohen, "Regimes of Private Tyranny: What Do They Mean to Morality and for the Criminal Law?" *University of Pittsburgh Law Review* 57 (1996): 757.

102. See Elshtain, *Women and War,* p. 244.

103. For a useful overview of these changes, see Madeline Morris, "By Force of Arms: Rape, War and Military Culture," *Duke Law Journal* 45 (1996): 732–38. For a recent expression of doubt by an anthropologist, see Anna Simons, "In War, Let Men Be Men," *New York Times,* April 23, 1997, p. A23.

104. On the parallel to African American integration, see Kauth and Landis, "Applying Lessons Learned from Minority Integration in the Military"; on the parallel to the integration of women, see Patricia J. Thomas and Marie D. Thomas, "Integration of Women in the Military: Parallels to the Progress of Homosexuals?" in Gregory M. Herek, Jared B. Jobe, and Ralph M. Carney, eds., *Out in Force: Sexual Orientation and the Military* (Chicago: University of Chicago Press, 1996), pp. 65–85.

105. See Paul A. Gade, David R. Segal, and Edgar M. Johnson, "The Experience of Foreign Militaries," in Gregory M. Herek, Jared B. Jobe, and Ralph M. Carney, eds., *Out in Force: Sexual Orientation and the Military* (Chicago: University of Chicago Press, 1996), pp. 106–30.

106. See Paul Koegel, "Lessons Learned from the Experience of Domestic Police and Fire Departments," in Gregory M. Herek, Jared B. Jobe, and Ralph M. Carney, eds., *Out in Force: Sexual Orientation and the Military* (Chicago: University of Chicago Press, 1996), pp. 131–56.

107. For discussion of how such policy changes should be understood and implemented, see Gail L. Zellman, "Implementing Policy Changes in Large Organizations: The Case of Gays and Lesbians in the Military," in Gregory M. Herek, Jared B. Jobe, and Ralph M. Carney, eds., *Out in Force: Sexual Orientation and the Military* (Chicago: University of Chicago Press, 1996), pp. 266–89; on the relevance of unit cohesion, properly analyzed, see Robert J. MacCoun, "Sexual Orientation and Military Cohesion: A Critical Review of the Evidence," in Gregory M. Herek, Jared B. Jobe, and Ralph M. Carney, eds., *Out in Force: Sexual Orientation and the Military* (Chicago: University of Chicago Press, 1996), pp. 157–76.

108. See, in general, Allan Berube, *Coming Out Under Fire: The History of Gay Men and Women in World War Two* (New York: Free Press, 1990).

109. See, in general, ibid.; Randy Shilts, *Conduct Unbecoming: Gays and Lesbians in the U.S. Military* (New York: St. Martin's Press, 1993).

110. See, in general, Berube, *Coming Out Under Fire.*

111. See, for relevant studies, Janet Lever and David E. Kanouse, "Sexual Orientation and Proscribed Sexual Behaviors," in Gregory M. Herek, Jared B. Jobe, and Ralph M. Carney, *Out in Force: Sexual Orientation and the Military* (Chicago: University of Chicago Press, 1996), pp. 15–38, at p. 22 (gay men); Thomas and Thomas, "Integration of Women in the Military: Parallels to the Progress of Homosexuals?" p. 72 (lesbians).

112. See, for example, *Watkins v. United States Army,* 837 F. 2d 1428 (9th Cir. 1988) (regulation barring gays violates equal protection by discriminating on basis of homosexual orientation); cf. *Watkins v. United States Army,* 875 F. 2d 699 (9th Cir. en banc 1989) (army estopped from barring soldier's enlistment solely because of his acknowledged homosexuality); *Cammermeyer v. Aspin,* 850 F. Supp. 910 (W. D. Wash. 1994) (National Guard officer's discharge for sexual orientation violated equal protection); *Pruitt v. Cheney,* 963 F. 2d 1160 (9th Cir. 1992) (discharged rev-

erend's First Amendment rights not violated but did state an equal-protection claim [discrimination on grounds of sexual orientation] on which relief could be granted, so case remanded to district court); *Dahl v. Secretary of U.S. Navy,* 830 F. Supp. 1319 (E.D. Cal. 1993) (homosexual exclusion policy violated equal protection in that it could not be based on anything but illegitimate prejudice).

113. See *Able v. United States,* 880 F. Supp. 968 (E.D.N.Y. 1995), at 974–75, *rev'd Able v. United States,* 1996 WL 391210 (2nd Cir.).

114. See *Able v. United States,* 1996 WL 391210 (2nd Cir.) (speech restriction of the policy not unconstitutional but remanded for consideration of constitutionality of act restriction of policy and reconsideration of speech restriction in light of that analysis); *Thomasson v. Perry,* 80 F. 3d 915 (4th Cir. 1996) ("Don't Ask, Don't Tell" policy subject to rational basis; there is no fundamental right to engage in homosexual acts, and there is legitimate interest in preventing them); *Philips v. Perry,* 1997 U.S. App. LEXIS 2646 (9th Cir.) (policy, including restrictions on speech, has adequate basis in prohibiting sex acts).

115. See *Able v. United States,* 1996 WL 391210 (2nd Cir.), p. 13, citing *City of Renton v. Playtime Theatres, Inc.,* 475 U.S. 41 (1986) (scattering zoning of adult theater held constitutional).

116. See *Thomasson v. Perry,* 80 F. 3d 915 (4th Cir. 1996), at 930, citing *Price Waterhouse v. Hopkins,* 490 U.S. 228 (1989) (discriminatory words may be basis for Title VII action) and *R.A.V. v. City of St. Paul,* 505 U.S. 377 (1992) (sexually derogatory fighting words may produce violation of Title IV).

117. See *Miller v. California,* 413 U.S. 15 (1973).

118. See *Chaplinsky v. New Hampshire,* 315 U.S. 568 (1942).

119. See *Philips v. Perry,* p. *52.

120. For support for this interpretation, see Theodore R. Sarbin, "The Deconstruction of Stereotypes: Homosexuals and Military Policy," in Gregory M. Herek, Jared B. Jobe, and Ralph M. Carney, eds., *Out in Force: Sexual Orientation and the Military* (Chicago: University of Chicago Press, 1996), pp. 177–96, at p. 181.

121. See, for an illuminating treatment of this issue, MacCoun, "Sexual Orientation and Military Cohesion: A Critical Review of the Evidence."

122. See Thomas and Thomas, "Integration of Women in the Military: Parallels to the Progress of Homosexuals?"; Kauth and Landis, "Applying Lessons Learned from Minority Integration in the Military."

123. See Gade, Segal, and Johnson, "The Experience of Foreign Militaries"; Koegel, "Lessons Learned from the Experience of Domestic Police and Fire Departments."

124. See, for an illuminating treatment of this issue, Lois Shawver, "Sexual Modesty, the Etiquette of Disregard, and the Question of Gays and Lesbians in the Military," in Gregory M. Herek, Jared B. Jobe, and Ralph M. Carney, eds., *Out in Force: Sexual Orientation and the Military* (Chicago: University of Chicago Press, 1996), pp. 226–46.

125. See *Thomasson v. Perry,* pp. 921–26; *Able v. United States,* 1996 WL 391210 (2nd Cir.), pp. 11–12; *Philips v. Perry,* pp. *13–*20 (Rymer, J.), *30–*39 (Noonan, J., concurring).

126. See *Rostker v. Goldberg* (women may constitutionally be excluded from requirement to register for draft).

127. See *Craig v. Boren* (intermediate-level standard of review applicable to gender-based classification, in age at which beer may be sold to men and women, and classification found unconstitutional).

128. See *United States v. Virginia*.

129. A different, perhaps closer case would be posed by a neutral military regulation requiring uniform dress regulations barring the wearing of headgear indoors (forbidding the wearing of a yarmulke by an Orthodox Jew). See *Goldman v. Weinberger*, 475 U.S. 503 (1986) (regulation held constitutional against free-exercise challenge). Even *Goldman* may be a doubtful constitutional result, as Congress apparently believed in reversing it. See 10 U.S.C. sec. 774 (1988) (granting relief from the regulation).

CHAPTER 9

1. See *Baehr v. Lewin*, 74 Haw. 645, 852 P. 2d 44 (1993).

2. *Baker v. State of Vermont*, 170 Vt. 194, 744 A. 2d 864 (Vt. 1999).

3. See *Goodridge v. Department of Public Health*, 440 Mass. 309, 798 N.E. 2d 941 (2003).

4. See 1 U.S.C.A. sec. 7, 28 U.S.C.A. sec. 1738C, as amended by Congress on September 21, 1996, PL 104–199, 110 Stat. 2419.

5. See Katherine Q. Seeyle and Janet Elder, "Strong Support Is Found for Ban on Gay Marriage," *New York Times*, December 21, 2003, p. A1 (discussing public and presidential support for a constitutional amendment).

6. See, for example, *Dean v. District of Columbia*, 653 A. 2d 307 (D.C. 1995) (District of Columbia marriage law prohibits clerk from issuing marriage license to same-sex couple and does not unlawfully discriminate against couples under D.C. Human Rights Act or U.S. Constitution); *DeSanto v. Barnsley*, 328 Pa. Super. Ct. 181, 476 A. 2d 952 (1984) (man could not seek divorce from other man because same-sex common-law marriages are not permitted in Pennsylvania); *Singer v. Hara*, 11 Wash. Ct. App. 247, 522 P. 2d 1187 (1974) (statutory prohibition of same-sex marriage not violative of Washington Equal Rights Amendment); *Jones v. Hallahan*, 501 Ky. Ct. App. S.W. 2d 588 (1973) (same-sex couple incapable of obtaining marriage license because same-sex marriage would not be a marriage); *Baker v. Nelson*, 291 Minn. 310, 191 N.W. 2d 185 (1971) (same-sex couple not permitted to marry and denial not violative of constitutional protections); *Anonymous v. Anonymous*, 67 Misc. 2d 982, 325 N.Y. Sup. Ct. 2d 499 (1971) (marriage between males a nullity despite fact husband thought wife was a female at time of marriage and she subsequently underwent reassignment surgery). But see *M.T. v. J.T.*, 140 N.J. Super. Ct. 77, 355 A. 2d 204 (1976) (absent fraud, man not allowed to void marriage to postoperative transsexual female); *In re Matter of Marley*, 1996 Del. Super. Ct. WL 280890 (1996).

7. See *Lilly v. City of Minneapolis*, Minn. Dist. Ct. WL 315620 (1994) (registered domestic partners are not spousal dependants for purposes of extending employee insurance coverage).

8. See *In re Matter of Cooper*, 187 A.D. 2d 128, 592 N.Y. App. Div. 2d 797 (1993) (surviving partner of same-sex relationship not entitled to spousal right of election against decedent's will).

9. See *Adams v. Howerton*, 673 F. 2d 1036 (9th Cir. 1982) (an Australian and an American male citizen who had been married by minister in Colorado not married for purposes of Immigration and Nationality Act).

10. See *McConnell v. Nooner*, 547 F. 2d 54 (8th Cir. 1976) (spousal veteran benefits denied to same-sex partner of veteran who had gone through same-sex marriage ceremony).

11. See William N. Eskridge, Jr., *The Case for Same-Sex Marriage: From Sexual Liberty to Civilized Commitment* (New York: Free Press, 1996).

12. See Mark Strasser, *Legallywed: Same-Sex Marriage and the Constitution* (Ithaca, N.Y.: Cornell University Press, 1997).

13. See Evan Gerstmann, *Same-Sex Marriage and the Constitution* (Cambridge: Cambridge University Press, 2004).

14. For example, as Eskridge argued, having children is not a constitutionally reasonable requirement for heterosexual marriage and, therefore, not having children could not be a compelling reason for excluding homosexuals from the institution. See Eskridge, *The Case for Same-Sex Marriage*, pp. 127–52. See, for judicial support of the premise of Eskridge's argument, *Turner v. Safley,* 482 U.S. 78 (1987) (state bar to marriage by prison inmates, on ground no opportunity sexually to consummate marriage and thus not able to procreate, held unconstitutional).

15. See *Goodridge v. Department of Public Health*, p. 948.

16. *Lawrence v. Texas,* 539 U.S. 558, 123 S. Ct. 2472 (2003), p. 2496 (footnotes and citations omitted).

17. Ibid., p. 2482.

18. Ibid., p. 2484.

19. See Yuval Merin, *Equality for Same-Sex Couples: The Legal Recognition of Gay Partnerships in Europe and the United States* (Chicago: University of Chicago Press, 2002), pp. 278–307.

20. See, on this point, Richards, *Women, Gays, and the Constitution: The Grounds for Feminism and Gay Rights in Culture and Law* (Chicago: University of Chicago Press, 1998), pp. 55–56.

21. See ibid., pp. 117–24.

22. See James Baldwin, *No Name in the Street* (New York: Dell, 1972), p. 63.

23. On this point, see Richards, *Women, Gays, and the Constitution,* pp. 141, 442.

24. On this point, see ibid., pp. 155–82.

25. See, on this point, Gregory M. Herek, "Why Tell If You're Not Asked? Self-Disclosure, Intergroup Contact, and Heterosexuals' Attitudes Toward Lesbians and Gay Men," in Gregory M. Herek, Jared. B. Jobe, and Ralph M. Carney, eds., *Out in Force: Sexual Orientation and the Military* (Chicago: University of Chicago Press, 1996), pp. 203, 207–8.

26. *Loving v. Virginia,* 388 U.S. 1 (1967) (striking down Virginia's laws banning interracial marriage).

27. See *Zablocki v. Redhail,* 434 U.S. 374 (1978) (striking down a Wisconsin statute that prohibited a person under a court order to support minor children from marrying without judicial permission on the ground that the means selected by the state to pursue legitimate interests of child support unduly abridged the basic right to marry).

28. *Turner v. Safley,* 482 U.S. 78 (1987) (Missouri state prison regulation forbidding inmates from marrying under most circumstances is unconstitutional abridgment of basic right to marry).

29. *Perez v. Sharp,* 32 Cal. 2d 711, 198 P. 2d 17 (1948).

30. *Loving v. Virginia.*

31. *Goodridge v. Department of Public Health*, p. 958.

32. See John Finnis, "Law, Morality, and 'Sexual Orientation,'" *Notre Dame Journal of Law, Ethics, and Public Policy* 9 (1995): 11.

33. See Hadley Arkes, "Testimony on the Defense of Marriage Act, 1996," Judiciary Committee, House of Representatives, 1996 WL 246693 (F.D.C.H.), p. 11;

see also Hadley Arkes, "Questions of Principle, Not Predictions," *Georgia Law Journal* 84 (1995): 321; and, to similar effect, Robert P. George and Gerard V. Bradley, "Marriage and the Liberal Imagination," *Georgia Law Journal* 84 (1995): 301. For cogent criticism, see Stephen Macedo, "Homosexuality and the Conservative Mind," *Georgia Law Journal* 84 (1995): 261; and "Reply to Critics," *Georgia Law Journal* 84 (1995): 329.

34. *Turner v. Safley,* 482 U.S. 78 (1987) (denial of marriage right to prison inmates, on ground no opportunity sexually to consummate marriage and thus not able to procreate, held unconstitutional). For discussion, see Eskridge, *The Case for Same-Sex Marriage,* pp. 128–30.

35. See Gerstmann, *Same-Sex Marriage and the Constitution,* p. 95.

36. Arguments of such sorts are based on appeals to nature of the sort that David Hume considered for similar reasons an illegitimate basis for public laws, including laws prohibiting suicide: "'Tis impious, says the *French* superstition to inoculate for the small-pox, or usurp the business of providence, by voluntarily producing distempers and maladies. 'Tis impious, says the modern *European* superstition, to put a period to our own life, and thereby rebel against our creator. And why not impious, say I, to build houses, cultivate the ground, and sail upon the ocean? In all these actions, we employ our powers of mind and body to produce some innovation in the course of nature, and in none of them do we any more. They are all of them, therefore, equally innocent or equally criminal." David Hume, "Of Suicide," *Essays Moral Political and Literary,* ed. by Eugene F. Miller (Indianapolis, Ind.: LibertyClassics, 1985 [1777]), p. 585.

37. Ibid.

38. See, in general, Anthony Giddens, *The Transformation of Intimacy: Sexuality, Love, and Eroticism in Modern Societies* (Cambridge: Polity, 1992); John D'Emilio and Estelle B. Freedman, *Intimate Matters: A History of Sexuality in America* (New York: Harper and Row, 1988), pp. 239–360; Barbara Ehrenreich, Elizabeth Hess, and Gloria Jacobs, *Remaking Love: The Feminization of Sex* (New York: Anchor, 1986); Ann Snitow, Christine Stansell, and Sharon Thompson, eds., *Powers of Desire: The Politics of Sexuality* (New York: Monthly Review Press, 1983); Carole S. Vance, ed., *Pleasure and Danger: Exploring Female Sexuality* (Boston: Routledge and Kegan Paul, 1984).

39. See Mark D. Jordan, *The Invention of Sodomy in Christian Theology* (Chicago: University of Chicago Press, 1997), p. 174.

40. Mark Jordan observed: "The Christian criterion of fertility, of parenting, of filiation, is not bodily. That much was worked out with painstaking care in the early Trinitarian debates," ibid., p. 174.

41. For important studies of the differences between human and animal sexuality, see Clellan S. Ford and Frank A. Beach, *Patterns of Sexual Behavior* (New York: Harper and Row, 1951); Irenaus Eibl-Eibesfeldt, *Love and Hate: The Natural History of Behavior Patterns,* trans. by Geoffrey Strachan (New York: Holt, Rinehart, and Winston, 1971). The insight is also central to Freud's exploration of the imaginative role of sexuality in human personality; see Sigmund Freud, "'Civilized' Sexual Morality and Modern Nervous Illness," *Standard Edition of the Complete Psychological Works of Sigmund Freud,* vol. 9, ed. and trans. by James Strachey (London: Hogarth Press, 1959), pp. 181, 187: "The sexual instinct . . . is probably more strongly developed in man than in most of the higher animals; it is certainly more constant, since it has almost entirely overcome the periodicity to which it is tied in animals. It places extraordinarily large amounts of force at the disposal of civilized

activity, and it does this in virtue of its especially marked characteristic of being able to displace its aim without materially diminishing its intensity. This capacity to exchange its originally sexual aim for another one, which is no longer sexual but which is physically related to the first aim, is called the capacity for sublimation."

42. See Andrew Koppelman, "The Miscegenation Analogy: Sodomy Laws as Sex Discrimination," *Yale Law Journal* 98 (1988): 145.

43. See ibid., pp. 159–60.

44. Germain Grisez, *The Way of the Lord Jesus, Volume Two: Living a Christian Life* (Quincy, Ill.: Franciscan Press, 1993), p. 570.

45. See, for fuller development of this critique of Grisez, Gareth Moore, *A Question of Truth: Christianity and Homosexuality* (London: Continuum, 2003), pp. 253–73.

46. See George Will, "Discussing Homosexual Marriage," 1996 WL 5541151, reprinted from *Washington Post*, Sunday, May 19, 1996.

47. See William Bennett, "Leave Marriage Alone (Legalizing Same-Sex Marriage Would Tamper with Centuries of Tradition and Demean the Institution of Marriage)," 1996 WL 9471473, reprinted from *Newsweek*, June 3, 1996.

48. See, for example, Andrew Sullivan, "Here Comes the Groom: A (Conservative) Case for Gay Marriage," in Bruce Bayer, ed., *Beyond Queer: Challenging Gay Left Orthodoxy* (New York: Free Press, 1996), pp. 252–58. See also Jonathan Rauch, "For Better or Worse?" *New Republic*, May 6, 1996, pp. 18–23.

49. See Eskridge, *The Case for Same-Sex Marriage*. For a similar argument by a gay man defending the humane need within gay and lesbian culture for institutional incentives for fidelity, see Gabriel Rotello, *Sexual Ecology: AIDS and the Destiny of Gay Men* (New York: Dutton, 1997), pp. 233–61.

50. But for an argument that some forms of polygamy, if based on modern values giving "perfect freedom and independence to women in their relation to men," would be consistent with rights-based feminism, see Edward Carpenter, *Love's Coming of Age: A Series of Papers on the Relations of the Sexes* (New York: Vanguard Press, 1926 [1896]), p. 134. It would, in this view, be a factual question whether any such form of polygamy could reasonably be proposed in contemporary circumstances. Many advocates of gay marriage might reasonably deny, consistent with Nancy Rosenblum's view cited in the text, that it could be. See Eskridge, *The Case for Same-Sex Marriage*, pp. 148–49.

51. See Nancy L. Rosenblum, "Democratic Sex: *Reynolds v. U.S.*, Sexual Relations, and Community," in David M. Estlund and Martha C. Nussbaum, eds., *Sex, Preference, and Family: Essays on Law and Nature* (New York: Oxford University Press, 1997), p. 80.

52. For the debate in social science and law surrounding what this development factually comes to and what normative sense we should make of it, see Lenore J. Weitzman, *The Divorce Revolution: The Unexpected Social and Economic Consequences for Women and Children in America* (New York: Free Press, 1985); Martha Albertson Fineman, *The Illusion of Equality: The Rhetoric and Reality of Divorce Reform* (Chicago: University of Chicago Press, 1991); Ira Mark Ellman, Paul M. Kurtz, and Katharine T. Bartlett, eds., *Family Law: Cases, Text, Problems,* 2nd ed. (Charlottesville, Va.: The Michie Company, 1991), pp. 292–301; Howard S. Erlanger, ed., "Review Symposium on Weitzman's *Divorce Revolution,*" *American Bar Foundation Research Journal* 4 (1986): 759–97; James B. McLindon, "Separate But Unequal: The Economic Disaster of Divorce of Women and Children," *Family Law Quarterly* 21 (1987): 351–409; Greg J. Duncan and Saul D. Hoffman, "A Reconsideration of

the Economic Consequences of Marital Dissolution," *Demography* 22 (1985): 485; Judith A. Seltzer and Irwin Garfinkel, "Inequality in Divorce Settlements: An Investigation of Property Settlements and Child Support Awards," *Social Science Research* 19 (1990): 82; Susan Moller Okin, "Economic Equality After Divorce," *Dissent* (summer 1991): 383; Martha A. Fineman, "Implementing Equality: Ideology, Contradiction and Social Change, A Study of Rhetoric and Results in the Regulation of the Consequences of Divorce," *Wisconsin Law Review* (1983): 789; Jane Rutherford, "Duty in Divorce: Shared Income as a Path of Equality," *Fordham Law Review* 58 (1990): 539; Joan Williams, "Is Coverture Dead? Beyond a New Theory of Alimony," *Georgia Law Journal* 82 (1994): 2227; Isabel Marcus, "Locked In and Locked Out: Reflections on the History of Divorce Law Reform in New York State," *Buffalo Law Review* 37 (1989): 375; Marsha Garrison, "Good Intentions Gone Awry: The Impact of New York's Equitable Distribution Law on Divorce Outcomes," *Brooklyn Law Review* 57 (1991): 621.

53. It is a different question whether such principles would justify, in contemporary circumstances, the use of criminal law against polygamous unions (in particular, such unions undertaken in accord with religious conscience). Legitimate state purposes, which might be sufficiently powerful to disallow the extension of marriage to such unions, might not be sufficient to justify the use of criminal sanctions in this arena for the same reasons that one might reasonably believe adultery should no longer be condemned by criminal law (such laws inflict a preponderance of harm over good in areas better regulated or addressed in other ways).

54. See John Stuart Mill and Harriet Taylor Mill, *Essays on Sex Equality,* ed. by Alice S. Ross (Chicago: University of Chicago Press, 1970).

55. See John Stuart Mill, *On Liberty,* ed. by Alburey Castell (New York: Appleton-Century-Crofts, 1947 [1859]), pp. 92–94.

56. Richard A. Epstein, "Live and Let Live," *Wall Street Journal,* July 13, 2004, p. A14.

57. See, in general, Edward O. Laumann, John H. Gagnon, Robert T. Michael, and Stuart Michaels, *The Organization of Sexuality: Sexual Practices in the United States* (Chicago: University of Chicago Press, 1994), pp. 172–224.

58. See 1 U.S.C.A. sec. 7, 28 U.S.C.A. sec. 1738C, as amended by Congress on September 21, 1996, PL 104–199, 110 Stat. 2419.

59. See Discussion Draft, May 2, 1996, H.R. 3396, 104th Congress, 2d Session.

60. The provision reads as follows: "Full faith and credit shall be given in each State to the public acts, records, and judicial proceedings of every other State. And the Congress may by general laws prescribe the manner in which such acts, records, and proceedings shall be proved, and the effect thereof." Art. IV, sec. 1, U.S. Constitution.

61. See Laurence H. Tribe, "Toward a Less Perfect Union," *New York Times,* May 26, 1966, E-11; letter of Laurence Tribe to Sen. Edward M. Kennedy, 142 Congressional Record S5931-01, pp. *S5932-33. See also Mark Strasser, *"Loving the Romer Out for Baehr:* On Acts in Defense of Marriage and the Constitution," *University of Pittsburgh Law Review* 58 (1997): 279.

CHAPTER 10

1. See *Doe v. Commonwealth's Attorney,* 425 U.S. 901 (1976), *aff'g mem.* 403 F. Supp. 1100 (E.D. Va. 1975).

2. *Bowers v. Hardwick,* 478 U.S. 186 (1986).

3. *Lawrence v. Texas*, 539 U.S. 558, 123 S. Ct. 2472 (2003).

4. For defense of this review, see David A. J. Richards, *Foundations of American Constitutionalism* (New York: Oxford University Press, 1989).

5. See, on this point, Yuval Merin, *Equality for Same-Sex Couples: The Legal Recognition of Gay Partnerships in Europe and the United States* (Chicago: University of Chicago Press, 2002).

6. See, on this point, William N. Eskridge, Jr., "United States: *Lawrence v. Texas* and the Imperative of Comparative Constitutionalism," *International Journal of Constitutional Law*, 2, 3 (July 2004): p. 560.

7. See, for critical discussion of these scholars, Evan Gerstmann, *Same-Sex Marriage and the Constitution* (Cambridge: Cambridge University Press, 2004), pp. 194–210.

8. See, in particular, Carol Gilligan, *The Birth of Pleasure: A New Map of Love* (New York: Vintage Books, 2003).

9. For fuller discussion of my father's voice and its role in my life, see David A. J. Richards, *Tragic Manhood and Democracy: Verdi's Voice and the Powers of Musical Art* (Brighton, U.K.: Sussex Academic Press, 2004).

10. See David A. J. Richards, *Disarming Manhood: Roots of Ethical Resistance in Jesus, Garrison, Tolstoy, Gandhi, King, and Churchill* (Athens: Ohio University Press, 2005 [forthcoming]).

11. See, on this point, Gilligan, *The Birth of Pleasure*, pp. 4–5.

12. See J. G. Peristiany, ed., *Honour and Shame: The Values of Mediterranean Society* (Chicago: University of Chicago Press, 1966), pp. 66–67.

13. See ibid., pp. 253–54, 256–57.

14. See ibid., pp. 42–53.

15. See David I. Kertzer, *Sacrifices for Honor: Italian Infant Abandonment and the Politics of Reproductive Control* (Boston: Beacon Press, 1993).

16. See David D. Gilmore, ed., *Honour and Shame and the Unity of the Mediterranean* (Washington, D.C.: American Anthropological Association, 1987), p. 110.

17. See Kertzer, *Sacrifices for Honor*, p. 125.

18. Ibid., p. 56.

19. Ibid., pp. 107, 122.

20. Ibid., p. 148.

21. See, on these points, Gilligan, *The Birth of Pleasure*, pp. 14–17, 89–91, 161–63, 178–79, 204.

22. I explore both this ethics and its associated moral psychology in David A. J. Richards, *A Theory of Reasons for Action* (Oxford: Clarendon Press, 1971).

23. Virginia Woolf, *Three Guineas* (San Diego: Harcourt Brace and Company, 1938), p. 102.

24. Sara Ruddick, *Maternal Thinking: Toward a Politics of Peace* (Boston: Beacon Press, 1989), p. 38.

25. Ibid., p. 41.

26. See ibid., pp. 119–23.

27. See, on this phenomenon in infancy, Daniel N. Stern, *The Interpersonal World of the Infant: A View from Psychoanalysis and Developmental Psychology* (New York: Basic Books, 1985).

28. See Ruddick, *Maternal Thinking*, pp. 148–51.

29. Ibid., p. 166.

30. Ibid., pp. 182–83.

31. Ibid., pp. 169–70.

32. See ibid., p. 176.

33. Such an attempt might show itself in reading this alternative developmental story as a narrative of the etiology of homosexuality. In my view, it would be a developmental strength in gay men if their development included a maternal care like that described by Ruddick, but it is clear that not all gay men come from such a background, and it is certainly quite clear that many straight men also profit from such backgrounds (as we see in Garrison, Tolstoy, Gandhi, King, and Churchill). For one plausible view of the character of gay men's close relations to their mothers, see Richard Green, *The "Sissy Boy Syndrome" and the Development of Homosexuality* (New Haven, Conn.: Yale University Press, 1987).

34. William Ian Miller, *Bloodtaking and Peacemaking: Feud, Law, and Society in Saga Iceland* (Chicago: University of Chicago Press, 1990), p. 305.

35. William Ian Miller, *Humiliation and Other Essays on Honor, Social Discomfort, and Violence* (Ithaca, N.Y.: Cornell University Press, 1993), p. 196.

36. See, in general, Kenneth S. Greenberg, *Honor and Slavery* (Princeton, N.J.: Princeton University Press, 1996); Pieter Spierenburg, *Men and Violence: Gender, Honor, and Rituals in Modern Europe and America* (Columbus: Ohio State University Press, 1998); Richard E. Nisbett and Dov Cohen, *Culture of Honor: The Psychology of Violence in the South* (Boulder, Colo.: Westview Press, 1996).

37. See Joanne B. Freeman, *Affairs of Honor: National Politics in the New Republic* (New Haven, Conn.: Yale University Press, 2001).

38. See Bertram Wyatt-Brown, *Southern Honor: Ethics and Behavior in the Old South* (New York: Oxford University Press, 1982).

39. See James Gilligan, *Violence: Reflections on a National Epidemic* (New York: Vintage Books, 1997).

40. See Chris Hedges, *War Is a Force That Gives Us Meaning* (New York: Public Affairs, 2002); Mark Juergensmeyer, *Terror in the Mind of God: The Global Rise of Religious Violence* (Berkeley: University of California Press, 2000); see also Amin Maalouf, *In the Name of Identity: Violence and the Need to Belong*, trans. by Barbara Bray (New York: Arcade Publishing, 2000); Michael Ignatieff, *The Warrior's Honor: Ethnic War and the Modern Conscience* (New York: Henry Holt, 1997).

41. Carol Gilligan, "Knowing and Not Knowing: Reflections on Manhood," *Psychotherapy and Politics International* 2, 2 (2004): 104.

42. See, for fuller discussion, Richards, *Tragic Manhood and Democracy.*

43. See, in particular, David A. J. Richards, *Women, Gays, and the Constitution: The Grounds for Feminism and Gay Rights in Culture and Law* (Chicago: University of Chicago Press, 1998).

44. See ibid.; David A. J. Richards, *Identity and the Case for Gay Rights: Race, Gender, Religion as Analogies* (Chicago: University of Chicago Press, 1999).

45. I defend this view at length in Richards, *Women, Gays, and the Constitution.*

46. See, for an example of a gay life caught in this transition, James McCourt, *Queer Street: Rise and Fall of an American Culture, 1947–1985* (New York: W. W. Norton, 2003).

47. See ibid.

48. See, for extended arguments in defense of this position, Richards, *Women, Gays, and the Constitution,* pp. 411–57.

49. See H. L. A. Hart, *Law, Liberty, and Morality* (Palo Alto, Calif.: Stanford University Press, 1963).

50. Nicola Lacey, *A Life of H. L. A. Hart: The Nightmare and the Noble Dream* (Oxford: Oxford University Press, 2004).

51. For the reflections of Hart's wife on him, their marriage, and her professional

life, see Jenifer Hart, *Ask Me No More: An Autobiography* (London: Peter Halban, 1998).

52. See Arthur Rimbaud, *Complete Works,* trans. by Paul Schmidt (New York: Perennial Classics, 2000), p. 228.

53. I am indebted for these points to Donald Levy.

54. See, for elaborations of this point in the cases of Gandhi and King, Richards, *Disarming Manhood,* pp. 92–180.

55. For further discussion, see Richards, *Tragic Manhood and Democracy.*

56. See Colm Toibin, *Love in a Dark Time* (New York: Scribner, 2001), pp. 185–213.

57. Ibid., p. 200.

58. See, for a general study of this gender issue in German fascism, Claudia Koonz, *The Nazi Conscience* (Cambridge, Mass.: The Belknap Press at Harvard University Press, 2003); see also Claudia Koonz, *Mothers in the Fatherland: Women, the Family, and Nazi Politics* (New York: St. Martin's Press, 1987).

59. See Robert Conquest, *Stalin: Breaker of Nations* (New York: Penguin, 1991), pp. 163–65.

60. See Walter Laqueur, *The Dream That Failed: Reflections on the Soviet Union* (New York: Oxford University Press, 1994), p. 13.

61. See, on all these points, Francois Furet, *The Passing of an Illusion: The Idea of Communism in the Twentieth Century,* trans. by Deborah Furet (Chicago: University of Chicago Press, 1999).

62. See ibid., pp. 174–75, 178, 189–90.

63. See, on these points, Arthur Koestler, *Darkness at Noon,* trans. by Daphne Hardy (New York: Bantam Books, 1968 [1941]), pp. 124–29, 134–37, 153, 182–85, 189–90, 205.

64. See, on these points, Hedges, *War Is a Force that Gives Us Meaning;* Ignatieff, *The Warrior's Honor;* Maalouf, *In the Name of Identity;* Daniel Pipes, *Militant Islam Reaches America* (New York: W. W. Norton, 2002); Kanan Makiya, *Cruelty and Silence: War, Tyranny, Uprising, and the Arab World* (New York: W. W. Norton, 1993); Avishai Margalit, "The Suicide Bombers," *New York Review of Books,* January 16, 2003, pp. 36–39; Bernard Lewis, *What Went Wrong? Western Impact and Middle Eastern Response* (Oxford: Oxford University Press, 2002).

65. Juergensmeyer, *Terror in the Mind of God,* p. 195.

66. Arundhati Roy, *War Talk* (Cambridge, Mass.: South End Press, 2003), p. 13.

67. See David L. Chappell, *A Stone of Hope: Prophetic Religion and the Death of Jim Crow* (Chapel Hill: University of North Carolina Press, 2004), p. 153.

68. See Roy, *War Talk,* pp. 18–19, 34, 50, 105.

69. See, in general, ibid.

70. See, on Churchill's rather racist way of dismissing the claims of the Palestinians, ibid., p. 58.

71. See, on ways of helping boys and men live outside patriarchy, Terrence Real, *I Don't Want to Talk About It: Overcoming the Secret Legacy of Male Depression* (New York: Fireside, 1997); William Pollack, *Real Boys: Rescuing Our Sons from the Myths of Boyhood* (New York: Henry Holt, 1998).

72. See, for development and support of this claim, Richards, *Women, Gays, and the Constitution,* pp. 297–310.

73. See, for development and support of this claim, ibid., pp. 173–78, 321, 329–30.

74. See, for development and support of this claim, ibid., pp. 317–27.

75. For fuller discussion of this point, see ibid., ch. 4.

76. See, on this point, ibid., pp. 329–30.

77. See, on these points, ibid., pp. 322–23, 326, 331, 358.

78. On Otto Weininger, see ibid., pp. 332–36.

79. See, on this point, ibid., pp. 342–46, 352.

80. See, for further development of this argument, ibid., ch. 6.

81. On "the narcissism of small differences," see Sigmund Freud, *Civilization and Its Discontents, Standard Edition of the Complete Psychological Works of Sigmund Freud*, ed. and trans. by James Strachey (London: Hogarth Press, 1961), vol. 21, p. 114; see also *Moses and Monotheism*, vol. 23 (1964), p. 91.

82. See, on the continuities among heterosexual and homosexual forms of intimacy in the modern world, in general, Anthony Giddens, *The Transformation of Intimacy: Sexuality, Love, and Eroticism in Modern Societies* (Cambridge, U.K.: Polity, 1992); John D'Emilio and Estelle B. Freedman, *Intimate Matters: A History of Sexuality in America* (New York: Harper and Row, 1988), pp. 239–360; Philip Blumstein and Pepper Schwartz, *American Couples* (New York: William Morrow, 1983), pp. 332–545. On declining fertility rates, see Claudia Goldin, *Understanding the Gender Gap: An Economic History of American Women* (New York: Oxford University Press, 1990), pp. 139–42; on childlessness, see, in general, Elaine Tyler May, *Barren in the Promised Land: Childless Americans and the Pursuit of Happiness* (New York: Basic Books, 1995); on rising divorce rates, see Carl N. Degler, *At Odds: Women and the Family in America from the Revolution to the Present* (New York: Oxford University Press, 1980), pp. 165–68, 175–86. See also Barbara Ehrenreich, Elizabeth Hess, and Gloria Jacobs, *Remaking Love: The Feminization of Sex* (New York: Anchor, 1986); Ann Anitow, Christine Stansell, and Sharon Thompson, eds., *Powers of Desire* (New York: Monthly Review Press, 1983); Carol S. Vance, ed., *Pleasure and Danger: Exploring Female Sexuality* (Boston: Routledge and Kegan Paul, 1984).

83. On this point, see Susan Moller Okin, "Sexual Orientation and Gender: Dichotomizing Differences," in David M. Estlund and Martha C. Nussbaum, eds., *Sex, Preference, and Family: Essays on Law and Nature* (New York: Oxford University Press, 1997), pp. 44–59.

84. On the need to make gay love tragic, see the analysis of Toibin, *Love in a Dark Time*, pp. 28, 30, 157, 199–200.

85. See, for development of this point, Richards, *Women, Gays, and the Constitution*, pp. 297–310.

86. See, in general, Susan Faludi, *Backlash: The Undeclared War Against American Women* (New York: Doubleday, 1991); Marilyn French, *The War Against Women* (London: Penguin, 1992).

87. For some sense of the range of such views and their supporting reasons, see Sherrye Henry, *The Deep Divide: Why American Women Resist Equality* (New York: Macmillan, 1994); Elizabeth Fox-Genovese, *"Feminism Is Not the Story of My Life": How Today's Feminist Elite Has Lost Touch with the Real Concerns of Women* (New York: Doubleday, 1996); *Feminism Without Illusions: A Critique of Individualism* (Chapel Hill: University of North Carolina Press, 1991).

88. For the antifeminism of the sectarian hard core, see Didi Herman, *The Antigay Agenda: Orthodox Vision and the Christian Right* (Chicago: University of Chicago Press, 1997), pp. 103–10; for its opposition to the civil rights agenda in general, see ibid., pp. 111–36, 140.

89. On the analogy of such contemporary homophobia to anti-Semitism, see

ibid., pp. 82–91, 125–28; Elaine Pagels, *The Origin of Satan* (New York: Random House, 1996), pp. 102–5. See also, for a useful study of the reactionary populist politics of this group, Chris Bull and John Gallagher, *Perfect Enemies: The Religious Right, the Gay Movement, and the Politics of the 1990's* (New York: Crown Publishers, 1999).

90. See, on this point, Esther Kaplan, "Onward Christian Soldiers: The Religious Right's Sense of Siege Is Fueling a Resurgence," *Nation*, July 5, 2004, pp. 33–36.

91. John Rawls, *Collected Papers,* ed. by Samuel Freeman (Cambridge, Mass.: Harvard University Press, 1999), p. 613.

92. See George M. Marsden, *Fundamentalism and American Culture: The Shaping of Twentieth Century Evangelicalism, 1870–1925* (New York: Oxford University Press, 1980).

93. See Raoul Berger, *Government by Judiciary* (Cambridge, Mass.: Harvard University Press, 1977); *Death Penalties* (Cambridge, Mass.: Harvard University Press, 1982).

94. *Brown v. Board of Education,* 347 U.S. 483 (1954).

95. See Robert H. Bork, *Tradition and Morality in Constitutional Law* (Washington, D.C.: American Enterprise Institute, 1984); "Neutral Principles and Some First Amendment Problems," *Indiana Law Journal* 47 (1971): 9.

96. See Richards, *Foundations of American Constitutionalism.*

97. See, on this point, ibid., pp. 102–5, 131–71.

98. For fuller discussion, see Nicholas Bamforth and David A. J. Richards, *New Natural Law, Sexuality, and Gender: A Defense of Patriarchal Religion?* (work in draft).

99. I am indebted for this point to Carol Gilligan.

100. See *Romer v. Evans,* 116 S. Ct. 1620 (1996).

101. On "the narcissism of small differences," see Freud, *Civilization and Its Discontents,* p. 114; *Moses and Monotheism,* p. 91.

102. Catharine R. Stimpson, "Marry, Marry, Quite Contrary: To Wed Is to Lose One's Precious Distance from Conformity," *Nation*, July 5, 2004, p. 39.

103. Cited in Toibin, *Love in a Dark Time,* p. 191.

104. See, on this point, Susan Moller Okin, *Justice, Gender, and the Family* (New York: Basic Books, 1989).

105. Walt Whitman, "In Paths Untrodden," *Calamus, Walt Whitman: The Complete Poems,* ed. by Francis Murphy (Harmondsworth, Middlesex, England: Penguin, 1975), p. 146.

BIBLIOGRAPHY

Abelove, Henry, Michele Aina Barale, and David M. Halperin, eds. *The Lesbian and Gay Studies Reader.* New York: Routledge, 1993.

Ahlstrom, Sydney E. *A Religious History of the American People.* New Haven, Conn.: Yale University Press, 1972.

Altman, Dennis. *Homosexual Oppression and Liberation.* New York: Avon, 1971.

———. *The Homosexualization of America, the Americanization of the Homosexual.* New York: St. Martin's Press, 1982.

Altman, Dennis, Carole Vance, Martha Vicinus, and Jeffrey Weeks, eds. *Homosexuality, Which Homosexuality? International Conference on Gay and Lesbian Studies.* London: GMP Publishers, 1989.

Amsterdam, Anthony G. "Thurgood Marshall's Image of the Blue-Eyed Child in *Brown.*" *N.Y.U. Law Review* 68 (1993): 226.

Aquinas, Thomas. *On the Truth of the Catholic Faith: Summa Contra Gentiles.* Trans. by Vernon Bourke. New York: Image, 1956.

Arendt, Hannah. *The Origins of Totalitarianism.* New York: Harcourt Brace Jovanovich, 1973.

Arkes, Hadley. "Questions of Principle, Not Predictions." *Georgia Law Journal* 84 (1995): 321.

———. "Testimony on the Defense of Marriage Act, 1996." Judiciary Committee, House of Representatives. 1996 WL 246693 (F.D.C.H.).

Augustine. *The City of God.* Trans. by Henry Bettenson. Harmondsworth, U.K.: Penguin, 1972.

Bacon, Margaret Hope. *Mothers of Feminism: The Story of Quaker Women in America.* San Francisco: Harper and Row, 1989.

Badinter, Elisabeth. *Man/Woman: The One Is the Other.* Trans. by Barbara Wright. London: Collins Harvill, 1989.

———. *On Masculine Identity.* Trans. by Lydia Davis. New York: Columbia University Press, 1995.

Bailey, Derrick S. *Homosexuality and the Western Christian Tradition.* New York: Longmans, Green, 1955.

Baldwin, James. *No Name in the Street.* New York: Dell, 1972.

Bamforth, Nicholas. *Sexuality, Morals and Justice: A Theory of Lesbian and Gay Rights Law.* London: Cassell, 1997.

Barkan, Elazar. *The Retreat of Scientific Racism: Changing Concepts of Race in*

Britain and the United States Between the World Wars. Cambridge: Cambridge University Press, 1992.

Barnett, Walter. *Sexual Freedom and the Constitution.* Albuquerque: University of New Mexico Press, 1973.

Bayer, Bruce, ed. *Beyond Queer: Challenging Gay Left Orthodoxy.* New York: Free Press, 1996.

Beauvoir, Simone de. *The Second Sex.* Trans. by H. M. Parshley. New York: Vintage, 1974 (1953).

Benedict, Ruth. *Race: Science and Politics.* New York: The Viking Press, 1945.

Benjamin, Jessica. *The Bonds of Love: Psychoanalysis, Feminism, and the Problem of Domination.* London: Virgo, 1988.

Bennett, William. "Leave Marriage Alone (Legalizing Same-Sex Marriage Would Tamper with Centuries of Tradition and Demean the Institution of Marriage)." 1996 WL 9471473. Reprinted from *Newsweek,* June 3, 1996.

Bentham, Jeremy. *An Introduction to the Principles of Morals and Legislation.* New York: Hafner Publishing Co., 1963.

———. "Offences Against One's Self: Paederasty" (part 1). *Journal of Homosexuality* 3 (1978): 389; "Jeremy Bentham's Essay on 'Paederasty,'" *Journal of Homosexuality* 4 (1978): 91.

———. *The Rationale of Reward,* cited at: http://jeromekahn123.tripod.com/ utilitarianismtheethicaltheoryforalltimes/id4.html.

Berger, Raoul. *Death Penalties.* Cambridge, Mass.: Harvard University Press, 1982.

———. *Government by Judiciary.* Cambridge, Mass.: Harvard University Press, 1977.

Bersani, Leo. *Homos.* Cambridge, Mass.: Harvard University Press, 1995.

Berube, Allan. *Coming Out Under Fire: The History of Gay Men and Women in World War Two.* New York: Free Press, 1990.

Blackstone, William. *Commentaries on the Laws of England 1765–1769,* vol. 4. Facsimile of first edition ed. by Thomas A. Green. Chicago: University of Chicago Press, 1979.

Blumstein, Philip, and Pepper Schwartz. *American Couples.* New York: William Morrow, 1983.

Boas, Franz. *The Mind of Primitive Man,* rev. ed. Westport, Conn.: Greenwood Press, 1983 (1911).

Bork, Robert H. "Neutral Principles and Some First Amendment Problems." *Indiana Law Journal* 47 (1971): 9.

———. *Tradition and Morality in Constitutional Law.* Washington, D.C.: American Enterprise Institute, 1984.

Boston Lesbian Psychologies Collective. *Lesbian Psychologies: Explorations and Challenges.* Urbana: University of Illinois Press, 1987.

Boswell, John. *Same-Sex Unions in Premodern Europe.* New York: Villard Books, 1994.

Branch, Taylor. *Parting the Waters: Martin Luther King and the Civil Rights Movement, 1954–63.* London: Papermac, 1990.

Braude, Ann. *Radical Spirits: Spiritualism and Women's Rights in Nineteenth-Century America.* Boston: Beacon Press, 1989.

Brown, Peter. *The Body and Society: Men, Women, and Sexual Renunciation in Early Christianity.* New York: Columbia University Press, 1988.

Bull, Chris, and John Gallagher. *Perfect Enemies: The Religious Right, the Gay Movement, and the Politics of the 1990's.* New York: Crown Publishers, 1999.

Campion, Nardi Reede. *Ann the Word: The Life of Mother Ann Lee, Founder of the Shakers.* Boston: Little, Brown, 1976.

Cantarella, Eva. *Bisexuality in the Ancient World.* Trans. by Cormac O Cuilleanain. New Haven, Conn.: Yale University Press, 1992.

Card, Claudia. *Lesbian Choices.* New York: Columbia University Press, 1995.

———. *The Unnatural Lottery: Character and Moral Luck.* Philadelphia: Temple University Press, 1996.

Carpenter, Edward. *Love's Coming of Age: A Series of Papers on the Relations of the Sexes.* New York: Vanguard Press, 1926 (1896).

Case, Mary Ann C. "Disaggregating Gender from Sex and Sexual Orientation: The Effeminate Man in the Law and Feminist Jurisprudence." *Yale Law Journal* 105 (1995): 90.

Cash, W. J. *The Mind of the South.* New York: Vintage Books, 1941.

Chafe, William H. *The Paradox of Change: American Women in the 20th Century.* New York: Oxford University Press, 1991.

———. *Women and Equality: Changing Patterns in American Culture.* New York: Oxford University Press, 1977.

Chamberlain, Houston Stewart. *The Foundations of the Nineteenth Century,* 2 vols. Trans. by John Lees. London: John Lane, 1911.

Chappell, David L. *A Stone of Hope: Prophetic Religion and the Death of Jim Crow.* Chapel Hill: University of North Carolina Press, 2004.

Chauncey, George. *Gay New York: Gender, Urban Culture, and the Making of the Gay Male World, 1890–1940.* New York: Basic Books, 1994.

Chesler, Ellen. *Woman of Valor: Margaret Sanger and the Birth Control Movement in America.* New York: Anchor, 1992.

Chodorow, Nancy. *Femininities Masculinities Sexualities: Freud and Beyond.* London: Free Association Press, 1994.

———. *Feminism and Psychoanalytic Theory.* London: Polity, 1989.

———. *The Reproduction of Mothering: Psychoanalysis and the Sociology of Gender.* Berkeley: University of California Press, 1978.

Cleaver, Eldridge. *Soul on Ice.* New York: Dell, 1968.

Cobb, Thomas R. R. *An Inquiry into the Law of Negro Slavery in the United States of America.* New York: Negro Universities Press, 1968 (1858).

Cohen, Jane Maslow. "Regimes of Private Tyranny: What Do They Mean to Morality and for the Criminal Law?" *University of Pittsburgh Law Review* 57 (1996): 757.

Cohen, Marcia. *The Sisterhood: The True Story of the Women Who Changed the World.* New York: Simon and Schuster, 1988.

Committee on Homosexual Offenses and Prostitution. *The Wolfenden Report.* New York: Stein and Day, 1963.

Conquest, Robert. *Stalin: Breaker of Nations.* New York: Penguin, 1991.

Cooper, Anna Julia. *A Voice from the South.* Ed. by Mary Helen Washington. New York: Oxford University Press, 1988 (1892).

Cory (pseud.), Donald Webster. *The Homosexual in America: A Subjective Approach.* New York: Castle Books, 1951.

Crimp, Douglas. *Cultural Analysis/Cultural Activism.* Cambridge: The MIT Press, 1988.

Crouch, Stanley. *Notes of a Hanging Judge: Essays and Reviews, 1979–1989.* New York: Oxford University Press, 1990.

Curry, Thomas J. *The First Freedoms: Church and State in America to the Passage of the First Amendment.* New York: Oxford University Press, 1986.

Davis, Peggy Cooper. *Neglected Stories: The Constitution and Family Values.* New York: Hill and Wang, 1997.

DeBerg, Betty A. *Ungodly Women: Gender and the First Wave of American Fundamentalism.* Minneapolis, Minn.: Fortress Press, 1990.

Degler, Carl N. *At Odds: Women and the Family in America from the Revolution to the Present.* New York: Oxford University Press, 1980.

————. *In Search of Human Nature: The Decline and Revival of Darwinism in American Social Thought.* New York: Oxford University Press, 1991.

D'Emilio, John. *Sexual Politics, Sexual Communities: The Making of a Homosexual Minority in the United States, 1940–1970.* Chicago: University of Chicago Press, 1983.

D'Emilio, John, and Estelle B. Freedman. *Intimate Matters: A History of Sexuality in America.* New York: Harper and Row, 1988.

Denfeld, Rene. *The New Victorians: A Young Woman's Challenge to the Old Feminist Order.* New York: Warner Books, 1995.

Desroche, Henri. *The American Shakers: From Neo-Christianity to Presocialism.* Trans. by John K. Savacool. Amherst: University of Massachusetts Press, 1971.

Devlin, Patrick. *The Enforcement of Morals.* London: Oxford University Press, 1965.

Dinnerstein, Dorothy. *The Mermaid and the Minotaur: Sexual Arrangements and Human Malaise.* New York: Harper and Row, 1976.

Donald, David Herbert. *Lincoln.* New York: Simon and Schuster, 1995.

Duberman, Martin. *Stonewall.* New York: Plume, 1993.

Duberman, Martin Bauml, Martha Vicinus, and George Chauncey, Jr., eds. *Hidden from History: Reclaiming the Gay and Lesbian Past.* New York: New American Library, 1989.

Du Bois, W. E. B. *Black Reconstruction in America, 1860–1880.* New York: Atheneum, 1969 (1935).

Dudziak, Mary L. "Desegregation as a Cold War Imperative." *Stanford Law Review* 41 (1988): 61.

Duggan, Lisa, and Nan D. Hunter. *Sex Wars: Sexual Dissent and Political Culture.* New York: Routledge, 1995.

Duncan, Greg J., and Saul D. Hoffman. "A Reconsideration of the Economic Consequences of Marital Dissolution." *Demography* 22 (1985): 485.

Dworkin, Ronald. *Life's Dominion: An Argument About Abortion, Euthanasia, and Individual Freedom.* New York: Knopf, 1993.

Ehrenreich, Barbara, Elizabeth Hess, and Gloria Jacobs. *Remaking Love: The Feminization of Sex.* New York: Anchor, 1986.

Eibl-Eibesfeldt, Irenaus. *Love and Hate: The Natural History of Behavior Patterns.* Trans. by Geoffrey Strachan. New York: Holt, Rinehart, and Winston, 1971.

Elliot, Jonathan. *The Debates in the Several State Conventions on the Adoption of the Federal Constitution,* vol. 2. Washington, D.C.: Printed for the Editor, 1836.

Ellman, Ira Mark, Paul M. Kurtz, and Katharine T. Bartlett, eds. *Family Law: Cases, Text, Problems,* 2nd ed. Charlottesville, Va.: The Michie Company, 1991.

Elshtain, Jean Bethke. *Women and War.* New York: Basic Books, 1987.

Ely, John Hart. *Democracy and Distrust: A Theory of Judicial Review.* Cambridge, Mass.: Harvard University Press, 1983.

————. "The Wages of Crying Wolf: A Comment on *Roe v. Wade.*" *Yale Law Journal* 82 (1974): 920.

Epstein, Richard A. "Live and Let Live." *Wall Street Journal*, July 13, 2004, p. A14.

Erlanger, Howard S., ed. "Review Symposium on Weitzman's *Divorce Revolution.*" *American Bar Foundation Research Journal* 4 (1986): 759–97.

Eskridge, William N., Jr. *The Case for Same-Sex Marriage: From Sexual Liberty to Civilized Commitment.* New York: Free Press, 1996.

———. *Gaylaw: Challenging the Apartheid of the Closet.* Cambridge, Mass.: Harvard University Press, 1999.

———. "United States: *Lawrence v. Texas* and the Imperative of Comparative Constitutionalism." *International Journal of Constitutional Law* 2, 3 (July 2004): 555–60.

Estlund, David M., and Martha C. Nussbaum, eds. *Sex, Preference, and Family: Essays on Law and Nature.* New York: Oxford University Press, 1997.

Evans, Sara. *Personal Politics: The Roots of Women's Liberation in the Civil Rights Movement and the New Left.* New York: Vintage, 1980.

Faderman, Lillian. *Odd Girls and Twilight Lovers: A History of Lesbian Life in Twentieth-Century America.* New York: Columbia University Press, 1991.

———. *Surpassing the Love of Men.* New York: William Morrow, 1981.

Faludi, Susan. *Backlash: The Undeclared War Against American Women.* New York: Doubleday, 1991.

Faust, Drew Gilpin, ed. *The Ideology of Slavery: Proslavery Thought in the Antebellum South, 1830–1860.* Baton Rouge: Louisiana State University Press, 1981.

Fineman, Martha A. *The Illusion of Equality: The Rhetoric and Reality of Divorce Reform.* Chicago: University of Chicago Press, 1991.

———. "Implementing Equality: Ideology, Contradiction and Social Change, A Study of Rhetoric and Results in the Regulation of the Consequences of Divorce." *Wisconsin Law Review* (1983): 789.

Finkelman, Paul. *Slavery and the Founders: Race and Liberty in the Age of Jefferson.* Armonk, N.Y.: M. E. Sharpe, 1996.

Finnis, John. "Law, Morality, and 'Sexual Orientation.'" *Notre Dame Journal of Law, Ethics, and Public Policy* 9 (1995): 11.

Flax, Jane. *Thinking Fragments: Psychoanalysis, Feminism, and Postmodernism in the Contemporary West.* Berkeley: University of California Press, 1990.

Ford, Clellan S., and Frank A. Beach. *Patterns of Sexual Behavior.* New York: Harper and Row, 1951.

Foster, Lawrence. *Women, Family, and Utopia: Communal Experiments of the Shakers, the Oneida Community, and the Mormons.* Syracuse, N.Y.: Syracuse University Press, 1991.

Fox-Genovese, Elizabeth. *"Feminism Is Not the Story of My Life": How Today's Feminist Elite Has Lost Touch with the Real Concerns of Women.* New York: Doubleday, 1996.

———. *Feminism Without Illusions: A Critique of Individualism.* Chapel Hill: University of North Carolina Press, 1991.

Franke, Katherine M. "The Central Mistake of Sex Discrimination Law: The Disaggregation of Sex from Gender." *University of Pennsylvania Law Review* 144 (1995): 1.

Frankenberg, Ruth. *The Social Construction of Whiteness: White Women, Race Matters.* Minneapolis: University of Minnesota Press, 1993.

Franklin, John Hope, and Alfred A. Moss, Jr. *From Slavery to Freedom: A History of Negro Americans,* 6th ed. New York: Knopf, 1988.

Fredrickson, George M. *The Black Image in the White Mind: The Debate on Afro-*

American Character and Destiny, 1817–1914. Middletown, Conn.: Wesleyan University Press, 1971.

———. *White Supremacy: A Comparative Study in American and South African History.* Oxford: Oxford University Press, 1981.

Freedman, Estelle B., Barbara C. Gelpi, Susan L. Johnson, and Kathleen M. Weston, eds. *The Lesbian Issue: Essays from Signs.* Chicago: University of Chicago Press, 1982.

Freeman, Jo. *The Politics of Women's Liberation: A Case Study of an Emerging Social Movement and Its Relation to the Policy Process.* New York: Longman, 1975.

Freeman, Joanne B. *Affairs of Honor: National Politics in the New Republic.* New Haven, Conn.: Yale University Press, 2001.

French, Marilyn. *The War Against Women.* London: Penguin, 1992.

Freud, Sigmund. *Standard Edition of the Complete Psychological Works of Sigmund Freud,* vol. 9. Ed. by James Strachey. London: Hogarth Press, 1959, Vol. 21: 1961, Vol. 23: 1964.

Fried, Charles. *Order and Law: Arguing the Reagan Revolution—A Firsthand Account.* New York: Simon and Schuster, 1991.

Friedan, Betty. *The Feminine Mystique.* London: Penguin, 1982 (1963).

Frye, Marilyn. *The Politics of Reality: Essays in Feminist Theory.* Trumansburg, N.Y.: Crossing Press, 1983.

———. *Willful Virgin: Essays in Feminism, 1976–1992.* Freedom, Calif.: Crossing Press, 1992.

Furet, Francois. *The Passing of an Illusion: The Idea of Communism in the Twentieth Century.* Trans. by Deborah Furet. Chicago: University of Chicago Press, 1999.

Garfield, Deborah M., and Rafia Zafar, eds. *Harriet Jacobs and Incidents in the Life of a Slave Girl.* Cambridge: Cambridge University Press, 1996.

Garrison, Marsha. "Good Intentions Gone Awry: The Impact of New York's Equitable Distribution Law on Divorce Outcomes." *Brooklyn Law Review* 57 (1991): 621.

Gebhard, Paul H. "Incidence of Overt Homosexuality in the United States and Western Europe." In J. M. Livingood, ed., *National Institute of Mental Health Task Force on Homosexuality.* Washington, D.C.: U.S. Government Printing Office, 1972.

Genovese, Eugene D. *Roll, Jordan, Roll: The World the Slaves Made.* New York: Vintage Books, 1974.

George, Robert P., and Gerard V. Bradley. "Marriage and the Liberal Imagination." *Georgia Law Journal* 84 (1995): 301.

Gerstmann, Evan. *Same-Sex Marriage and the Constitution.* Cambridge: Cambridge University Press, 2004.

Giddens, Anthony. *The Transformation of Intimacy: Sexuality, Love, and Eroticism in Modern Societies.* Cambridge: Polity, 1992.

Giddings, Paula. *When and Where I Enter … : The Impact of Black Woman on Race and Sex in America.* New York: William Morrow, 1984.

Gilligan, Carol. *The Birth of Pleasure.* New York: Vintage Books, 2003.

———. *In a Different Voice: Psychological Theory and Women's Development.* Cambridge, Mass.: Harvard University Press, 1982.

———. "Knowing and Not Knowing: Reflections on Manhood." *Psychotherapy and Politics International* 2, 2 (2004): 99–114.

Gilligan, James. *Violence: Reflections on a National Epidemic.* New York: Vintage Books, 1997.

Gilmore, David D., ed. *Honour and Shame and the Unity of the Mediterranean.* Washington, D.C.: American Anthropological Association, 1987.

Goldin, Claudia. *Understanding the Gender Gap: An Economic History of American Women.* New York: Oxford University Press, 1990.

Goldman, Nancy Loring. *Female Soldiers—Combatants or Noncombatants?* Westport, Conn.: Greenwood Press, 1982.

Goldstein, Anne B. "History, Homosexuality, and Political Values: Searching for the Hidden Determinants of *Bowers v. Hardwick.*" *Yale Law Journal* 97 (1988): 1073.

————. "Reasoning About Homosexuality: A Commentary on Janet Halley's 'Reasoning About Sodomy: Act and Identity in and After *Bowers v. Hardwick.*'" *Virginia Law Review* 79 (1993): 1781.

Gossett, Thomas F. *Race: The History of an Idea in America.* New York: Schocken Books, 1965.

Gould, Stephen Jay. *The Mismeasure of Man.* New York: W. W. Norton, 1981.

Grant, Jacquelyn. *White Women's Christ and Black Women's Jesus: Feminist Christology and Womanist Response.* Atlanta, Ga.: Scholars Press, 1989.

Grant, Madison. *The Passing of the Great Race or The Racial Basis of European History.* New York: Charles Scribner's Sons, 1919.

Green, Richard. *The "Sissy Boy Syndrome" and the Development of Homosexuality.* New Haven, Conn.: Yale University Press, 1987.

Greenawalt, Kent. *Religious Convictions and Political Choice.* New York: Oxford University Press, 1988.

Greenberg, David F. *The Construction of Homosexuality.* Chicago: University of Chicago Press, 1988.

Greenberg, Jack. *Crusaders in the Courts: How a Dedicated Band of Lawyers Fought for the Civil Rights Revolution.* New York: Basic Books, 1994.

Greenberg, Kenneth S. *Honor and Slavery.* Princeton, N.J.: Princeton University Press, 1996.

————. *Masters and Statesmen: The Political Culture of American Slavery.* Baltimore: The Johns Hopkins University Press, 1985.

Grisez, Germain. *The Way of the Lord Jesus, Volume Two: Living a Christian Life.* Quincy, Ill.: Franciscan Press, 1993.

Gutman, Herbert G. *The Black Family in Slavery and Freedom, 1750–1925.* New York: Vintage Books, 1976.

Hacker, Andrew. *Two Nations: Black and White, Separate, Hostile, Unequal.* New York: Charles Scribner's Sons, 1992.

Halevy, Elie. *The Growth of Philosophic Radicalism.* Trans. by Mary Morris. Boston: Beacon Press, 1960.

Haller, John S., Jr. *Outcasts from Evolution: Scientific Attitudes of Racial Inferiority, 1859–1900.* New York: McGraw-Hill Book Company, 1971.

Halley, Janet E. "Reasoning About Sodomy: Act and Identity in and After *Bowers v. Hardwick.*" *Virginia Law Review* 79 (1993): 1721.

Hart, H. L. A. *Law, Liberty, and Morality.* Palo Alto, Calif.: Stanford University Press, 1963.

————. "Social Solidarity and the Enforcement of Morals." *University of Chicago Law Review* 35 (1967): 1.

Hart, Jenifer. *Ask Me No More: An Autobiography.* London: Peter Halban, 1998.

Hay, Harry. *Radically Gay.* Ed. by Will Roscoe. Boston: Beacon Press, 1996.

Hedges, Chris. *War Is a Force That Gives Us Meaning.* New York: Public Affairs, 2002.

Henry, Sherrye. *The Deep Divide: Why American Women Resist Equality.* New York: Macmillan, 1994.

Herdt, Gilbert. *Third Sex, Third Gender: Beyond Sexual Dimorphism in Culture and History.* New York: Zone Books, 1994.

Herek, Gregory M., Jared B. Jobe, and Ralph M. Carney, eds. *Out in Force: Sexual Orientation and the Military.* Chicago: University of Chicago Press, 1996.

Herman, Didi. *The Antigay Agenda: Orthodox Vision and the Christian Right.* Chicago: University of Chicago Press, 1997.

Higginbotham, Evelyn Brooks. *Righteous Discontent: The Women's Movement in the Black Baptist Church, 1880–1920.* Cambridge, Mass.: Harvard University Press, 1993.

Higham, John. *Strangers in the Land: Patterns of American Nativism, 1860–1925.* New Brunswick, N.J.: Rutgers University Press, 1988.

Hilberg, Raul. *The Destruction of the European Jews,* vol. 3. New York: Holmes and Meier, 1985.

Hoagland, Sarah Lucia. *Lesbian Ethics: Toward New Value.* Palo Alto, Calif.: Institute of Lesbian Studies, 1988.

Hole, Judith, and Ellen Levine. *Rebirth of Feminism.* New York: Quadrangle, 1971.

Holmes, Oliver Wendell. "The Path of the Law." *Harvard Law Review* 10 (1897): 457.

Honore, Tony. *Sex Law.* London: Duckworth, 1978.

hooks, bell. *Ain't I a Woman: Black Women and Feminism.* Boston: South End Press, 1981.

———. *Feminist Theory: From Margin to Center.* Boston: South End Press, 1984.

———. *Killing Rage: Ending Racism.* New York: Henry Holt, 1995.

Horsman, Reginald. *Race and Manifest Destiny: The Origins of American Racial Anglo-Saxonism.* Cambridge, Mass.: Harvard University Press, 1981.

Huggins, Nathan, ed. *W. E. B. Du Bois.* New York: Library of America, 1986.

Hume, David. *Essays Moral Political and Literary.* Ed. by Eugene F. Miller. Indianapolis, Ind.: LibertyClassics, 1985 (1777).

Humez, Jean M. *Mother's First-Born Daughters: Early Shaker Writings on Women and Religion.* Bloomington: Indiana University Press, 1993.

Hunter, Nan D. "Identity, Speech, and Equality." *Virginia Law Review* 79 (1993): 1695.

———. "Life After *Hardwick*." *Harvard Civil Rights–Civil Liberties Law Review* 27 (1992): 531.

Hutcheson, Francis. *A System of Moral Philosophy,* 2 vols. in 1. New York: Augustus M. Kelley, 1968 (1755).

Ignatieff, Michael. *The Warrior's Honor: Ethnic War and the Modern Conscience.* New York: Henry Holt, 1997.

Ireland, Patricia. *What Women Want.* New York: Dutton, 1996.

Jacobs, Harriet A. *Incidents in the Life of a Slave Girl.* Ed. by Jean Fagan Yellin. Cambridge, Mass.: Harvard University Press, 1987 (1861).

Jefery-Poulter, Stephen. *Peers, Queers, and Commons: The Struggle for Gay Law Reform from 1950 to the Present.* London: Routledge, 1991.

Jeffries, John C., Jr. *Justice Lewis F. Powell, Jr.: A Biography.* New York: Fordham University Press, 2001.

Johnson, John W., *Griswold v. Connecticut: Birth Control and the Constitutional Right to Privacy.* Lawrence: University Press of Kansas, 2005.

McPherson, James M. *The Abolitionist Legacy: From Reconstruction to the NAACP.* Princeton, N.J.: Princeton University Press, 1975.

———. *The Struggle for Equality: Abolitionists and the Negro in the Civil War and Reconstruction.* Princeton, N.J.: Princeton University Press, 1964.

Merin, Yuval. *Equality for Same-Sex Couples: The Legal Recognition of Gay Partnerships in Europe and the United States.* Chicago: University of Chicago Press, 2002.

Michael, Robert T., John H. Gagnon, Edward O. Laumann, and Gina Kolata. *Sex in America: A Definitive Survey.* Boston: Little, Brown, 1994.

Mill, John Stuart. *On Liberty.* Ed. by Alburey Castell. New York: Appleton-Century-Crofts, 1947 (1859).

———. *Utilitarianism.* Ed. by Oskar Piest. Indianapolis, Ind.: The Library of Liberal Arts, 1957 (1861).

Mill, John Stuart, and Harriet Taylor Mill. *Essays on Sex Equality.* Ed. by Alice S. Rossi. Chicago: University of Chicago Press, 1970.

Miller, William Ian. *Bloodtaking and Peacemaking: Feud, Law, and Society in Saga Iceland.* Chicago: University of Chicago Press, 1990.

———. *Humiliation and Other Essays on Honor, Social Discomfort, and Violence.* Ithaca, N.Y.: Cornell University Press, 1993.

Miller, William Lee. *The First Liberty: Religion and the American Republic.* New York: Knopf, 1987.

Mitchell, Brian. *Weak Link: The Feminization of the American Military.* Washington, D.C.: Regnery Gateway, 1989.

Mixner, David. *Stranger Among Friends.* New York: Bantam Books, 1996.

Mohr, Richard D. *A More Perfect Union: Why Straight America Must Stand Up for Gay Rights.* Boston: Beacon Press, 1994.

———. *Gay Ideas: Outing and Other Controversies.* Boston: Beacon Press, 1992.

———. *Gays/Justice: A Study of Ethics, Society, and Law.* New York: Columbia University Press, 1988.

Moore, Gareth. *A Question of Truth: Christianity and Homosexuality.* London: Continuum, 2003.

Morris, Aldon D. *The Origins of the Civil Rights Movement: Black Communities Organizing for Change.* New York: Free Press, 1984.

Morris, Madeline. "By Force of Arms: Rape, War and Military Culture." *Duke Law Journal* 45 (1996): 651.

Myrdal, Gunnar. *An American Dilemma: The Negro Problem and Modern Democracy,* 2 vols. New York: Pantheon Books, 1972 (1944).

Nava, Michael, and Robert Dawidoff. *Created Equal: Why Gay Rights Matter to America.* New York: St. Martin's Press, 1994.

Niblock, John F. "Anti-Gay Initiatives: A Call for Heightened Judicial Scrutiny." *UCLA Law Review* 41 (1993): 153.

Nieman, Donald G. *Promises to Keep: African-Americans and the Constitutional Order, 1776 to the Present.* New York: Oxford University Press, 1991.

Nisbett, Richard E., and Dov Cohen. *Culture of Honor: The Psychology of Violence in the South.* Boulder, Colo.: Westview Press, 1996.

Noddings, Nel. *Caring: A Feminine Approach to Ethics and Moral Education.* Berkeley: University of California Press, 1984.

———. *Women and Evil.* Berkeley: University of California Press, 1989.

Nomination of Robert H. Bork to Be Associate Justice of the Supreme Court of the United States: Hearings Before the Senate Committee on the Judiciary, 100th Congress, 1st Session (1987), at 3047 (statement of David A. J. Richards).

Nussbaum, Martha. "Objectification." *Philosophy and Public Affairs* 24 (1995): 249.
Okin, Susan Moller. "Economic Equality After Divorce." *Dissent* (summer 1991): 383.
———. *Justice, Gender, and the Family.* New York: Basic Books, 1989.
Pagels, Elaine. *The Origin of Satan.* New York: Random House, 1996.
Paglia, Camille. *Sex, Art, and American Culture: Essays.* New York: Vintage Books, 1992.
———. *Sexual Personae: Art and Decadence from Nefertiti to Emily Dickinson.* New York: Vintage, 1991.
———. *Vamps and Tramps: New Essays.* New York: Vintage Books, 1994.
Patai, Daphne, and Noretta Koertge. *Professing Feminism: Cautionary Tales from the Strange World of Women's Studies.* New York: Basic Books, 1994.
Pellauer, Mary D. *Toward a Tradition of Feminist Theology: The Religious Social Thought of Elizabeth Cady Stanton, Susan B. Anthony, and Anna Howard Shaw.* Brooklyn, N.Y.: Carlson Publishing, 1991.
Peristiany, J. G., ed. *Honour and Shame: The Values of Mediterranean Society.* Chicago: University of Chicago Press, 1966.
Pharr, Suzanne. *Homophobia: A Weapon of Sexism.* Inverness, Calif.: Chardon Press, 1988.
Pipes, Daniel. *Militant Islam Reaches America.* New York: W. W. Norton, 2002.
Plato. *The Collected Dialogues of Plato.* Ed. by Edith Hamilton and Huntington Cairns. New York: Pantheon, 1964.
Pollack, William. *Real Boys: Rescuing Our Sons from the Myths of Boyhood.* New York: Henry Holt, 1998.
Presidential Commission on the Assignment of Women in the Armed Forces. *Women in Combat: Report to the President.* Washington, D.C.: Brassey's, 1991.
Procter-Smith, Marjorie. *Women in Shaker Community and Worship: A Feminist Analysis of the Uses of Religious Symbolism.* Lewiston, N.Y.: Edwin Mellen Press, 1985.
Proust, Marcel. *Cities of the Plain.* Trans. by C. K. Scott Moncrieff. New York: Vintage, 1970.
Rauch, Jonathan. "For Better or Worse?" *New Republic,* May 6, 1996, pp. 18–23.
Rawls, John. *Collected Papers.* Ed. by Samuel Freeman. Cambridge, Mass.: Harvard University Press, 1999.
———. *A Theory of Justice.* Cambridge, Mass.: Harvard University Press, 1971.
Real, Terrence. *I Don't Want to Talk About It: Overcoming the Secret Legacy of Male Depression.* New York: Fireside, 1997.
Rhode, Deborah. *Justice and Gender.* Cambridge, Mass.: Harvard University Press, 1989.
Rich, Adrienne. *Of Woman Born: Motherhood as Experience and Institution.* New York: W. W. Norton, 1976.
———. *On Lies, Secrets, and Silence: Selected Prose, 1966–1978.* New York: W. W. Norton, 1979.
Richards, David A. J. *A Theory of Reasons for Action.* Oxford: Clarendon Press, 1971.
———. "Commercial Sex and the Rights of the Person: A Moral Argument for the Decriminalization of Prostitution." *University of Pennsylvania Law Review* 127 (1979): 1195.
———. *Conscience and the Constitution: History, Theory, and Law of the Reconstruction Amendments.* Princeton, N.J.: Princeton University Press, 1993.

————. "Constitutional Legitimacy and Constitutional Privacy." *New York University Law Review* 61 (1986): 800.

————. "Constitutional Privacy, the Right to Die, and the Meaning of Life: A Moral Analysis." *William and Mary Law Review* 22 (1981): 327.

————. *Disarming Manhood: Roots of Ethical Resistance in Jesus, Garrison, Tolstoy, Gandhi, King, and Churchill.* Athens: Ohio University Press, 2005 (forthcoming).

————. "Drug Use and the Rights of the Person: A Moral Argument for the Decriminalization of Certain Forms of Drug Use." *Rutgers Law Review* 33 (1981): 607.

————. *Foundations of American Constitutionalism.* New York: Oxford University Press, 1989.

————. *Free Speech and the Politics of Identity.* Oxford: Oxford University Press, 1999.

————. "Homosexuality and the Constitutional Right to Privacy." *New York University Review of Law and Social Change* 8 (1978–1979): 311.

————. *Identity and the Case for Gay Rights: Race, Gender, Religion as Analogies.* Chicago: University of Chicago Press, 1999.

————. *The Moral Criticism of Law.* Encino, Calif.: Dickenson-Wadsworth, 1977.

————. "Public Reason and Abolitionist Dissent." *Chicago-Kent Law Review* 69 (1994): 787.

————. *Sex, Drugs, Death and the Law: An Essay on Human Rights and Overcriminalization.* Totowa, N.J.: Rowman and Littlefield, 1982.

————. "Sexual Autonomy and the Constitutional Right to Privacy: A Case Study in Human Rights and the Unwritten Constitution." *Hastings Law Journal* 30 (1979): 957.

————. "Sexual Preference as a Suspect Religious Classification: An Alternative Perspective on the Unconstitutionality of Anti-Lesbian/Gay Initiatives." *Ohio Law Review* 55 (1994): 491.

————. *Toleration and the Constitution.* New York: Oxford University Press, 1986.

————. *Tragic Manhood and Democracy: Verdi's Voice and the Powers of Musical Art.* Brighton, U.K.: Sussex Academic Press, 2004.

————. "Unnatural Acts and the Constitutional Right to Privacy: A Moral Theory." *Fordham Law Review* 45 (1977): 1282.

————. *Women, Gays, and the Constitution: The Grounds for Feminism and Gay Rights in Culture and Law.* Chicago: University of Chicago Press, 1998.

Rimbaud, Arthur. *Complete Works.* Trans. by Paul Schmidt. New York: Perennial Classics, 2000.

Robb, Graham. *Strangers: Homosexual Love in the Nineteenth Century.* New York: W. W. Norton, 2003.

Roiphe, Katie. *The Morning After: Sex, Fear, and Feminism.* Boston: Little, Brown, 1993.

Rosenberg, Rosalind. *Beyond Separate Spheres: Intellectual Roots of Modern Feminism.* New Haven, Conn.: Yale University Press, 1982.

Rotello, Gabriel. *Sexual Ecology: AIDS and the Destiny of Gay Men.* New York: Dutton, 1997.

Rothblum, Esther D., and Kathleen A. Brehony. *Boston Marriages: Romantic but Asexual Relationships Among Contemporary Lesbians.* Amherst: University of Massachusetts Press, 1993.

Roy, Arundhati. *War Talk.* Cambridge, Mass.: South End Press, 2003.

Ruddick, Sara. *Maternal Thinking: Toward a Politics of Peace.* Boston: Beacon Press, 1989.

Rutherford, Jane. "Duty in Divorce: Shared Income as a Path of Equality." *Fordham Law Review* 58 (1990): 539.

Scanlon, T. M. *What We Owe to Each Other.* Cambridge, Mass.: Harvard University Press, 1998.

Scheman, Naomi. *Engenderings: Constructions of Knowledge, Authority, and Privilege.* London: Routledge, 1993.

Seeyle, Katherine Q., and Janet Elder. "Strong Support Is Found for Ban on Gay Marriage." *New York Times,* December 21, 2003, p. A1.

Seligman, Edwin R. A., ed. *Encyclopaedia of the Social Sciences,* vol. 7. New York: Macmillan, 1937.

Seltzer, Judith A., and Irwin Garfinkel. "Inequality in Divorce Settlements: An Investigation of Property Settlements and Child Support Awards." *Social Science Research* 19 (1990): 82.

Sered, Susan Starr. *Priestess, Mother, Sacred Sister: Religions Dominated by Women.* New York: Oxford University Press, 1994.

Shaw, Brent D. "A Groom of One's Own?" *New Republic,* July 18 and 25, 1994, pp. 33–41.

Shilts, Randy. *Conduct Unbecoming: Gays and Lesbians in the U.S. Military.* New York: St. Martin's Press, 1993.

Silverman, Kaja. *Male Subjectivity at the Margins.* New York: Routledge, 1992.

Simons, Anna. "In War, Let Men Be Men." *New York Times,* April 23, 1997, p. A23.

Smith-Rosenberg, Carroll. *Disorderly Conduct: Visions of Gender in Victorian America.* New York: Knopf, 1985.

Snitow, Anne, Christine Stansell, and Sharon Thompson, eds., *Powers of Desire.* New York: Monthly Review Press, 1983.

Sollors, Werner. *Beyond Ethnicity: Consent and Descent in American Culture.* New York: Oxford University Press, 1986.

Sommers, Christina Hoff. *Who Stole Feminism: How Women Have Betrayed Women.* New York: Simon and Schuster, 1994.

Southern, David W. *Gunnar Myrdal and Black-White Relations: The Use and Abuse of an American Dilemma, 1944–1969.* Baton Rouge: Louisiana State University Press, 1987.

Spierenburg, Pieter. *Men and Violence: Gender, Honor, and Rituals in Modern Europe and America.* Columbus: Ohio State University Press, 1998.

Stampp, Kenneth M. *The Peculiar Institution.* New York: Vintage, 1956.

Stanton, William. *The Leopard's Spots: Scientific Attitudes Toward Race in America, 1815–59.* Chicago: University of Chicago Press, 1960.

Stein, Stephen J. *The Shaker Experience in America.* New Haven, Conn.: Yale University Press, 1992.

Stern, Daniel N. *The Interpersonal World of the Infant: A View from Psychoanalysis and Developmental Psychology.* New York: Basic Books, 1985.

Stimpson, Catharine R. "Marry, Marry, Quite Contrary: To Wed Is to Lose One's Precious Distance from Conformity." *Nation,* July 5, 2004, pp. 38–40.

Stimpson, Catharine R., and Ethel Spector Person. *Women: Sex and Sexuality.* Chicago: University of Chicago Press, 1980.

Stocking, George W., Jr. *A Franz Boas Reader: The Shaping of American Anthropology, 1883–1911.* Chicago: University of Chicago Press, 1974.

———. *Race, Culture, and Evolution: Essays in the History of Anthropology.* New York: Free Press, 1968.

Strasser, Mark. *Legallywed: Same-Sex Marriage and the Constitution.* Ithaca, N.Y.: Cornell University Press, 1997.

———. *"Loving* the *Romer* Out for *Baehr:* On Acts in Defense of Marriage and the Constitution." *University of Pittsburgh Law Review* 58 (1997): 279.

Sundquist, Eric J. *To Wake the Nations: Race in the Making of American Literature.* Cambridge, Mass.: Belknap Press of Harvard University Press, 1993.

Takaki, Ronald. *Iron Cages: Race and Culture in 19th-Century America.* New York: Oxford University Press, 1990.

Tamir, Yael. *Liberal Nationalism.* Princeton, N.J.: Princeton University Press, 1993.

Thomas, Kendall. "The Eclipse of Reason: A Rhetorical Reading of *Bowers v. Hardwick.*" *Virginia Law Review* 79 (1993): 1805.

Toibin, Colm. *Love in a Dark Time.* New York: Scribner, 2001.

Tribe, Laurence H. *"Lawrence v. Texas:* The 'Fundamental Right' That Dare Not Speak Its Name." *Harvard Law Review* 117 (2004): 117.

———. "Toward a Less Perfect Union." *New York Times,* May 26, 1966, p. E11; letter of Laurence Tribe to Sen. Edward M. Kennedy, 142 Cong. Rec. S5931-01, p. *S5932-33.

Tushnet, Mark V. *Making Civil Rights Law: Thurgood Marshall and the Supreme Court, 1956–1961.* New York: Oxford University Press, 1994.

———. *The NAACP's Legal Strategy Against Segregated Education, 1925–1950.* Chapel Hill: University of North Carolina Press, 1987.

Tussman, Joseph, and Jacobus tenBroek. "The Equal Protection of the Laws." *California Law Review* 37 (1949): 37.

Vaid, Urvashi. *Virtual Equality: The Mainstreaming of Gay and Lesbian Liberation.* New York: Anchor, 1995.

Vance, Carole S., ed. *Pleasure and Danger: Exploring Female Sexuality.* Boston: Routledge and Kegan Paul, 1984.

Vidal, Gore. *The City and the Pillar.* London: Andre Deutsch, 1994 (1948).

Walters, Ronald G. *The Antislavery Appeal: American Abolitionism After 1830.* New York: W. W. Norton, 1978.

Warner, Michael, ed. *Fear of a Queer Planet: Queer Politics and Social Theory.* Minneapolis: University of Minnesota Press, 1993.

Weeks, Jeffrey. *Coming Out: Homosexual Politics in Britain from the Nineteenth Century to the Present.* London: Quartet, 1990.

———. *Against Nature: Essays on History, Sexuality and Identity.* London: Rivers Oran, 1991.

Weitzman, Lenore J. *The Divorce Revolution: The Unexpected Social and Economic Consequences for Women and Children in America.* New York: Free Press, 1985.

Weld, Theodore Dwight. *American Slavery as It Is.* New York: Arno Press and The New York Times, 1968 (1839).

West, Cornel. *Race Matters.* Boston: Beacon Press, 1993.

White, Edmund. *Genet: A Biography.* New York: Knopf, 1993.

Whitman, Walt. *Walt Whitman: The Complete Poems.* Ed. by Francis Murphy. Harmondsworth, U.K.: Penguin, 1975.

Will, George. "Discussing Homosexual Marriage." 1996 WL 5541151. Reprinted from *Washington Post,* Sunday, May 19, 1996.

Williams, Joan. "Gender Wars: Selfless Women in the Republic of Choice." *N.Y.U. Law Review* 66 (1991): 1559.

———. "Is Coverture Dead? Beyond a New Theory of Alimony." *Georgia Law Journal* 82 (1994): 2227.

Williams, Walter L. *The Spirit and the Flesh: Sexual Diversity in American Indian Culture.* Boston: Beacon Press, 1986.

Wintemute, Robert. *Sexual Orientation and Human Rights: The United States Constitution, the European Convention, and the Canadian Charter.* Oxford: Clarendon Press, 1995.

Witherspoon, John. *Lectures of Moral Philosophy.* Ed. by Jack Scott. East Brunswick, N.J.: Associated University Presses, 1982.

Wolf, Naomi. *The Beauty Myth: How Images of Beauty Are Used Against Women.* New York: Anchor, 1991.

Wollstonecraft, Mary. *A Vindication of the Rights of Woman. The Works of Mary Wollstonecraft.* Ed. by Janet Todd and Marilyn Butler. New York: New York University Press, 1989 (1790), vol. 5, pp. 237–60.

Woodward, C. Vann. *Origins of the New South, 1877–1913.* Baton Rouge: Louisiana State University Press, 1971.

———. *Reunion and Reaction: The Compromise of 1877 and the End of Reconstruction.* New York: Oxford University Press, 1966.

———. *The Strange Career of Jim Crow,* 3d rev. ed. New York: Oxford University Press, 1974.

Woodward, C. Vann, and Elisabeth Muhlenfeld. *The Private Mary Chesnut: The Unpublished Civil War Diaries.* New York: Oxford University Press, 1984.

Woolf, Virginia. *Three Guineas.* San Diego: Harcourt Brace and Company, 1938.

Wyatt-Brown, Bertram. *Southern Honor: Ethics and Behavior in the Old South.* New York: Oxford University Press, 1982.

Young-Bruehl, Elisabeth. *The Anatomy of Prejudices.* Cambridge, Mass.: Harvard University Press, 1996.

INDEX OF CASES

CONSTITUTIONS, LEGISLATION, REGULATIONS

SUBJECT INDEX

Abolitionist feminists, 52, 54, 55, 155
  racism/slavery and, 53, 63
Abolitionist movement, 28, 74
Abortion, 10, 11, 70, 166, 168, 190n21
  criminalization of, 71, 77, 90, 113
  decriminalization of, 75
  right to, xii, 32, 72, 75, 132
Addams, Jane, 187n108
Adultery, 81, 85, 86, 139, 141, 209n53
African Americans, 28
  political/moral community and, 121
AIDS, 33, 113
Altman, Dennis, 34
American Dilemma, An (Myrdal), 46
Americanism, religion of, 119
American Law Institute, 97
American Revolution, 48, 66
Amerindian homosexuals, 33
Andrews, Stephen, 66
Antiabortion laws, 70, 72, 81, 135, 136
Anticontraception laws, 70, 72, 81, 135
Antidiscrimination laws, 91, 94, 107, 157
Antiestablishment principle, 108, 117,189–
  90n11
Anti-gay marriage amendment, 128, 141,
  147, 172
Anti-lesbian/gay initiatives, 116-20
Antimiscegenation laws, 40, 51, 54, 55, 65,
  81, 115, 135, 137
  arguments for, 138
  intimate life and, 131
  privacy and, 102
  unconstitutionality of, 31, 50, 72
Antiobscenity laws, 33
Antipolygamy movement, 139, 140
Antiracism, 32, 34, 55, 57
  abolitionist, 42–50
  gender roles in, 35

Anti-Semitism, 10, 52, 115, 172, 200n64,
  201n72, 214n89
  condemnation of, 49, 119, 155, 159, 171
  dehumanization of, 96
  gay identity and, 108
  homophobia and, 118
  intolerance and, 39
  political, 118, 119, 162
  racism and, 47
  unconstitutionality of, 24
Antisexism, 34, 57
Antiwar movement, 6, 28
Apartheid, 31, 55, 84
Aristotle, 15
Aryan brotherhood, 127
Aspen Institute, 193n25
Association, freedom of, 94, 120, 140
Atlanta race riots (1906), 44
Augustine, 40, 168, 191n47
  sexual morality of, 69, 83

Baehr v. Lewin (1993), 128, 137
Baker, Ella, 54
Baker v. State of Vermont (1999), 128, 130
Baldwin, James, 31, 34, 148, 162
  on masculinity, 172
  protest by, 161
  on sexual exploitation, 131
Ballard, Guy, 196n12
Bayle, Pierre, 39, 104, 105, 182n2
Bayless, H. Jeffrey, 200n56
Beauvoir, Simone de, 52
Beecher, Catharine, 35, 56, 58
Benedict, Ruth, 46, 47, 53
Bennett, William, 139
Bentham, Jeremy, 18, 19, 176nn4, 7
Berger, Raoul, 167
Bersani, Leo, 113

235